HOW TO WIRE 1947–1987

Chevy & GMC Trucks

Dennis W. Parks

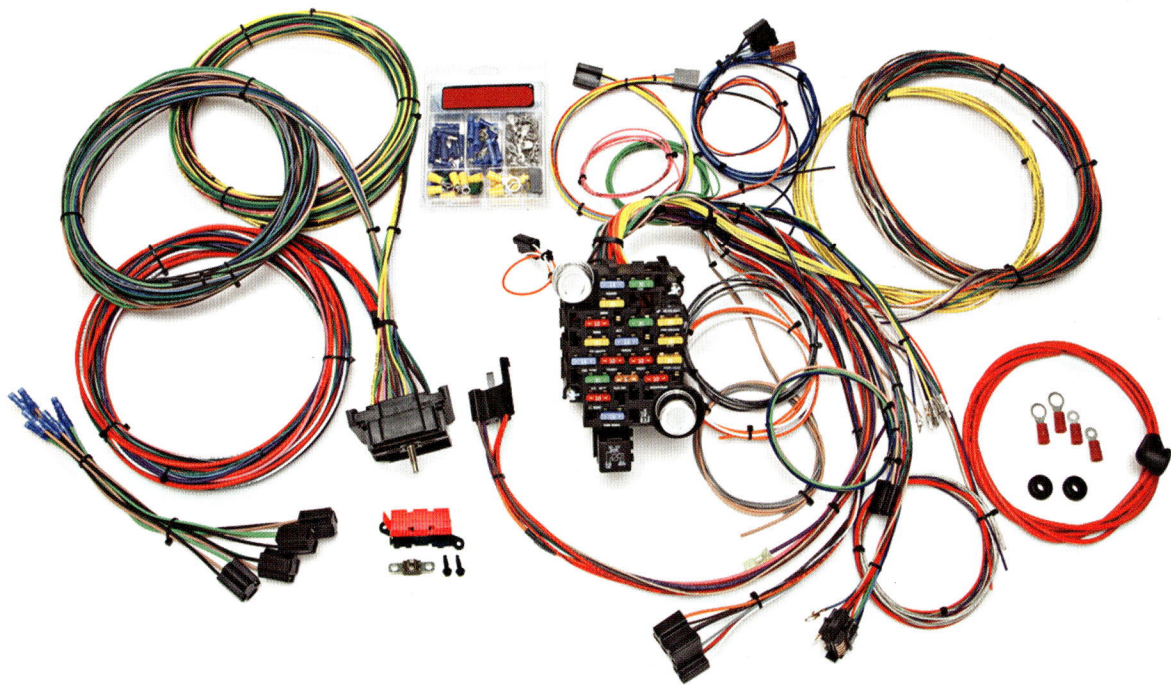

S·A DESIGN

*Car*Tech®

CarTech®

CarTech®, Inc.
6118 Main Street
North Branch, MN 55056
Phone: 651-277-1200 or 800-551-4754
Fax: 651-277-1203
www.cartechbooks.com

© 2024 by Dennis W. Parks

All rights reserved. No part of this publication may be reproduced or utilized in any form or by any means, electronic or mechanical, including photocopying, recording, or by any information storage and retrieval system, without prior permission from the Publisher. All text, photographs, and artwork are the property of the Author unless otherwise noted or credited.

No portion of this book may be reproduced, transferred, stored, or otherwise used in any manner for purposes of training any artificial intelligence technology or system to generate text, illustrations, diagrams, charts, designs or other works or materials.

The information in this work is true and complete to the best of our knowledge. However, all information is presented without any guarantee on the part of the Author or Publisher, who also disclaim any liability incurred in connection with the use of the information and any implied warranties of merchantability or fitness for a particular purpose. Readers are responsible for taking suitable and appropriate safety measures when performing any of the operations or activities described in this work.

All trademarks, trade names, model names and numbers, and other product designations referred to herein are the property of their respective owners and are used solely for identification purposes. This work is a publication of CarTech, Inc. and has not been licensed, approved, sponsored, or endorsed by any other person or entity. The Publisher is not associated with any product, service, or vendor mentioned in this book and does not endorse the products or services of any vendor mentioned in this book.

Edit by Wes Eisenschenk
Layout by Ella Nordrum

ISBN 978-1-61325-796-8
Item No. SA543

Library of Congress Cataloging-in-Publication Data Available

Written, edited, and designed in the U.S.A.
Printed in China
10 9 8 7 6 5 4 3 2 1

CarTech books may be purchased at a discounted rate in bulk for resale, events, corporate gifts, or educational purposes. Special editions may also be created to specification. For details, contact Special Sales at 6118 Main Street, North Branch, MN 55056 or by email at sales@cartechbooks.com.

DISTRIBUTION BY:

Europe
PGUK
63 Hatton Garden
London EC1N 8LE, England
Phone: 020 7061 1980 • Fax: 020 7242 3725
www.pguk.co.uk

Australia
Renniks Publications Ltd.
3/37-39 Green Street
Banksmeadow, NSW 2109, Australia
Phone: 2 9695 7055 • Fax: 2 9695 7355
www.renniks.com

Canada
Login Canada
300 Saulteaux Crescent
Winnipeg, MB, R3J 3T2 Canada
Phone: 800 665 1148 • Fax: 800 665 0103
www.lb.ca

CONTENTS

DEDICATION

To my neighbor Tom Kuhn, who served as a hand model for some of the photos in this book and as a technical advisor for portions of the wiring of both trucks that were involved with this project. He also served as a primary consultant for the construction of my new garage that took place while this book was being written.

ACKNOWLEDGMENTS

A very sincere thank-you to everyone who helped with this book, as I could not have done it without your help. In no particular order, thanks to Sam Kimbrough, John Kimbrough, Keith Moritz, Rich Fox, and Rex Watson for sharing your knowledge of automotive wiring over the years.

— Dennis W. Parks

In case you have not noticed, vintage pickup trucks are currently enjoying immense popularity. There are multiple reasons for this, and one of them is that they have been cool all along due to their simplicity. Some people are just now making that realization. Another reason for the popularity is the manufacturer's suggested retail price (MSRP) of new trucks. While new trucks are selling very well, sticker shock currently has a much longer effect on a buyer's wallet than it had in the past. Everything was less expensive when these trucks were new. While a two- or three-year loan used to be the normal duration, a seven-year loan is now common.

Pickup trucks are very convenient, especially for homeowners. It is difficult to haul a few 2x4s, a sheet of plywood or drywall, or a new couch in a four-door sedan. It's not a good idea to take the chance of spilling potting soil or other landscaping supplies onto the carpet of the family car. Whether you purchase one of these trucks to use purely as a beast of burden to haul something or as a boulevard cruiser, pickup trucks are hot, and that shows no sign of slowing down. In addition, they are versatile, and the current market prices reflect that notion.

Vintage trucks are easier and, therefore, less expensive to maintain than modern trucks. For the purposes of this book, I am speaking of Chevrolet and GMC trucks that were originally manufactured from 1947 to 1987. This was the pre-computer era, and there was less wiring. While these trucks were basic and had few options in the early years, they matured into a product that had something for everyone in the mid-1960s. A vast array of options regarding drivetrains and creature comforts made them more desirable and socially acceptable.

These GM pickup trucks have been the recipients of various engine swaps, suspension modifications, outrageous paint jobs, and plush interiors by hobbyists and professionals. However, the wiring, being out of sight and forgotten, is usually left untouched. Of course, over the years, that stock wiring has been tapped into for the installation of aftermarket stereos, fog lights, CB radios, tachometers, etc. While any of those installations are relatively simple, there is a high probability that the original wiring has been butchered by multiple owners with poorly installed accessories. Even if the original wiring has not been modified, it is a candidate for replacement because it is more than 40 years old.

Automotive enthusiasts are often hesitant to jump into the unknown depths of wiring replacement. However, this should no longer be a concern, as the automotive aftermarket for these trucks has been growing by leaps and bounds. Several companies now manufacture complete wiring kits for the most popular of these trucks. In addition, universal kits are widely available for the less-common trucks and for those who are building one-off custom trucks.

With the availability of wiring kits and the fact that installing one does not require an extensive list of specialized or expensive tools, this is an upgrade that you can do yourself. Patience is necessary because it will take a while to remove the existing wiring and install the new wiring. You must be committed to the project because there is no stopping in the middle—but that is true with any automotive project. A major advantage of doing the wiring yourself is that with this experience, you will be more knowledgeable and able to make a roadside repair if the electrical system goes awry.

The first chapter of this book provides basic electrical theory for two reasons: 1) It expands your knowledge, and with some knowledge and the electrical devices that are available, there is no limit to what you can accomplish, and 2) I do not want you to hurt yourself or burn up your truck.

In chapters two through six, I discuss the theory and the various components that are involved with the ignition system, gauges, lighting system, accessory circuits, and audio/video applications, respectively.

Finally, in chapter seven, I dive into two complete wiring projects. The first project is the complete rewiring of my 1970 Chevrolet C10, using a vehicle-specific wiring kit from Painless Wiring. The second project is wiring the frame-off rebuild of my 1955 Chevrolet pickup using a universal fuse panel and wiring kit from Affordable Street Rods. Unlike reality television shows, there are no free parts and no one is doing the work other than me.

BASIC AUTOMOTIVE WIRING

With the availability of commercially available wiring kits, rewiring a vintage GM pickup truck is not the big problem that many people may presume that it is. It certainly does not require an electrical engineering degree or a licensed electrician. However, it requires patience, the ability to use some very simple hand tools, some manual dexterity, and the ability to follow directions. Having some organizational skills and the ability to lay things out in a systematic manner to do neat, tidy work is a plus. Pay attention to the details and work in a methodical manner.

As your automotive wiring skills develop, you will become the hero to many of your automotive-inclined friends because few people learn this valuable skill. Many enthusiasts are willing to do mechanical work, bodywork, paint, or even upholstery because these tasks can be used to personalize a vehicle and make it stand out. However, when an electrical fuse blows or the binary switch of an electric fan goes bad 50 miles from home, knowing how to override or bypass the issue can save the day. Even if the repair is admittedly temporary in nature, it beats waiting for a tow rig and paying the fee.

Principles of Automotive Electricity

When troubleshooting an existing system or designing a custom electrical system, Ohm's Law and Kirchhoff's Law are important to know and understand. Fortunately, as long as you are using a wiring kit and can follow the directions, you will not need to know this information. Still, inquiring minds may want to know, so here it is.

Ohm's Law describes the relationship of voltage, current, and resistance. It states that current is equal to voltage divided by resistance.

Voltage is simply the difference in potential and is measured in volts (V). Current is the flow of electrons and is measured in amperes (commonly referred to as amps) (A). Voltage is a measure of the pressure that allows electrons to flow, while an ampere is a measure of the volume of electrons.

In other words, volts measure real power, while amps measure apparent power. Resistance is the opposition to the flow of electrons and is measured in ohms (Ω).

As an equation, this is Ohm's Law:
Current (A) =
Voltage (V) ÷ Resistance (Ω).

This equation can be reworked to find the other values as long as two of the three are known.

Voltage (V) =
Current (A) x Resistance (Ω)

Resistance (Ω) =
Voltage (V) ÷ Current (A)

Use Watt's Law to convert volts to amps. Watt's Law states that Current (A) = Power (W) ÷ Voltage (V).

Kirchhoff developed two laws that are important to know. Kirchhoff's Voltage Law states that the sum of voltages applied to a circuit equals the sum of the voltage drops across the components within that circuit. Kirchhoff's Current Law states that current entering a junction in a circuit equals the current leaving a junction.

Wire and Wire Size

Wire used in automotive wiring is referred to as primary wire. Most auto parts stores have primary wire in a variety of colors and in various lengths of rolls. Other than being able to reach from one point to the other, the important part of any primary wire is the thickness, which is referred

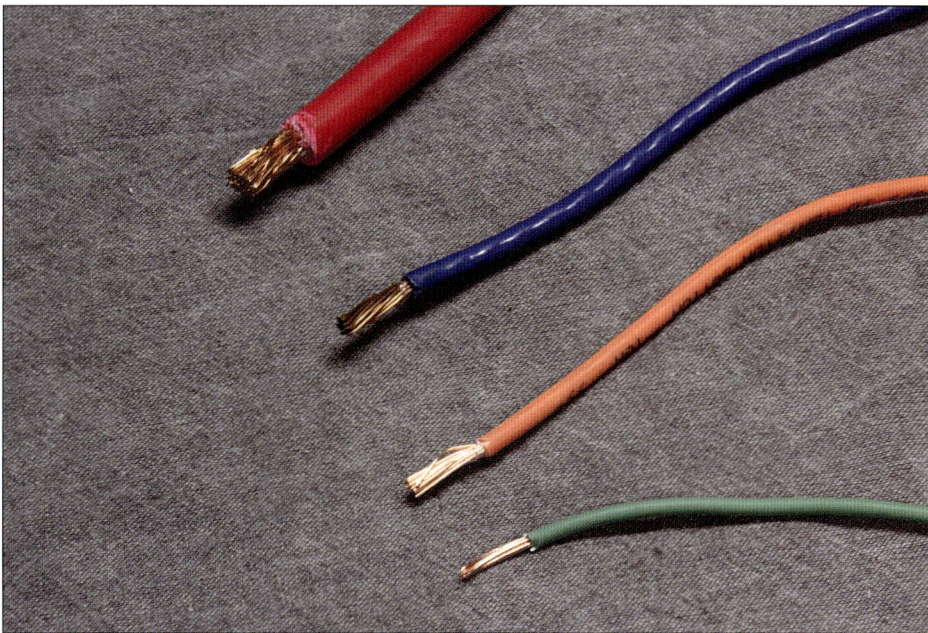

The various gauges (thickness) of wire is shown. From top to bottom, there is a 6-gauge red wire, a 10-gauge blue wire, a 12-gauge orange wire, and a 14-gauge green wire. The smaller the gauge number (the bigger the wire), the more strands of copper are in the wire.

to as gauge, or "gage." For automotive wiring, common gauges are between 2 and 22. In the United States, electrical wire is listed in standardized American wire gauge (AWG).

Contrary to conventional wisdom, 2-gauge wire is large and 22-gauge wire is small. Simply put, the larger the gauge number, the smaller the wire.

Table 1-1: Wire Size and Capacity	
Wire Size (AWG)	**Current Capacity (Amps)**
4	59.626
8	18.696
10	14.834
12	9.327
14	5.870
18	2.320
22	0.914

The smaller the wire, the greater the resistance (Ω) in the wire. According to Ohm's Law, the greater resistance, the less capacity current (amps) the wire can safely carry. For example, to determine the correct size of wire to use in a 12-volt system with an accessory that requires 10 amps, use the following equation:

$$\text{Resistance } (\Omega) =$$
$$\text{Voltage (V)} \div \text{Current (A)}$$

$$\text{Resistance } (\Omega) = 12 \div 10 = 1.20 \text{ Ohms}$$

Table 1-1 shows that 1.20 Ohms falls between 22 gauge and 18 gauge. To prevent the wire from being overloaded and potentially burning, use the larger of the two wires. In this case, use 18-gauge wire.

To further demonstrate this, the wire used between the truck's battery and starter or to the chassis ground is most likely a 2-gauge wire. To power the lights of the instrument panel, a 22-gauge wire would typically be used. The more amps that run through an electrical circuit, the larger the wire must be.

The overall length of wires in the circuit is also a factor in the required size of the wire. As the length of the wires increases, the wire size must also increase. For the most part, this additional length will not come into play

in a vintage pickup. However, wire length may be an issue if the battery is relocated to the extreme rear of the truck instead of being in the engine compartment (close to the starter). Still, since a 2-gauge wire will be used, that should not be a problem. Just remember that in any situation where you are sizing a wire, a bigger wire is safer than a smaller wire.

Why You Should Rewire a Vintage Pickup

To rewire a truck from scratch, it is necessary to accurately determine the current load on each wire. Then, before selecting the size of the wire, determine the length of wire necessary to run from the fuse panel through the entire circuit. While this would be elementary to an electrical engineer, it would be very time-consuming for someone who plans to rewire a vintage truck.

Fortunately, a very strong aftermarket has embraced the fact that these trucks are very popular. That has allowed them to justify the expense of engineering wiring kits that make the life of the hobbyist significantly easier. This convenience does come with an expense, but it is minimal when compared to a new engine, a paint job, or even a new set of wheels and tires. In addition, with bad wiring being a safety issue, buying a manufactured wiring harness may actually save you money.

Whether the truck is a bare-bones stocker or if it has been updated with power windows, doors, and a killer stereo, its electrical needs are met by electrical current passing through multistrand copper wire. Most of these vintage trucks are more than 25 years old, and some are pushing 70 years.

Many of these trucks are still on the road with their original wiring,

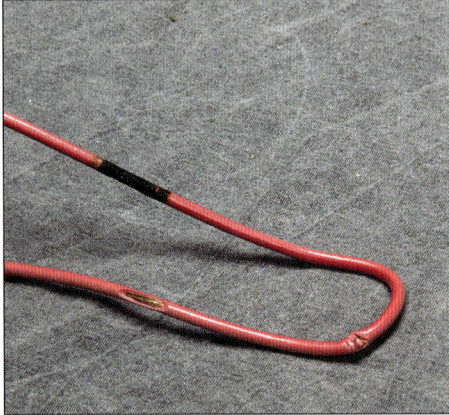

This piece of wire has common damage that is cause for replacement. On the lower side is an example of where the protective insulation has been scraped off. This could be due to not using a rubber grommet when passing through sheet metal. The wire also has a spot that indicates that it has been pinched and a black spot where it has been burned.

The type of wire that was originally installed in these trucks on the assembly line is stiff and holds its shape after being bent. As it gets older, it becomes somewhat brittle.

Newer wire, whether purchased at an auto parts store or as part of a wiring kit, is flexible. This makes it less brittle and less likely to crack or break any of the strands of copper inside the insulation.

but they could probably all benefit from new wiring. Old wires can become brittle, allowing them to crack and/or break. They may have become abraded by rubbing on a metal surface or by passing through a metal surface that is no longer protected by a rubber grommet. Either of these situations could cause an electrical short that could leave you stranded alongside the road. In some situations, it could leave you stranded alongside the road as your truck burns. My intent is not to scare anyone but merely open your eyes to reality.

Use XL-Series Wire

When rewiring part or all of a truck, use XL-series wire rather than GPT-series wire. The XL-series wire has a cross-linked (thermoset) polyolefin insulation. This wire has a high melting point and stays flexible during its life. The high melting point is especially important in underhood applications or any time that wires are near the exhaust. Remaining flexible simply makes the wire easier to work with and less likely to break when a maintenance procedure may necessitate that the wiring be moved out of the way.

The GPT-series wire is older and has thermoplastic insulation. This wire has a very low melting point and gets stiff and brittle as it ages.

Unlike Romex wire, which is used in residential wiring (a solid piece of copper wire about 1/8-inch in diameter wrapped in insulation), primary wire consists of several small strands of copper wire wrapped in insulation. More strands provide more surface area on which the current can flow. This combination of thin wires and thin insulation is far superior to the original wire that was thicker. The wire is less brittle and will be less likely to cause a bulge beneath carpet or upholstery.

Wire Color

TECH TIP

Always document the color and the size of the wire for every wire in the vehicle. ∎

Primary wire is available in a wide variety of colors at local auto parts stores or other retail outlets. An even wider variety of colors and wires with various color stripes are available to original equipment manufacturers (OEMs) and aftermarket suppliers. OEMs typically have their own color codes for the vehicles that they manufacture. Manufacturers of vehicle-specific wiring kits typically follow the OEM color codes. However, many manufacturers of universal aftermarket wiring kits seem to follow the GM color codes.

The electric current does not care what color the wire is as long as the wire is big enough to handle the current load without causing a fire. When creating your own wiring system, use whatever colors you want, but be sure to document which size of wire is in each color. Not having documentation of the wiring color codes will make troubleshooting and repair a nightmare, especially alongside a deserted highway in the dark.

Aftermarket wiring systems typically have plenty of wire for each circuit that the kit supports. In most cases, you will route the wire from the fuse panel to its destination and then cut off the excess wire. The only situ-

Regardless of the gauge of the wire, automotive wiring consists of several strands of copper wire. These strands are covered with a non-conductive insulation material.

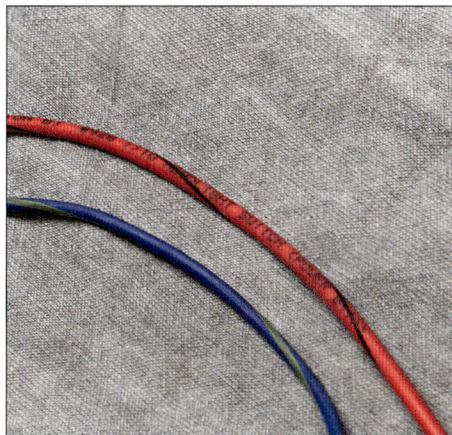

To further differentiate wires, a stripe of a different color is often included on the wire's insulation. This is very common on universal accessories that may have the same color as existing wires on the vehicle.

ation where this is not true is in the case of a stretched limousine.

For wiring any accessories that are not included in the kit, there will probably be enough wire cut off from another circuit. For this reason, hang on to any scrap wire until the project has been completed. Additional wire in rolls up to about 25 or 30 feet long is also available at auto parts stores.

The wires in many aftermarket wiring kits include printing on the insulation that identifies the circuit to which the wire applies. This information may be a wire number, what the wire connects to, or other pertinent information.

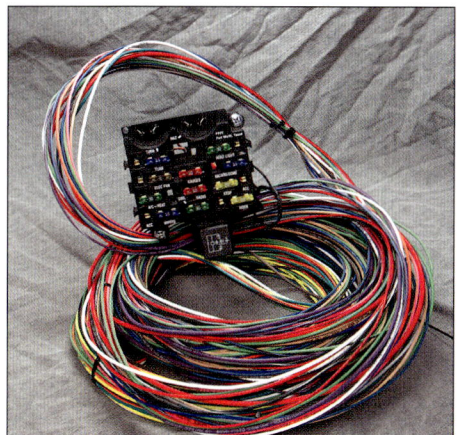

In most (if not all) vehicle-specific wiring kits, the wires are already connected to the fuse panel. Mount the fuse panel, route the wires to where they terminate, cut the wires to the appropriate length, apply the appropriate connector, and make the connection.

If you choose to go into the hobby or business of wiring vehicles on a regular basis, much longer spools of wire are available through wholesale outlets. These sources also supply other electrical components, such as connectors, switches, and fuses, at a more economical price.

Fuses and Fuse Panels

Any electric current generates heat. When it is in the form of a lightning bolt, the heat is not felt, as that heat is not confined. However, when that current is confined within a wire, the amount of heat generated can potentially cause a fire if the wire is too small. Safety devices, such as fuses, fusible links, diodes, and circuit breakers, can be installed within a circuit to prevent overheating. Each of these devices is designed for certain situations and conditions.

Fuses are available in different types, but regardless of size or type, they typically have a strip of metal or wire contained within them. The amperage rating of the fuse determines the size of the metal or wire within the fuse. When a fuse is rated for 5 amps, the wire inside the fuse will break when more than 5 amps are transmitted through the circuit. This breaks the circuit, effectively shutting down that circuit and any accessories that are powered by that circuit. A 20-amp fuse has a larger wire or a strip of metal inside of it than a 5-amp fuse has. However, in similar fashion, when more than 20 amps are sent through the fuse, the metal breaks, shutting down the circuit.

The fuse's rating is always printed on the outside of the fuse. The rating number is usually easy to find on the newer blade-type fuses but can be difficult to see or read on the old glass tube-type fuses. With fuses, the larger the number, the more current the fuse can withstand before it breaks the circuit.

All circuits should be protected by the required or recommended fuse size. For example, say that the total amperage required for a particular circuit is 12 amps. From Table 1-1 on page 7, this requires a 10-gauge

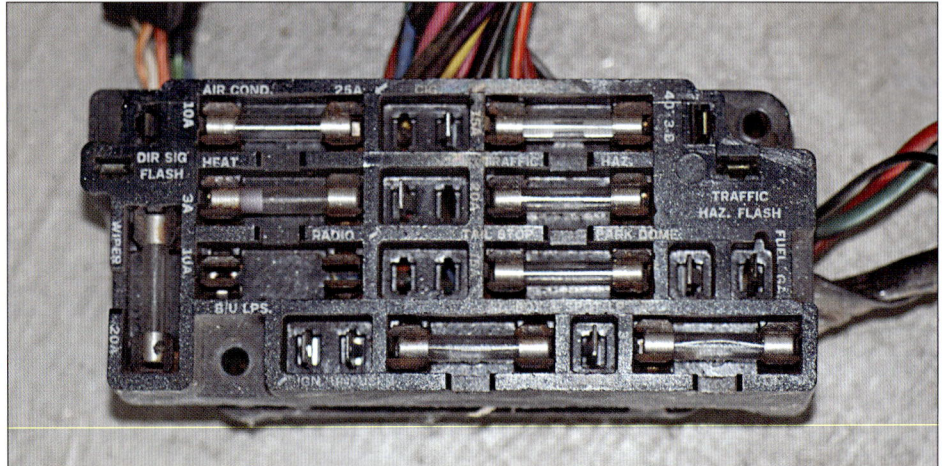

Most original fuse panels for these vintage trucks used glass fuses. Each space for a fuse had a contact at each end to work with the design of the fuse. Spade connectors were also available to connect auxiliary wires. The size of the fuse is typically stamped in the metal cap of the fuse and is often difficult to read.

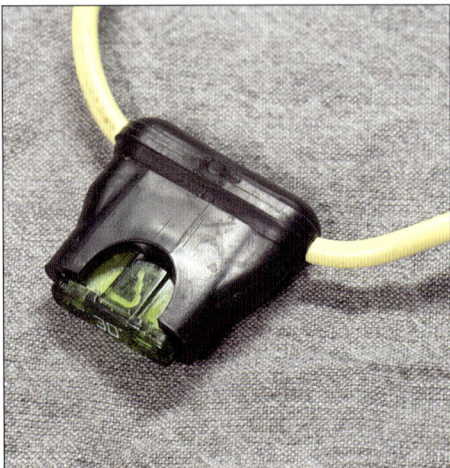

The metal filament (a thin Z-shaped wire) is visible inside the little window of this blade-type fuse. If too much current passes through this fuse, the filament will break, shutting down all current through the circuit.

Blade-type fuses push into a slot in the fuse panel. Blade fuses are color coded to distinguish their size, and their amp rating is clearly stamped on the end. The horseshoe filament between the two blades breaks when the fuse blows.

wire. This circuit must be protected by a 15-amp fuse. If you would use a 10-amp fuse instead, the fuse would blow under normal operation, even though the circuit would have been operating correctly. If you would use a 20-amp fuse, the wire could potentially burn before the fuse blows.

Fuses should be replaced only with fuses of the same amp rating. For these reasons, it is always a good idea to carry several fuses (with at least one for every size of fuse in the truck) at all times.

Most (if not all) of the trucks that this book pertains to were originally equipped with glass fuses. They are roughly a 1/4 inch in diameter and are available in different lengths and amp ratings. Glass fuses are comprised of a glass tube with a metal cap on each end to make contact with the fuse panel. These metal caps are a design flaw, as rust could form on them. Even though the fuse did not blow, this can cause problems that are difficult to diagnose.

Around 1980, auto manufacturers began using blade-type fuses. This type of fuse is made of plastic with two metal blades that fit into the fuse panel. Blade-type fuses are more durable than their glass counterparts. Operationally, blade-type fuses work the same as glass fuses.

Fuse panels are designed for either glass fuses or one of the three sizes of blade-type fuses: Mini ATC, ATC, or Maxi. Glass fuses cannot be used in a blade-type fuse panel, and blade-type fuses cannot be used in a glass-type fuse panel. In addition, the three different blade-type fuses are not interchangeable with a fuse panel of a different size.

Whenever you are rewiring a vehicle, either type of fuse panel can be used—as long as the appropriate fuses

are used. While there may be exceptions, most aftermarket wiring kits use blade-type fuses and fuse panels.

Regardless of the type of fuse, the fuses plug into a fuse panel, which serves as a central point for all wiring in a truck. Most fuse panels have

some type of identification for each circuit. For vehicle-specific wiring kits, the panel is commonly labeled with the name of the circuit, such as "A/C-Heat," "Gauges," or "Horn." The wires are also already connected to the fuse panel. Any wires for circuits

This is the universal Wiremaster Power Panel II from Affordable Street Rods, which features 24 circuits, including a few for whatever you want them to be. Affordable Street Rods also offers the Wiremaster Power Panel, which includes 32 circuits, including power windows, power doors, and an electric fuel pump. The complete process of wiring of my 1955 Chevy pickup using this kit is documented in this book.

This is the Painless Wiring 21-circuit fuse panel for 1967–1972 GM pickups, and it is mounted in my 1970 Chevy Stepside. The complete process of rewiring of this truck is documented in this book.

that you do not use must be tied up and out of the way (for possible future use) or cut off (never to be used again).

When choosing to keep any wires that are not connected, those wires should be capped off with a butt connector. This ensures that no bare wires make contact with anything when the fuse panel is energized.

Fuse panels for universal applications sometimes do not have any wires connected to them. They do have the fuses in place and the appropriate internal wiring to the predetermined terminals. These fuse panels typically number each terminal and assign specific terminals to specific circuits. Each wire comes pre-crimped with a forked terminal that is secured in place on the terminal block with a screw.

The instructions for this type of kit tell the installer which circuit terminal #1 provides power to, as well as what color and size of wire connects to it. An advantage of this type of wiring kit is that a truck can be wired sufficiently for it to run and have the necessary lighting. Other accessories, such as a stereo, air conditioning, or power windows could be added later without the wires being in the way right now.

Regardless of which type of wiring kit and fuse panel is chosen, installation is fairly easy. It includes mounting the fuse panel, running the wires to their destination, cutting the wires to the appropriate length, crimping on the correct connector, and connecting to the accessory.

Several aftermarket wiring kits are available, including vehicle-specific kits or those that are more universal in design. Each type has its pros and cons. Most kits are available with about 21 circuits or with about 28 circuits. The kits with 21 circuits cover all of the necessities, while the 28-circuit

kits include power windows, power doors, and other circuits that are for modern conveniences or creature comforts.

While there may be some exceptions, using an electric fuel pump typically requires the panel with more circuits. However, if you know that you are never going to use power doors and power windows, you could service the electric fuel pump with an auxiliary fuse panel if desired. Going this route probably will not save you any money, but if the basic wiring is already installed and you later decide to run an electric fuel pump, this allows an option other than rewiring the entire truck.

Flashers

Flashers are used to generate the flashing capability for the turn signals and hazard flashers. The flasher begins its operating cycle when the turn signal or hazard flasher is switched on, causing electrical current to begin passing through the flasher. This causes the resistance wire to heat up, making electrical contact with the output side of the flasher. This provides power to the turn-signal switch and on to the turn-signal lights, causing the lights to illuminate.

As this contact is made, there is no longer any resistance, so the wire begins to cool. As the resistance wire cools, it loses electrical contact with the switch, causing the light to turn off. When there is no contact, resistance begins to build and heats the resistance wire, restarting the process. This flashing process continues until the turn-signal or hazard switch is turned off.

Fusible Links

Fusible links perform the same basic task that fuses do but in a dif-

ferent manner and for different situations. Instead of being plugged into the fuse panel, a fusible link is installed inline. This allows a fusible link to be installed almost anywhere simply by cutting the wire in the desired circuit and splicing the fusible link into place by using two butt connectors.

Fusible links are available in various sizes. The fusible link itself consists of wire that is typically four sizes smaller than the circuit that it is used in and is surrounded by non-flammable insulation. Just like the wire within a fuse, the wire within the fusible link melts or breaks when too much current passes through it. When the wire breaks, the flow of current is stopped.

Fusible links are typically found in heavy load situations. This situation calls for larger wire, such as the 8- or 10-gauge wire that provides power to the starter solenoid.

Whenever a fuse or a fusible link

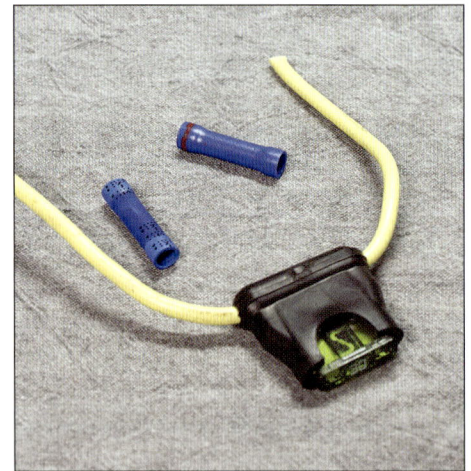

A fusible link can be thought of as an inline fuse. To install one, strip each end of the wire and crimp on an appropriately sized butt connector to each end. Cut the wire where you want to install the fusible link, strip each end of that wire, and crimp the fusible link in place.

does its intended job and shuts down a circuit (rather than allowing a fire to start), the situation should be resolved sooner than later. However, fuses usually do not blow while in the spacious and well-lit confines of a garage. Therefore, the issue may not be diagnosed and resolved immediately.

When the circuit is protected by a fuse, the situation may not be as dire as you first thought. If the accessory that was powered by the blown circuit is merely a creature comfort, fixing it can probably wait until you get back home. However, if the circuit is needed to get back home and you do not have any new fuses with you, you may be able to find a fuse of the same size in a non-essential circuit that you can move to the essential circuit. Just remember that it is critical to use a fuse of the same size as the one being replaced. If the fuse has a smaller rating than needed, it will simply blow out again. If the fuse has a larger rating than needed, you will not be protected.

While there may be situations where a fusible link would be ideal, be careful where you install them. Installing a fusible link requires a new fusible link, two butt connectors, and the tools to strip wire and to crimp on the two butt connectors. Access to the wire on which the fusible link is installed is also needed. If you are broken down along the side of the highway, you may not be able to meet all those requirements.

Diodes

Diodes are used to prevent spikes in voltage and to isolate current. Working as a one-way valve, diodes allow electric current to flow only one way. Electrical current flows from the anode end toward the cathode end (designated by a white stripe)

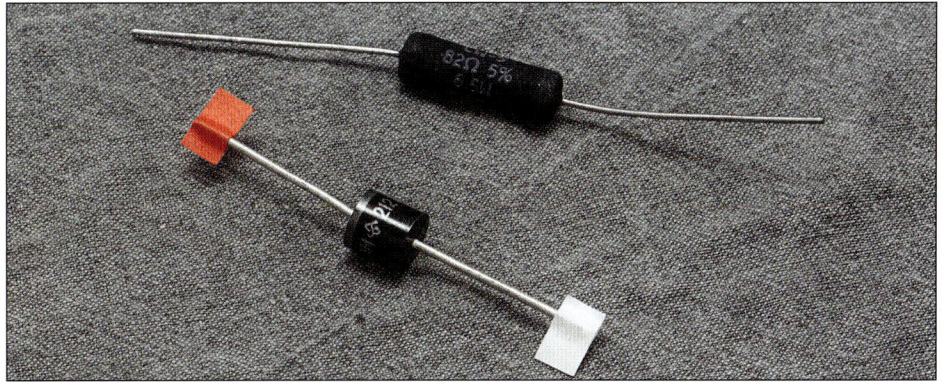

Diodes serve as a one-way valve to prevent electrical current from flowing backward and damaging a circuit during a voltage spike. All diodes have a stripe on the cathode end. Verify that the anode end (no stripe) is connected to the wire that is providing electrical current and that the cathode end is connected to the wire that is to receive electrical current. On the diode in the foreground, current will flow from the end with the white tag toward the end with the red tag. On the diode in the background, current will flow in the opposite direction.

and, therefore, must be installed correctly.

A common application for a diode is in the wiring for a GM alternator. Whenever residual current exists in a circuit when power is shut off, a diode prevents a power surge from flowing backward, which would damage the circuit.

Circuit Breakers

Circuit breakers can be thought of as a momentary fuse because they stop current flow only temporarily. Much like a fuse, the contacts are connected by a metal strip, but it does not break. Instead, the metal strip changes shape when it gets hot, breaking the electrical connection. When the metal strip cools, it returns to its original shape, and electric current is restored within the circuit.

There are two types of circuit breakers: automatic (auto) resetting or manual resetting. The auto resetting type is typically used in circuits that require high current, such as headlights, fog lights, power win-

dows, and power seats. The manual resetting type is commonly found only in circuits that power safety or security devices because they must be pushed back into place when they are tripped. This can include a system

A circuit breaker is typically placed in line between the positive terminal of the battery and the fuse panel. If anything in the electrical system goes awry, this temporarily shuts down electrical current to the fuse panel until it is safe to resume.

that shuts off an electric fuel pump in the case of an impact. It can also be used in anti-theft devices.

Relays

There are multiple circuits in automobiles that require a large amount of electrical current for a short period of time. Common examples are headlights, fog lights, electric fans, and a hydraulic brake-light switch. These accessories require continuous electric current to operate, but the demand for significantly higher current is for a relatively short period of time when they are turned on initially. It is not necessary or even desired to send that large amount of current through the entire circuit (even for just a short time).

Relays and solenoids are devices that are used to control the flow of electrical current. They perform similar tasks but do them differently. Therefore, there are some situations that call for a relay, while other situations call for a solenoid.

Relays are simply low-current devices that are used to control a high-current accessory. When a large amount of current is passed through a normal switch, it overloads the circuit. This typically results in a switch being destroyed or a fire started. Using a relay allows for passing lots of current to an accessory without risk to the circuit. Any time that an electrical circuit requires 10 amps or more, a relay should be used to protect the circuit.

Electrical relays contain two circuits. One circuit carries the required current to the powered device and the second circuit switches the flow of that current on and off. As a relatively low current from the battery is supplied to the relay, it throws the switch

Most automotive wiring relays are a cube that is approximately 1 inch in all dimensions with four or five spade terminals. The printing on the relay indicates how to wire it.

within the relay to provide the high current directly to the powered device without going through the complete wiring harness.

An electrical relay can be thought of as an electromagnetic switch. When power is applied to a relay, it switches to direct electrical current to a device. When power is removed from the relay, it prevents electrical current from flowing to the device.

Since the relay is simply a type of switch, it can be a single pole, single throw (SPST) or a single pole, double throw (SPDT). An SPST type of relay would be used to turn an accessory on or off. An SPDT type of relay would be used to provide power all the time to one device or another, such as in a dimmer switch.

Automotive electrical relays typically have a number printed near each terminal, along with a schematic printed on the side. An SPST relay has four terminals (labeled 85, 86, 30, and 87). An SPDT relay has five terminals (labeled 85, 86, 30, 87, and 87a).

When wiring a relay, power connects to terminals 85 and 30. When a switch is used in the circuit, the wire from the switch connects to terminal 85. Connect a wire from terminal 87 (which is now hot) to the power input side of the accessory that is being powered. Connect a ground wire to terminal 86 of the relay.

Table 1-2: Relay Terminal and Connection		
Relay Terminal	**Connection**	**Flow through Relay**
85*	Coil Input (+12 VDC)	Power In
86*	Coil Input (to Ground)	Ground
30	Common	Power In (Trigger)
87	Normally Open	Power Out
87a	Normally Closed	Power Out

*Terminals 85 and 86 can be interchanged.

When working with relays, the relay does not care which way the electricity is flowing. Therefore, terminals 86 and 85 can be interchanged with each other and terminals 87 and 30 can be interchanged with each other. Throughout this book and other sources, schematics may reflect this.

12-Volt Activated Relay

When a relay is required for a high-amperage component that must run continuously, the 12-volt power source to the relay must be from an ignition-switched, 12-volt wire to receive power whenever the ignition is in the on position. It must not be from a battery constant-hot source.

When a relay is required whether the ignition is in the on position or not, a switch can be installed between the relay and a constant battery source. This allows the high-amperage component to be turned on or off, regardless of the position of the ignition switch.

Ground-Activated Relay

The opposite of this is a ground-activated relay, which uses an uninterrupted power supply to provide 12 volts from a battery constant

hot or a switched circuit. The ground wire is switched, allowing the component to function whenever a ground source is provided. A common example is the horn relay. Pressing the horn activation button provides the ground, causing the horn to sound.

Solenoids

Solenoids are not used to direct the flow of electrical current but are used to move an object via an electromagnetic field. Common examples in contemporary vehicles are power door and trunk locks. Whenever the remote key fob is pressed to lock or unlock the doors, the click that you hear is from the movement of the solenoid. Of course, a solenoid is commonly used in the starting system of most pickup trucks.

Regardless of the solenoid's use, it includes a coil of wire around a

metallic armature. A magnetic field is created when power is applied to the coil. The armature is situated with a stop at the end in a way to limit its movement in a back-and-forth direction. The solenoid is wired so that the stop will act as a north pole and the armature as a south pole when power is applied, attracting both components together.

As both components are pulled together, the electrical terminals make contact to complete the electrical circuit. When power is removed, there is no magnetic attraction, causing the armature to move in the opposite direction, breaking the electrical circuit.

Ground

The return path to ground is as important as the incoming power to an electrical component. When the

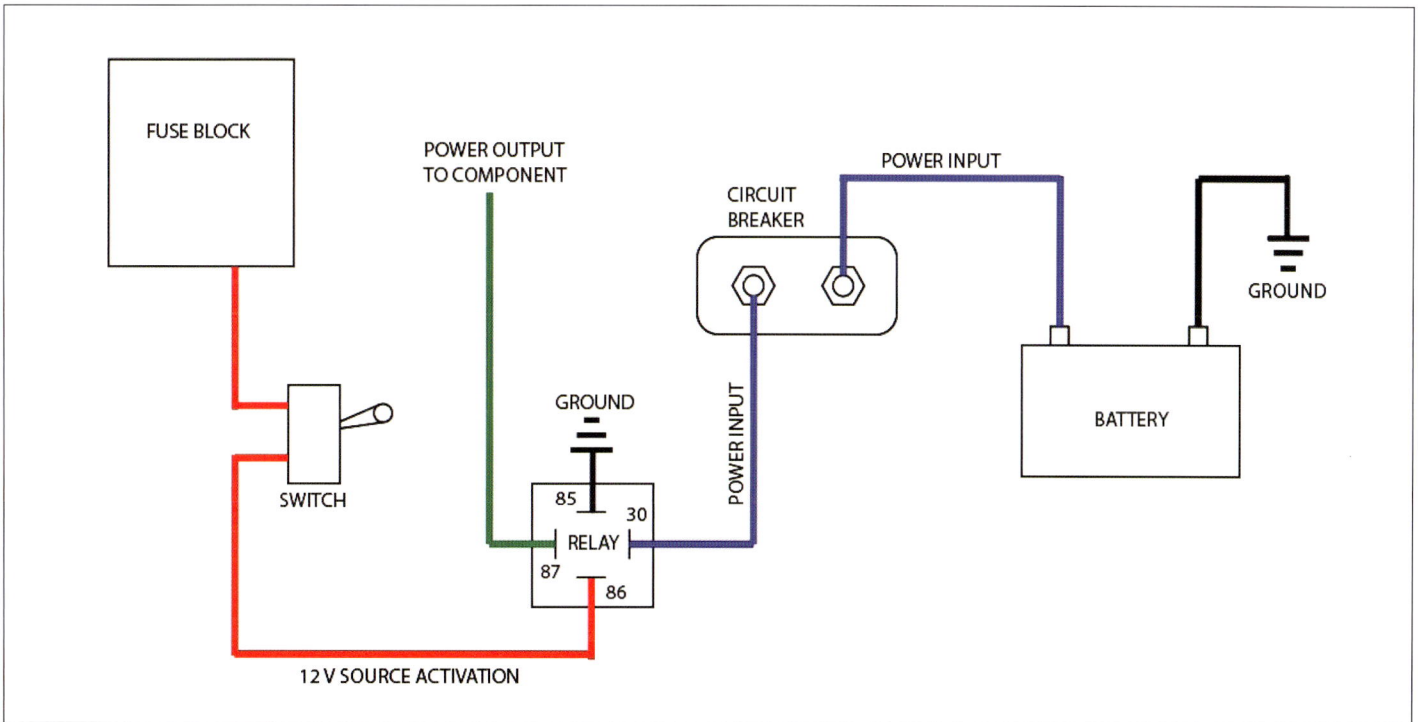

A 12-volt-activated relay is used to provide electrical current to a high-amperage device continuously whenever the ignition switch is in the on position and the engine is running. Examples that use a 12-volt-activated relay include fog lights, a snowplow blade, or a winch.

The GM starter solenoid typically sits atop the starter and is the site for electrical connections. Electrical power causes the solenoid to begin spinning, which then causes the starter motor to turn.

electrical component does not have adequate ground, it will not work, or, worse yet, it will work sporadically. The first two things to check when attempting to diagnose an electrical problem is to verify that it has power and that it has good ground. When a circuit is not working, there is a distinct possibility that it is not getting power. However, when it is not working properly, it is most likely a ground issue.

Vintage pickup trucks, as well as their passenger-carrying counterparts, all came from the factory with the chassis serving as the vehicle's starter circuit ground. This was done by running a battery cable between the negative terminal of the battery and a location on the chassis. As long as the connections were kept tight and no rust formed or dirt and grease collected, this worked pretty well.

However, it does not take long for the underside of a pickup truck to be contaminated, reducing the integrity of the ground in the process.

A better method to provide good ground is to run a battery cable between the negative terminal of the battery and a bolt between the engine block and transmission. The engine and transmission are not as susceptible to rust as the truck's frame.

To provide an adequate ground for the chassis, run a 6- or 8-gauge ground wire between the chassis and engine block. With the chassis grounded, a 10-gauge ground wire between each accessory and the chassis should be sufficient.

For pickup trucks that are now between 40 and 70 years old and had few electronics, this system of providing adequate ground worked well. With all of the electronic conveniences found in today's vehicles,

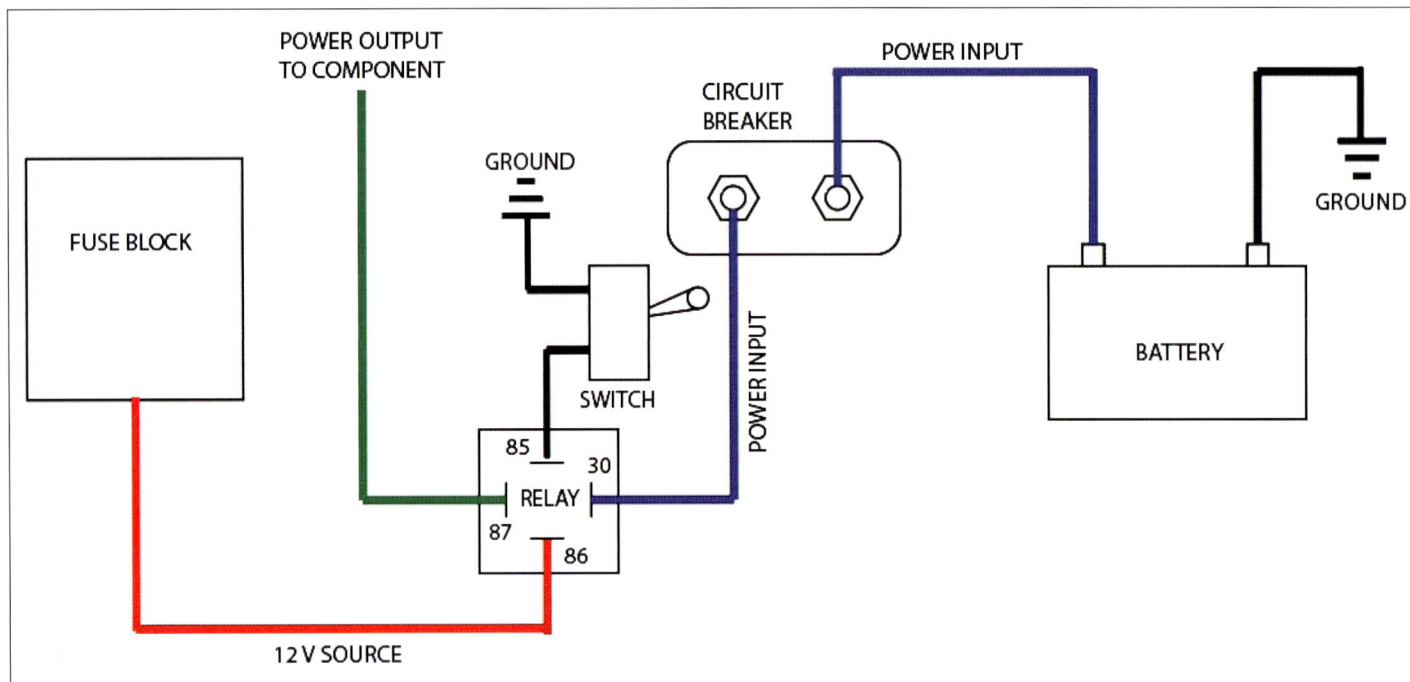

A ground-activated relay is used whenever the component always has power (regardless of the position of the ignition switch). Grounding the circuit is what closes the circuit and allows the component to operate. Examples that use a ground-activated relay include the horn, interior courtesy lights, and some power windows or door locks.

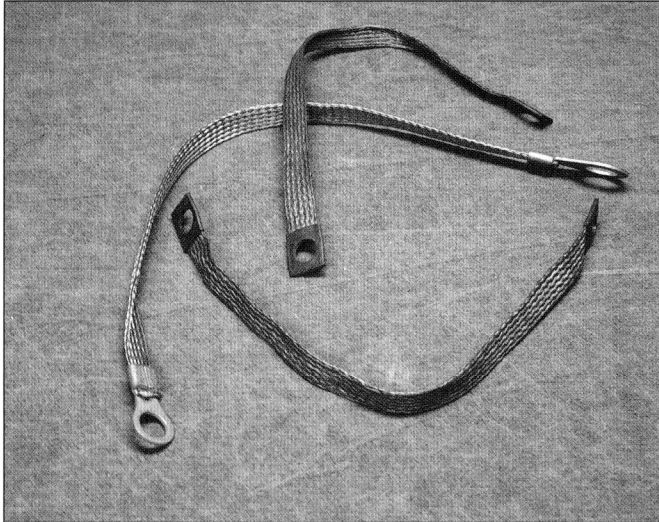

Ground straps, such as these, are typically used between an engine/transmission bolt and the truck's frame to ground the frame. They can be used in other locations as well. They are available in various lengths and with holes for a various size of bolts.

proper ground is more important than ever. Newer methods of grounding are provided in the wiring installations elsewhere in this book.

Required Tools

Unlike an automobile mechanic, an auto body technician, an auto painter, or even an auto upholsterer, wiring a car or truck does not require much expensive specialized equipment. Working on newer vehicles requires additional equipment, but for vintage trucks and hot rods, the tools are pretty basic.

A pair of universal electrical pliers that cut and strip wire and crimp-on connectors can be found for about $10. Screwdrivers and a socket set are also needed, but if you are reading this book, you probably already have those tools. While they are not absolutely necessary, a test light, multimeter, and battery charger will come in handy when troubleshooting and doing diagnostic work.

Wire Cutters

Wire cutters are used for cutting the electrical wire to length. While universal electrical pliers work to cut wire, they are cheap and become dull quickly. A good pair of diagonal side cutters last considerably longer and will make your life easier. You will cut a lot of wire when rewiring a vintage truck.

Diagonal side cutters are available in different sizes, and 8-inch pliers are pretty common and applicable for most wire-cutting tasks. This size is not too big for any automotive wire but is still adequate for cutting 2-gauge wire used for connecting the battery to the starter. Craftsman and Kobalt offer good diagonal side cutters.

Wire Strippers

Wire strippers are used for cutting the insulation from a wire before installing an electrical connector. A convenient aspect about universal electrical pliers is that the stripper portion is marked for the appropriate wire size so that only the insulation is stripped off. This is important so that none of the stranded wire that actually carries the current is broken. Find a pair that you like and fits in your hand nicely. You will be stripping lots of wire.

Wire Crimpers

Wire crimpers are for attaching the solderless connector onto the wire after the insulation has been stripped off. Some wire strippers also double as crimpers. It is important to use a pair that crimps the connector adequately but not too much. If a connector is crimped too much, it can damage the connection. Ratcheting wire crimpers help to make consistent crimps but are a bit more expensive. When having trouble making correct crimps, try using ratcheting-type crimpers.

Connectors

While some soldering is still done in automotive wiring, crimp-on connectors are much more common. For most people, crimp-on connectors are easier to use than a soldering iron. They are also easier to use for roadside repair when necessary. With a variety of connectors and a pair of universal electrical pliers in your glove box or stashed under the seat, almost any emergency repair that is needed can be made. A soldering iron probably won't be in anyone's tool bag in their truck. Even if you brought one, where would you plug it in?

Crimp-on, or solderless, connectors connect wires in a variety of situations. They can be used for a permanent connection or for a removable connection. They can be used to connect two wires to one wire. There are non-insulated and insulated crimp-on terminals.

The insulated connectors are color coded so they can be easily associated with the correct wire sizes. Remember that the smaller the wire gauge number, the larger the wire. For large wire (gauges 6 through 10), use yellow connectors. For medium wire (gauges 12 through 16), use blue connectors. For small wire (gauges 18 through 22), use red connectors. While you are rewiring a vintage pickup truck, you will begin to

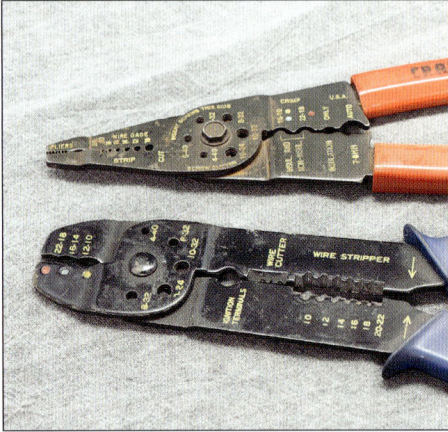

Either of these universal electrical pliers can be used to perform almost any wiring task, including cutting, stripping, or crimping wire. They are not expensive and can be found at automotive parts stores, hardware stores, or even some convenience stores. However, they are not of any use if you cannot find them when they are needed, so buy a pair and stash them in the truck.

These diagonal wire cutters are nearly identical (both are Craftsman), except the pair on the left is bent slightly. In some instances, that little bend is just enough to access a wire that cannot be reached with the straight pair.

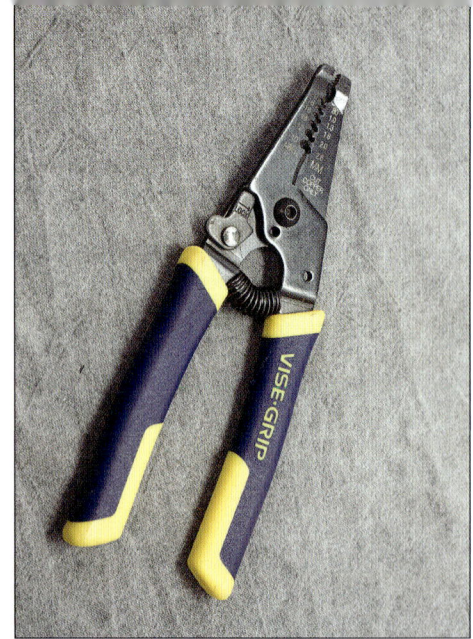

While rewiring a vehicle, many wires need to be stripped. Find a pair of wire strippers that are comfortable in your hand. Unlock the pliers by flipping the lever down, slide the wire into the appropriate notch (based on the wire gauge), close the pliers, and strip off the wire's insulation by sliding the pliers toward the end of the wire.

These are ratcheting crimpers, which apply the correct amount of pressure to crimp the connector each time they are used. Providing a correct and consistent crimp is important.

These are non-insulated ring terminals. All terminals (insulated or not) have a split in the metal part of the connector. When crimping any connector, ensure that the split is facing the groove of the crimping pliers. When using non-insulated connectors, use shrink-wrap tubing on the connector.

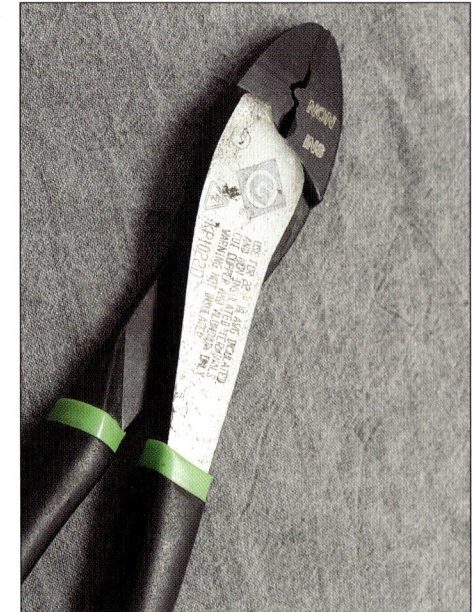

These Greenlee crimping pliers are a delight to use. They can crimp insulated and non-insulated terminals. Place the connector over the wire and in the appropriate notch and squeeze the handles together to make the crimp.

remember this. The appropriate wire size is typically shown on any package of wire connectors, so as long as you know which wire gauge you are working with, you do not necessarily need to commit this to memory.

Wires used for battery cables (as well as any other use) that are gauges 2 through 4 commonly use a much larger red connector. The size of these connectors is significantly larger than those for 18- through 22-gauge wire, so there is no real concern of anyone using the wrong red connector.

To crimp the larger connectors usually requires a bench-mounted crimper that operates similarly to a bench vise. When it is time to replace battery cables, new ones can be purchased at an auto parts store. However, if they do not have pre-crimped wires in the length that is needed, they will probably be able to sell the wire and the connectors and then crimp them together. Any auto parts store that is worthy of your business will do this for no additional cost.

To install a crimp-on connector, begin by cutting the wire to the proper length. Slide a length of heat-shrink tubing over the end of the wire and push it out of the way. Use wire strip-pers to remove 1/4 inch of the insulation from the end of the wire. Slide the wire into the crimp-on connector so that the exposed portion of wire is within the connector. Place the wire and the connector between the jaws of the wire crimper. The connectors have a split running lengthwise in them.

When crimping the connector, ensure that the split is in the grooved side of the crimper. Squeeze the crimpers together to secure the connector. After removing the wire and connector from the crimping pliers, give the connector a slight tug to ensure that it is securely crimped in place.

For non-insulated terminals, slide heat-shrink tubing into place over the shank of the connector. Using a heat gun, heat the heat-shrink tubing until it shrinks around the connector. While heat-shrink tubing is required to insulate the connection on non-insulated terminals, it is not required on insulated terminals.

Factory-style terminals are slightly different, as they have two terminal straps. Use wire strippers to remove 1/4 inch of the insulation from the end of the wire. Slide the wire into the crimp-on connector so that the exposed portion of wire is within the connector. Crimp the first strap (the one closest to the end of the wire) onto the copper wire strands

It is important to use the correct size of connector or terminal when wiring. If the connector is too large for the wires, it may not crimp down tight enough and the connection will not last. If the connector or terminal is too small, the wire will not fit properly.

These are ring connectors for 1- or 0-gauge wire. For automotive use, this size of wire is used for the battery cables where they connect to the starter or a chassis ground. The terminals on the other end of the battery cables must match the specific battery (with top posts or side posts).

Connectors (insulated and non-insulated) are available in various configurations and for various sizes of wire. Fork connectors are designed to slide around a screw that secures the wire to the terminal. These can be connected or disconnected by loosening the screw, inserting the form connector, and tightening the screw. Male and female spade connectors can be used in conjunction for use in a connection that can be disconnected.

Properly Crimping Electrical Connectors onto Wires

1 On a non-insulated connector, it is easier to get a better look at the split that is formed when the terminal is rolled into a three-dimensional shape.

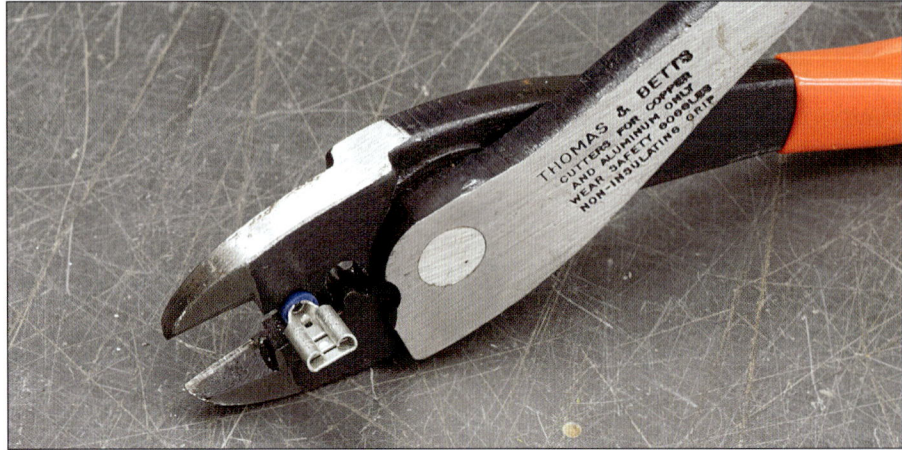

2 Position the connector so that the split is in the groove of the crimper pliers. This places the tongue portion of the crimper pliers so that it pushes the metal of the connector into the wire.

3 Prep the wire by stripping 1/4 inch of insulation from the wire.

4 Insert the stripped end of wire into the connector so that the bare portion of the wire is slightly sticking out the opposite end of the insulation. Ensure that the wire and connector are properly placed into the crimper and squeeze the handle. Remove the connector from the crimper and give the wire a slight tug to verify that the crimp is sufficient.

5 Connectors are available with heat-shrink material already secured to the connector. These are comparably priced to other connectors and eliminate the need to purchase heat-shrink tubing separately.

6 Strip the wire, insert the bare end of the wire into the connector, and crimp it.

7 With the connector properly crimped, use a heat gun to shrink the heat-shrink material. Heat-shrink material minimizes the possibility of moisture getting into the connection, which causes a common electrical failure.

of the wire. Then, crimp the second strap onto the insulation of the wire. Both ends of the metal strap should fold into the wire's insulation, rather than overlap.

Common connectors include butt connectors, ring connectors, fork connectors, push-on terminals (male

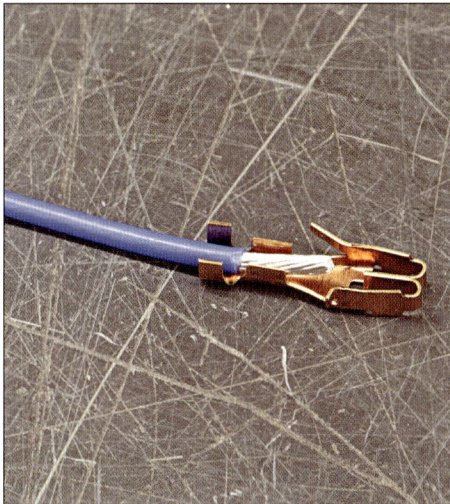

Factory-style terminals require the use of rollover crimping pliers. This requires making two separate crimps. First, crimp the copper part of the connector that secures the bare wire.

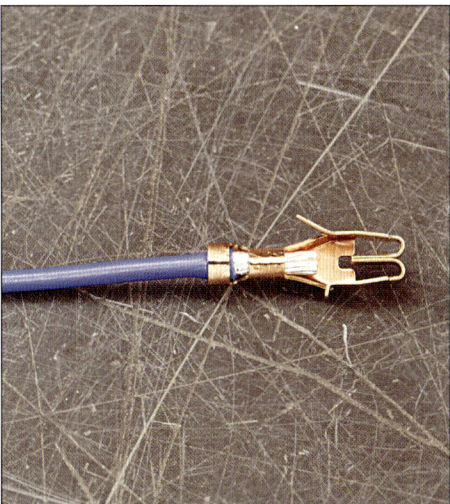

Next, crimp the copper portion of the connector that secures the connector to the insulated portion of the wire.

and female), and bullet connectors (male and female). While these are all designed to connect one wire to a terminal, two wires can be connected to a terminal by using the next larger ring or fork connector.

Butt Connectors

Butt connectors are used to permanently connect two pieces of wire. Examples of this are used in any situation when the electrical device already has wire pigtails connected to it, such as a horn or a third brake light. The wire supplying power to the accessory is crimped into one end of the butt connector. The hot (power) wire pigtail is crimped into the opposite end of the butt connector. The ground wire pigtail is connected to an appropriate ground with an appropriate connector.

Another example of a butt connector is the connection of the three wires included in a headlight plug. The prongs on the back of the head-

These three butt connectors show the colors for the size of wire that they are compatible with. This color code is universal for all automotive electrical connectors. Red connectors are for 18- through 22-gauge wire. Blue connectors are for 12- through 16-gauge wire. Yellow connectors are for 6- through 10-gauge wire.

light fit into the headlight plug, allowing easy removal of the headlight when it must be replaced. However, the headlight plug itself can be connected permanently to the high beam, low beam, and ground wires that come from the dimmer switch.

Although the best practice is to use only one piece of wire between terminals with no splices, butt connectors are used whenever two pieces of wire must be joined to effectively make a piece of wire longer.

Bullet Connectors

Bullet connectors are used very much like butt connectors but allow for a quick disconnect of the circuit. Examples of this are each wire that connects to the gauges to allow for removal of the dash panel for service.

The male portion of a bullet connector is shown in the lower left, and the female portion of the bullet connector is directly to its right. A completed connection is shown at the top. A significant difference between a butt connector and a bullet connector is that the bullet connector can be disconnected when necessary.

Ring connectors must be selected to fit the wire and the screw that secures it to the connection. Select the connector by the color of the insulation for the correct wire size. Then, select the appropriate hole size.

Ring Connectors

Ring connectors are used to provide a permanent connection to a terminal stud but can still be removed without damaging the wiring. Common occurrences of this are where the sender wire connects to the fuel-level sender, the oil-pressure sending unit, and the water-temperature sender. Each of these senders typically has a small stud on them.

A ring connector attached to the wire that runs from the gauge slips over this stud on the sender and is secured in place by a washer and a nut. Another common example is the power wire that is secured to the back of the alternator by a bolt. Requiring a wrench to remove, the connection is secure but easily disconnected when desired.

Push-on Connectors

Push-on connectors allow for easy connection and disconnection to an electrical device. When a push-on connector is securely crimped onto

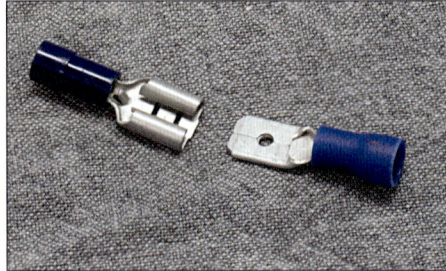

While spade terminals can be used together to connect two wires, they are intended to be used to terminate a wire that connects to an accessory or a fuse panel. When the accessory has a male terminal, use a female connector on the wire. When the fuse panel has a female terminal, use a male connector on the wire.

a wire, it can easily be pushed on or pulled off. These are commonly found on gauges, lighting for gauges, horns, and stoplight switches. As a safety precaution, male and female connections should be designed so that no male connector is energized while that same wire is disconnected.

Quick-Disconnect Plugs

Quick-disconnect plugs are commonly used whenever a collection of wires (albeit separate circuits) may need to be connected or disconnected as a group. A common example of this on GM trucks is where the ignition-switch wires connect on the steering column. Another example is the trailer wiring at the back of the truck where the taillights, brake lights, and electric brakes are connected or disconnected via a plug when the trailer is hitched or unhitched.

Each half of the connector fits with the other half in only one orientation. This is done so that the wires, when installed properly, connect only to the wire they are supposed to. When wiring this type of connector, install a wire on one end of the plug and then install the same wire in the corresponding terminal on the other half of the plug. Then, install both ends of the next wire into the next position on the plug.

Quick-disconnect plugs are used when connecting one group of wires to another group of wires, such as when connecting wires to the steering column for the turn signals, horn, and ignition. Male terminals go into one side of the plug and female terminals go into the other side of the plug.

Creating Weathertight Connections

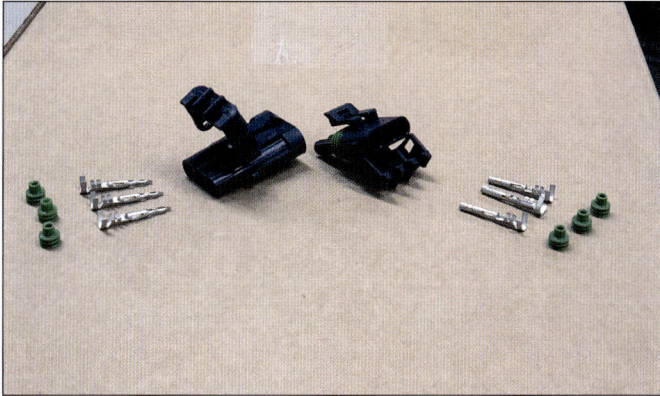

1 This example of a weathertight plug will accommodate three wires. There are two body halves, three male terminals, three female terminals, and six rubber grommets. The grommets are the key to making the connection weathertight.

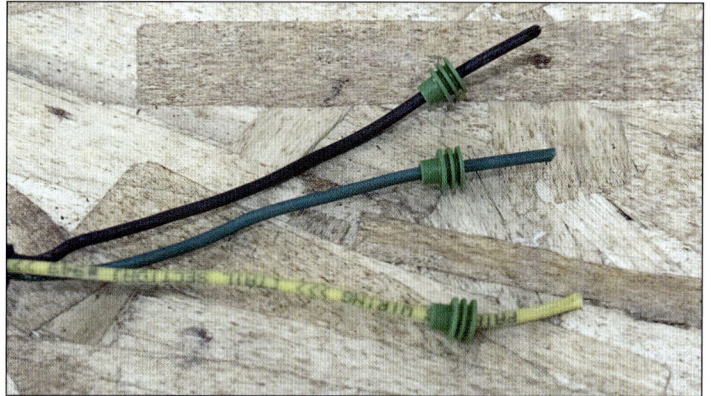

2 With the wires cut to the desired length, slide a rubber grommet over each wire. Orient the grommets so that the flat disc portion is closest to the end of the wire.

3 Strip the end of the wire approximately 3/8 inch and slide the appropriate terminal (male or female) onto the bare part of the wire. The terminal should cover the bare wire. Using rollover crimpers or needle-nose pliers, crimp the metal tangs over the wire's insulation. Then, give the wire and terminal a slight tug to ensure that they are properly crimped.

4 Push the terminated wires into the body of the plug until they snap or click into position. Then, fold the retaining clip into place to secure the wires.

5 Typically, an identifier is stamped into each of the corresponding wire locations on the plug. In this example, the green wire is in slot A, the brown wire is in slot B, and the yellow wire is in slot C. On the opposite half of the body, the same color of wires will go with the same identifier.

6 When both halves of the weathertight connection are wired and secure, slide them together until the retainer snaps into place. It is normal for the weathertight connection to be difficult to squeeze together at first.

Weathertight Connections

When using quick-disconnect plugs in any situation where they could get wet, a weathertight connection must be used. These are available at local auto parts stores, and they are available for a various number of wires. However, connectors for three wires seem to be common. Each plug comes with two body halves, a male terminal for each wire, a female terminal for each wire, and two rubber grommets for each wire.

To use these weathertight connections, determine where to locate the connection and cut each wire to the proper length. Slide a rubber grommet over the powered wire and strip 3/8 inch of insulation off the wire. Crimp the female terminal onto the wire. Push the terminal and wire into the body of the connector. Repeat this process for each wire that will go into the first half of the connector.

Using the remaining wire for the circuit you are wiring, slide a rubber grommet over the unpowered wire and strip 3/8 inch of insulation off the wire. Crimp the male terminal onto the wire. Push the terminal and wire into the body of the remaining connector. Ensure that the connector and wires are orientated so that the wires match up correctly. When all of the wires have grommets and terminals installed, push the two halves of the connector together until they are fully seated.

Conventional wisdom says that powered wires that can be unplugged should be terminated with a female terminal with the mating unpowered wires terminated with a matching male plug. That is still a good practice, but with the weathertight plugs, the connections are recessed on both ends, so there is no risk of coming in contact with the terminal of a powered wire.

Heat Gun

Heat guns are essential for securing heat-shrink tubing properly. They are available as electric models that must be plugged in during use or as cordless with a rechargeable battery. These can also be used to thaw frozen locks, which makes the cordless ones a bit more convenient.

Using a heat gun is the only safe way to properly shrink heat-shrink tubing. A consumer-quality hair dryer will not get hot enough to shrink the tubing. This corded electric heat gun was purchased several years ago at an auto parts store for less than $50.

DeWalt makes a very nice battery-powered heat gun. Being battery powered, it is cordless and portable. In addition to shrinking heat-shrink tubing, it works well to thaw frozen door locks.

Whether you are thawing frozen locks or heating shrink tubing, do not use a match, as it is dangerous. A hair dryer simply does not get warm enough.

Required Test Equipment

Although they may be considered to be test equipment, a test light and test meter are actually diagnostic equipment. The vintage GM truck that was just rewired serves as the best piece of test equipment that you can have. Does it start, stop, and drive without catching on fire? Will it start easily after having been driven for a while and then shut off? Do the electrical features, such as lights, radio, and the heating, ventilation, and air conditioning (HVAC) systems work as they should? If the answer to all these questions is yes, it passes the test, plain and simple. You passed, so now enjoy the truck.

When the answer to any of these questions is no, the real test begins. It is time to diagnose the problem and determine the correct course of action to resolve the issue.

Test Light

There are two questions to ask when troubleshooting an electrical device that is not working: 1) Is it getting power? and 2) Is it grounded? A test light, as simple as it is, provides answers to those questions. Electricity is basic, so there is no need to make it more difficult. Ask the simple questions first.

A test light looks much like an ice pick with a light bulb and a piece of wire with an alligator clip on the end. To verify that electrical current is passing through a specific point, connect the alligator clip to a known ground and touch the questionable

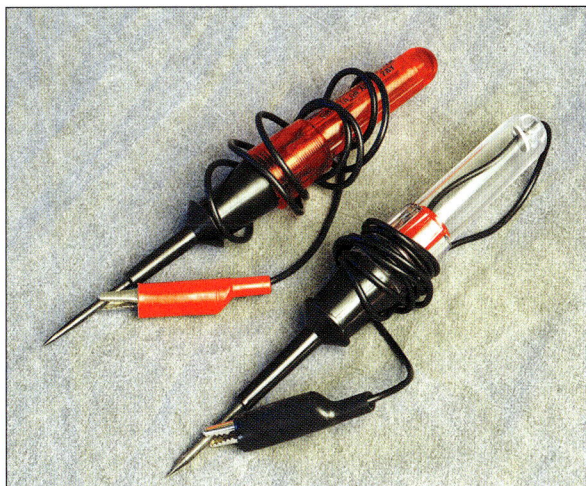

A test light can be used to determine if electrical power is flowing through a point or if the point is a suitable ground. If the alligator clip is secured to a known ground, the test light illuminates when the probe touches anything that has current flowing through it. If the alligator clip is secured to a point with power flowing through it, the test light will illuminate when the probe touches a suitable ground.

point with the pointed end. When the circuit is switched on and current is flowing through it, the light will illuminate. When the light does not illuminate, either there is no electrical current flowing through the point being tested or the ground is not adequate.

When performing diagnostic tests such as this, remember that paint, grease, and dirt do not conduct electricity very well. Therefore, it may need to be removed from the points that are being tested. The same basic process can be used to test for a good ground. Connect the alligator clip to a known power source and probe the area with the pointed end of the test light. When the light illuminates, a ground source has been found.

Keep in mind that a test light cannot determine how much current is flowing through a circuit. It can only tell if it is flowing or not. In some instances, the amount of current may dictate how bright the light illuminates, but the test light has no way to provide any number. To determine how much current is flowing, use a test meter, which is also known as a multimeter.

Multimeter (Test Meter)

Unlike a test light, which merely indicates the presence of current (or the lack thereof), a multimeter can measure ohms, volts DC, volts AC, and battery voltage. Turn the dial to the chosen unit of measure and then use

the power and ground probes to test the circuit. Determining if there is an unexpected voltage drop between two points or not enough amps to power a device is valuable information while diagnosing electrical issues.

Battery Charger

In addition to simply charging a weak battery, a battery charger can also be used as a known power source when testing electrical components, such as when installing power windows. When the riser mechanism is installed, connect the positive and negative cables of the battery charger to the respective wires of the power window motor. Then, plug in the battery charger to operate the power windows to verify that the mechanism operates as it should prior to installing glass that could be broken if something did not work properly.

A multimeter can measure the various aspects of an electrical circuit, making it very handy to use when diagnosing electrical issues.

Since the battery will be disconnected while doing any electrical work, a battery charger is handy to have as a temporary power source for testing the operation of a circuit. This could be used for testing power windows, lights, a cooling fan, or a variety of other circuits. However, it will not be of full use when accessories require the engine to be running, such as gauges or some lights that are controlled by the headlight switch.

IGNITION SYSTEMS

Although a truck requires lights to be street legal, begin with the ignition system instead when rewiring a vehicle. If the wiring is part of a complete rebuild, having a functioning ignition system provides an opportunity to run the engine on occasion, even when the truck cannot be driven yet. Speaking from experience, the sound of a healthy motor coming to life can rekindle enthusiasm on a stalled project.

The ignition system provides the most complicated component of the air-plus-fuel-plus-spark equation that results in a running engine. Air and fuel are ultimately addressed by a carburetor or fuel injection, and both usually require only minor adjustments to work properly.

LS engine swaps have been and continue to be popular upgrades to vintage trucks. For those engines to work properly, the entire electrical system for the specific engine must be included as part of the swap. Doing so is an important and complicated task—so much so that numerous books have been written on that topic alone, including CarTech's *LS Swaps: How to Swap GM LS Engines into Almost Anything* by Jefferson Bryant. Therefore, LS engine swaps are not covered in this book.

For the non-computer engines that typically go into these trucks, the ignition system consists of the ignition switch, a starter, a distributor, and a coil. While the battery and alternator are not technically part of the ignition system, they make up the charging system, which is closely connected to the ignition system. Optional accessories are a neutral safety switch and a master disconnect switch. The neutral safety switch plays a critical part in starting the engine safely. A master disconnect switch can minimize troublesome electrical issues and also be implemented as a theft deterrent.

Regardless of how simple or complex the components may be, the ignition system is simple. Activating the ignition causes electrical power to be fed to the starter via the starter solenoid. When the starter engages with

While electrical wiring is a necessity for these trucks to run and operate, that wiring can distract from the appearance of the engine compartment. This truck is a very nice example of a clean wiring installation. Wires are neatly routed and contained within the wiring loom.

the flywheel, the crankshaft causes the pistons to move up and down in the cylinders. At the same time, the camshaft causes the distributor to turn, sending spark to the combustion chamber via the spark-plug wires and spark plugs. When this spark meets up with the correct mixture of fuel and air, the engine starts, and the cycle continues.

Starters

The starter solenoid on all GM starters is located on the starter itself. If you install a Ford engine in a GM truck, you will discover that the starter solenoid is often mounted remotely. If you install a Chrysler Hemi engine in a GM truck, the starter solenoid is located directly on the starter but is controlled by a relay. Other than these locational differences in the starter solenoid, all automotive starters are basically the same.

All automotive starters are simply an electric motor. The starter's cylindrical case includes a number of field windings. Inside of that is an armature that also includes its own set of windings of copper wire that connect to a copper commutator. This armature/commutator assembly rotates around an axis within the cylindrical case.

When the ignition switch moves to the start position, a small amount of electrical current flows to the starter solenoid. This causes two electric contacts to close, sending electric current to the starter motor. As electric current begins flowing through the field windings of the starter and the armature, it creates a magnetic field, which causes the armature to turn and builds up torque within the starter. When enough torque is created, the engine turns over.

Three conditions make the engine starting process difficult: voltage drop, excessive ambient heat, and excessive ambient cold.

Voltage Drop

When insufficient electric current reaches the starter solenoid, the starter-motor circuit remains open and the starter motor does not turn, resulting in a clicking noise. This clicking noise is an indication of voltage drop, which means that the starter is receiving some power but not enough to turn the starter motor.

To minimize voltage drop, verify that the electrical connections at the starter, starter solenoid, and battery are kept clean from corrosion and are properly tightened. The starter must be connected to an adequate ground source, such as by connecting the negative battery cable directly to the engine block.

In addition, it is imperative that both battery cables are large enough to carry the momentary-but-heavy current load. Battery cables should never be smaller than 4-gauge wire, with 2-gauge wire being better. When all of these checks look good, it is a distinct possibility that the battery is low or dead. If it is low, it can be recharged, but if it is dead, it must be replaced.

Excessive Ambient Heat

As the ambient temperature increases, so does the electrical resistance within a circuit. To compensate for this, the electrical circuit (the starting circuit in this case) must be well maintained and kept in good working order.

Some Chevrolet engines have been known to exhibit a hot-start issue on occasion. Sometimes, this is a result of the exhaust being too close to the starter. One method to eliminate or minimize this issue (other than moving the exhaust) is to install a 30-amp relay in the ignition circuit between the ignition switch and the starter.

Excessive Ambient Cold

As ambient temperature decreases significantly, engine oil becomes thicker and more sluggish. When the ignition system is in less-than-perfect condition, the starter may not be able to create enough torque to turn over the engine. Since this is not really an electrical problem, using an engine heater and/or a high-torque starter are possible solutions if this becomes a concern.

As the starter solenoid receives electrical power, the starter motor begins to turn, rotating the gear that is shown near the end of the shaft. This gear engages with the flywheel to turn the engine's crankshaft, which gets the engine running when spark and fuel ignite.

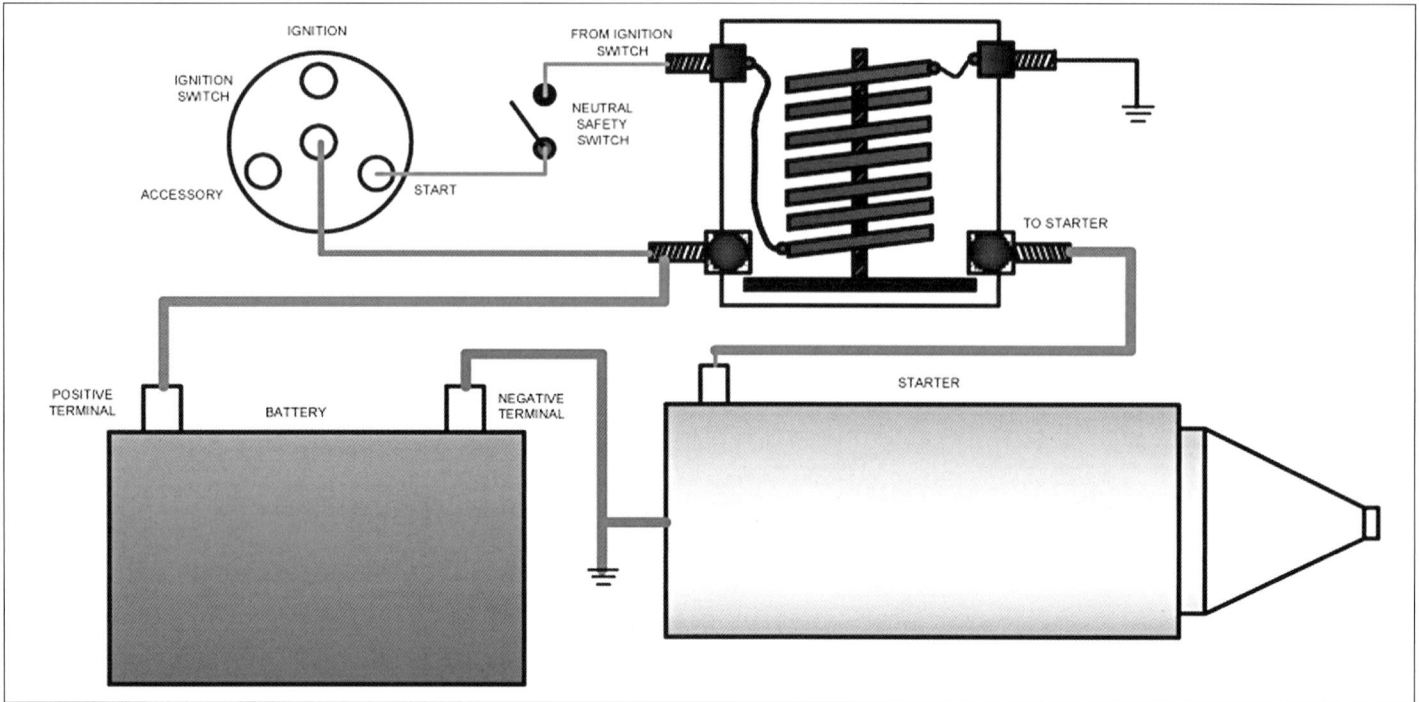

Although it happens quickly in a system that is working properly, the ignition system requires several things to happen before the engine starts. The battery must have a sufficient charge and a sufficient ground. When the key is turned to the start position on the ignition switch and the neutral safety switch closes the circuit, electrical current flows to the starter solenoid. This causes the solenoid to move, closing the portion of the circuit that causes the starter motor to turn. Of course, the starter solenoid and the starter must also both be grounded.

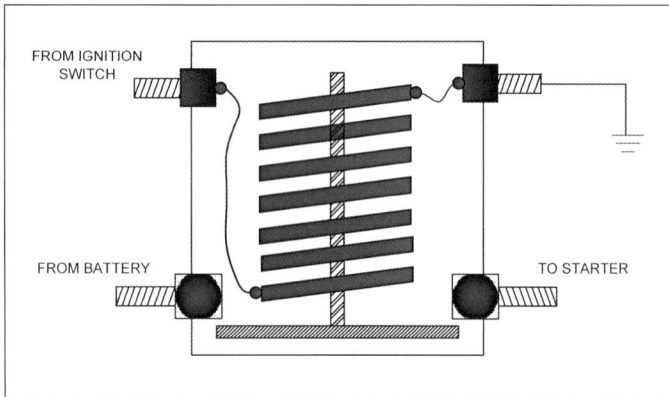

When the ignition switch is in any position other than start, the starter solenoid should not be energized. Therefore, no electrical current is flowing to the starter solenoid or the starter.

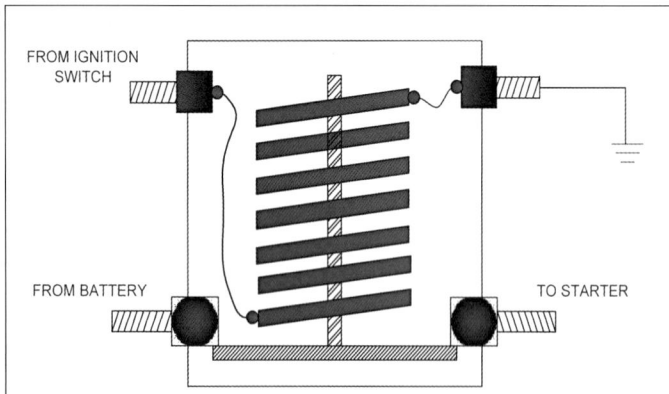

When the ignition switch is in the start position, the starter solenoid is energized, causing the ignition circuit to close and allowing the starter to start the engine.

Generators and Alternators

It is common knowledge that the battery provides the power that is required to start the engine. It is also common knowledge that power from the battery is required for the stereo, lights, air conditioning, and any other electrical devices. The expectation of every driver is for the engine to start and for the electrical devices to operate immediately. For this reason, there must be a method to recharge the battery quickly and efficiently.

The purpose of a generator or alternator is to recharge the vehicle's battery. They are both like a starter motor, as they include armatures, windings, field coils, and magnetic fields. As with all other electrical components, they must be grounded to operate properly.

Generators

Generators (also known as dynamos) convert mechanical energy into electrical energy and were standard equipment in automobiles until the early 1960s. While a generator does not produce electricity by itself, electrical current can be extracted from it.

A belt from the engine's crankshaft turns the armature within the generator, producing electrical current in the process. The faster the armature turns, the more electric current it will produce. The amount of current that is produced is limited by a voltage regulator that is placed in line between the generator and the battery.

The advantage of a generator is that there is always some amount of magnetic field present in the generator. Therefore, if the battery was dead, the vehicle could be pushed to get it running. The disadvantages of generators are that the electric contacts (also known as brushes) frequently require replacement. In addition, bearing failure is common, but this is typically due to improper belt tension.

Alternators

In 1962, General Motors began using an alternator instead of a generator in its new vehicles. However, alternators, as they are known today, date back to World War II. Unlike a generator, an alternator provides a useful charge even at idle speed. Overall improvements have all but eliminated the need to replace the contact brushes.

When generators were common, lighting was minimal and other electrical devices were rare. So, a generator only needed to produce roughly 30 amperes. Due to common electrical loads in contemporary vehicles

The alternator has one mounting point that solidly attaches to a mounting bracket. Another mounting point attaches to an adjustable arm that allows for proper belt tension. The pulley can be for a V-belt (shown) or for a serpentine belt. To switch the pulley, use an impact wrench to remove the nut and washer that secures the pulley, remove the pulley, and install the new pulley. Secure the new pulley with a washer and nut.

(regardless of vintage), including air conditioning, stereo, and additional lighting, alternators are commonly rated at 50 to 70 amps.

The advantage of an alternator is that it can produce large amounts of power that can be made at low speed. In addition, an alternator can also run at a high speed without suffering any damage. Alternators are virtually maintenance free.

The disadvantage of an alternator is that it does not retain any amount of a magnetic field, so it will not create any power on its own. Be cognizant of the fact that the alternator charge stud is always hot (in the electrical sense). An inadvertent connection between this stud and ground at the same time will possibly damage the alternator, as well as possibly the distributor and starter. The wire that connects to the charge stud must also be sized correctly to carry the full capacity of the alternator.

An alternator will never put out more power than is required. Whether an alternator is rated at 100 amps or 50 amps, it will put out only

45 amps if that is all that is required. Unless you plan to be blasting the stereo through several speakers, bouncing the truck up and down the boulevard using an air ride suspension, and running the air conditioning at full blast all at the same time, you probably do not require a 100-amp alternator for your vintage Chevrolet pickup.

Three-Wire Alternator

Three-wire alternators communicate with the vehicle's electrical monitoring system via three wires. One wire connects to the alternator charge output stud. This is commonly a red 6-gauge wire that connects to the battery via the fuse panel. This wire always has power. This applies to the one-wire alternator also.

The two other wires are what make the difference between a one-wire and a three-wire alternator. These two wires typically connect to two studs near the back of the alternator via a plug. On a 10-SI or 12-SI (also known as Delco) alternator, the plug is on the outside of the alterna-

This alternator is a 10-SI type (as identified by the two spade terminals near the edge of the back). Power from the battery connects to the alternator charge output stud, which is located slightly counterclockwise from the two spade terminals when looking from the back of the alternator. These alternators were commonly used on mid-1970s to mid-1980s GM vehicles.

The CS-130 and CS-144 alternators operate the same as the 10-SI type but have a different type of plug. The plug has more connections than the 10-SI type. These alternators were commonly used on mid-1980s to 1990s GM vehicles.

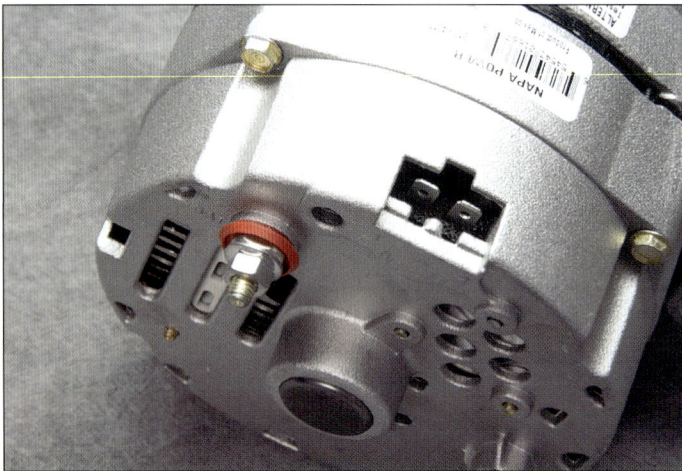

A 6-gauge wire connects to the alternator charge output stud (the stud with the red washer). The opposite end of this wire connects to the positive side of the battery or to the starter. This is the alternator output wire. The alternator regulator exciter wire connects to terminal 1 (as labeled on the alternator). The regulator power battery wire connects to terminal 2 (as labeled on the alternator).

This is the backside of the external voltage regulator that is commonly known as a one-wire alternator. It uses one 6-gauge wire between the alternator output stud and the battery. The regulator power (battery) wire from the fuse panel connects to terminal 3 on the voltage regulator, while the alternator regulator exciter wire from the fuse panel connects to terminal 4. A 14-gauge wire from terminal 2 of the voltage regulator connects to terminal R on the alternator, while a 14-gauge wire connects terminal 4 on the regulator to terminal F on the alternator. A 14-gauge ground wire must also be run from the G post on the alternator to a chassis ground.

tor near the back edge. On a CS-130 or CS-144 alternator (commonly found on late-1980s to mid-1990s GM vehicles, including TPI and LT1 engines), the plug is on the back of the alternator. Note that this later application uses a different type of plug.

Regardless of the type of alternator, the alternator regulator exciter wire (also known as ignition sense, which is usually white) has switched ignition power and is connected to the ignition/run terminal on the ignition switch. At the alternator, this wire connects to terminal 1.

In some instances, this configuration could cause/allow engine run-on (the engine continuing to run after the ignition has been shut off), as voltage back-feeds from the alternator. To avoid this, install a diode in line with the alternator regulator exciter wire. Remember that a diode is simply a one-way device, so the stripe on the diode must be closer to the alternator. This allows current to flow toward the alternator but not back toward the ignition system.

The regulator power battery wire (also known as battery sense, which is usually red) connects to the fuse panel and has power at all times. At the alternator, this wire connects to terminal 2. This battery-sense wire is what tells the alternator to make more or less power based on the amount that is required by the electrical system at the time.

One-Wire Alternator

On a one-wire alternator, that one wire is commonly a red 6-gauge wire. It connects to the battery via the fuse panel on one end and to the alternator charge output stud on the other. This one-wire alternator requires an external voltage regulator, which is connected via the two spade terminals located at the top of the back of the alternator.

Ignition Coils

As the starter begins to turn, fuel is pumped into the combustion chamber. For this fuel to be of any use, it must be ignited by a spark. The ignition coil converts the 12 volts that are sent from the battery into a higher voltage that can ignite the fuel. For the engine to start and run, the ignition coil must receive power.

When using a coil that is not internally resisted, a ballast resistor must be used, otherwise the coil will overheat very quickly (just a few minutes), rendering the coil useless. The ballast resistor can be installed in line between the fuse panel and the positive side of the coil or between the fuse panel and the "R" or "I" stud on the starter solenoid. As with an internally resisted coil, the tachometer signal wire (when used) connects to the negative side of the coil.

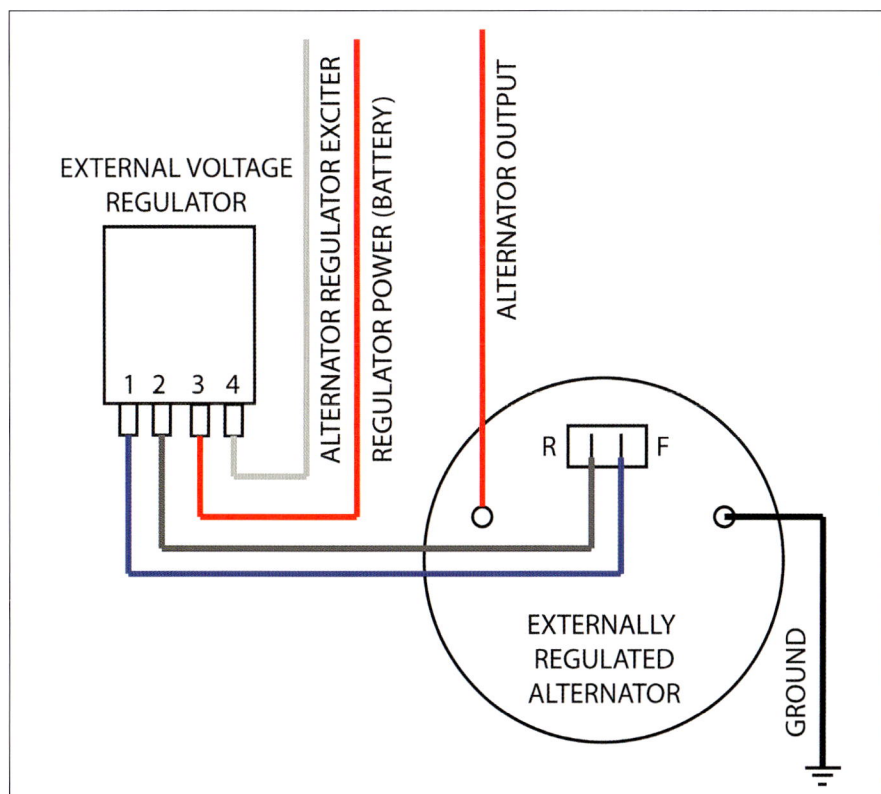

Connect one 6-gauge wire between the alternator output stud and the battery. Connect two wires from the fuse panel to the external voltage regulator. These two wires are the regulator power (battery) wire to terminal 3 on the voltage regulator and the alternator regulator exciter wire to terminal 4. Connect a 14-gauge wire from terminal 2 of the voltage regulator to terminal R on the alternator. Connect a 14-gauge wire to terminal 4 on the voltage regulator to terminal F on the alternator. Connect a 14-gauge ground wire from the G post on the alternator to a chassis ground.

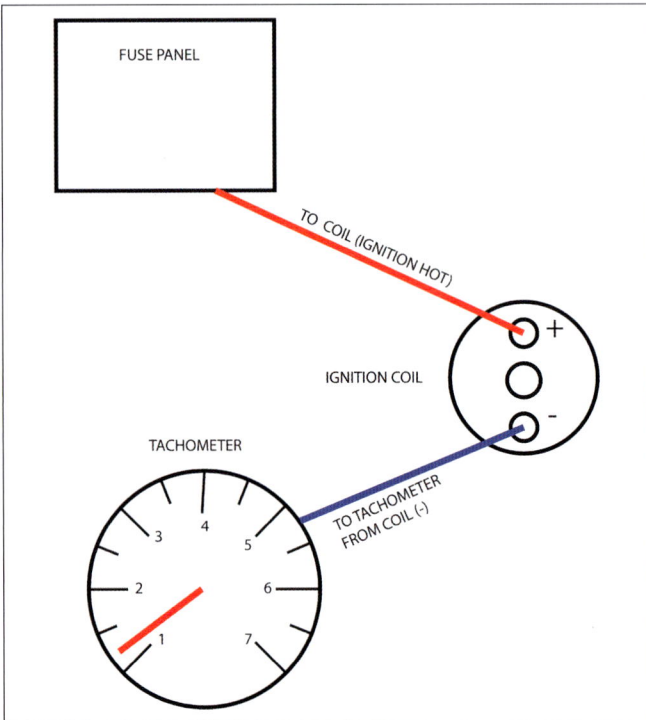

Whether the ignition coil is external to the distributor or included in a high-energy ignition (HEI)-type distributor, the ignition wire from the fuse panel connects to the positive side of the coil. When using a tachometer, connect the tachometer to the negative side of the coil.

Ignition switches, whether they are mounted in the dash or the steering column, typically have four distinct positions regarding wiring. If someone wanted to wire these differently, it could be done, but it could be harmful to the electrical system and may be confusing or even dangerous to the person who is driving the vehicle.

The ignition system in modern automobiles is self-contained. There is no longer a need for a passenger to get out of the vehicle and hand crank the engine while the driver manipulates the throttle and choke.

After the fuse panel, the ignition switch may be the single component that has the most wires connected to it. That may be directly or indirectly, as many of these accessories have their own dedicated on/off switch, but the overall ability to function is determined by the position of the ignition switch.

Like the headlight switch that directs electrical current to different circuits depending on its position, the ignition switch does as well. However, the difference is that the ignition switch has a lock cylinder in addition to the electrical switch. The tumblers in the lock cylinder hold the key in position. When those tumblers become worn excessively, the key may fall out even while the engine is running, or another key (anyone's key) may be able to start the engine. This happened to me and my 1957 GMC in high school, when one of my old friends had a 1955 Chevy pickup. He started my truck and left. When I arrived at the parking lot, my truck was already running.

On the other hand, if the tumblers are worn out, the lock cylinder may not turn at all, which makes starting the engine impossible. If the

When using an aftermarket ignition box, the switched ignition power wire connects to the ignition box and not to the coil. The ignition box will then provide the positive coil connection. Since these systems may vary from one manufacturer to another, refer to the instructions provided with the ignition box that you are using. The tachometer signal wire (when used) connects to the designated tachometer output terminal or wire.

When using a fuel-injection system and a standalone wiring harness, the switched ignition power wire connects to the fuel-injection harness wire labeled "Ignition" or "Fuse Block Ignition." The tachometer signal wire (when used) connects to the tachometer output terminal or wire from the engine-control module (ECM).

Ignition Switches

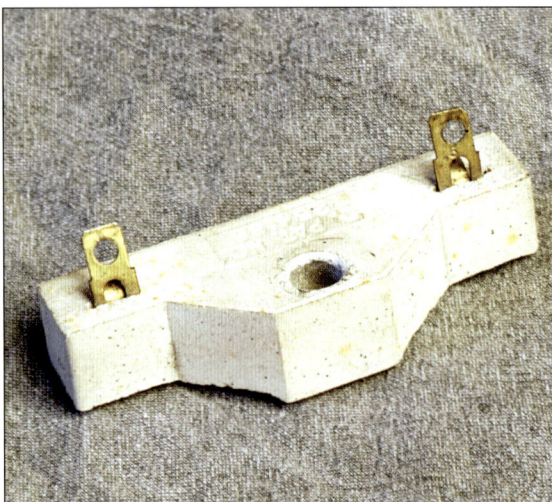

Mount the ballast resistor in a convenient location by placing a bolt through the hole near the middle of the ballast resistor. Secure a female spade connector to the wire from the fuse panel and slide it onto one of the terminals on the ballast resistor. Secure a female spade connector to the wire that connects to the coil and slide it onto the remaining terminal on the ballast resistor.

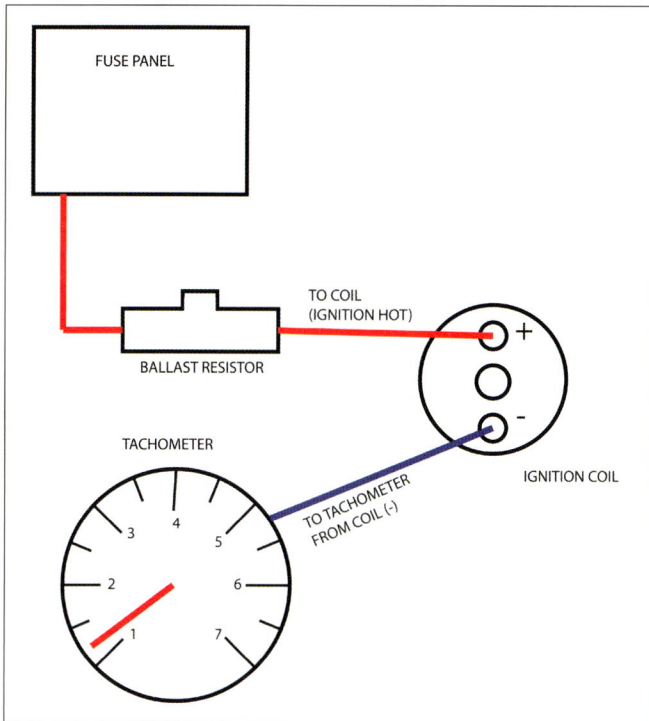

FUSE PANEL

TO COIL
(IGNITION HOT)

BALLAST RESISTOR

TACHOMETER

TO TACHOMETER
FROM COIL (-)

IGNITION COIL

After determining that the ignition coil is not internally resisted, install a ballast resistor somewhere between the fuse panel and the ignition coil. Simply cut the wire that connects the fuse panel and the ignition coil. Secure a female spade connector onto both ends of the wire and connect each wire to a spade connector on the ballast resistor.

electrical switch is worn out, that can make it impossible to start the engine as well. Either situation calls for the ignition switch to be replaced. If the ignition switch must be replaced, verify that the negative and positive battery cables are both disconnected from the battery. Without doing this, the danger of live wires would exist.

When the ignition switch is initiated (turned with a conventional key switch or a button pushed with a

push-button switch) and everything is wired correctly and is in good working order, the engine starts. The key position in a conventional ignition switch controls the various options that the ignition-switch controls. In most vehicles, including vintage GM pickup trucks, there are four positions: off, accessory, start, and ignition/run.

Off

An aftermarket ignition box can be used with various types of ignition systems, so refer to the instructions with those specific components to ensure that everything is wired correctly.

The switch should be in the off position whenever the ignition key is inserted or removed. With the key in this position, the ignition circuit is open, which means that the circuit will not operate. In this case, that is the intent. A possible exception is that an electric fan can be wired to continue running to cool the engine down to a predetermined temperature, even after the ignition switch has been shut off and the key has been removed.

Accessory

The accessory position is typically one step forward or one step backward from the off position. With the key in the accessory position, the ignition/run and start circuits are still open, so the engine will not be running.

In this position, the accessory circuit is closed, allowing the accessories to operate. Those accessories must be wired accordingly for them to operate when the key is in this position. Almost any accessory could be wired to operate in this mode, or you could be very selective as to what is available. However, when operating with the key in this position, the electric current is coming straight from the battery, so you could run your battery down far enough that it would not start your truck.

Start

With the key in the start position, the start and ignition circuits are closed. This position is used only for starting the engine and is the farthest away from the off position. To prevent the ignition switch from staying in the start position and burning up the starter, the ignition switch is spring loaded in this position. Whether the engine starts or not, when the key is

The ignition switch of some of these vintage trucks is a four-piece assembly. This one is from a 1970 C10 and is comprised of an ignition switch, a collar, a tumbler, and a bezel. The slotted collar indexes over the ignition switch and mounts behind the dash. Prior to inserting the tumbler, thread the bezel into the collar to secure the assembly to the dash.

The wiring end of the ignition switch is where the electrical connections are made. Beginning at the top, the first terminal is for the accessory connection, and the solenoid connection is just below it. On the left is the ignition terminal, and the two battery connections are to the right. The two terminals at the bottom are labeled G-2 and G-1.

released, it will return to the ignition/ run position.

Ignition/Run

After starting the engine, the ignition switch returns to the ignition/ run position and stays there until the engine is shut off. The ignition and accessory circuits are closed.

Mounting Locations

For early vintage GM pickup trucks, the stock location for the ignition switch is in the dash. It is secured by a collar that threads onto the body of the ignition switch. To remove the

The ignition switch on this Task Force truck is in the dash (to the right and down from the instrument panel) and is secured in place by a collar that is threaded on from the back. While the components are new, the dash layout is basically stock, except for the air-conditioning outlets.

For older trucks that have the ignition switch in the dash but do not have the conical bezel, a replacement ignition switch is most likely available at a local auto parts store. It may not look exactly like the vintage GM piece, but when it is installed, it will not be seen anyway. To connect wires to this switch, terminate the appropriate wires with insulated female spade connectors.

For this ignition switch, the necessary wires must be terminated with ring terminals. While either one of these switches will serve the purpose if a stock ignition switch fails, it shows that you should always leave the wires a bit long for any components that may require a replacement and may also require different connectors.

To remove the dash-mounted ignition switch, a paper clip or a tiny Allen wrench and the ignition key is necessary. With either of the first two items and the ignition key, it is easy to remove. Without those, it is a pain.

This quick-disconnect plug allows for a clean connection to the wires within the steering column. From left to right on the bottom portion of this photo, the wires are as follows: horn activation, front left turn and parking light, front right turn and parking light, hazard-light power, turn-signal power, rear left turn, rear right turn, and brake-light power.

Based on the steering wheel, this non-tilt steering column is most likely out of a 1980s–1990s pickup truck. It has the ignition key on the column, so the steering-column wiring will be somewhat different than if the key was on the dash. Depending on which wiring kit is used, the vendor will need to know which ignition key location you have.

ignition switch, remove the collar and pull the switch through the dash panel. Mark or tag each wire regarding the terminal to which is should be connected.

If you already have the replacement switch in hand, replace each wire one terminal at a time. When the wires are reconnected, slide the ignition switch through the dash panel and secure it with the collar. To be able to turn the key in the lock cyl-

BROWN, ACCESSORY.
GOOD SOURCE FOR
ALTERNATOR
EXCITER WIRE

IGNORE

IGNORE, GOES TO GROUND
DURING CRANKING.

PINK, IGNITION AND
ACCESSORY

PURPLE, START.

RED, POWER AND
BATTERY

PHYSICALLY LARGER TERMINAL,
NO POWER WHEN IN ACCESSORY
POSITION, GOES DEAD DURING
CRANKING. GOOD POWER
SOURCE FOR ACCESSORIES WITH
HEAVY CURRENT DRAW.

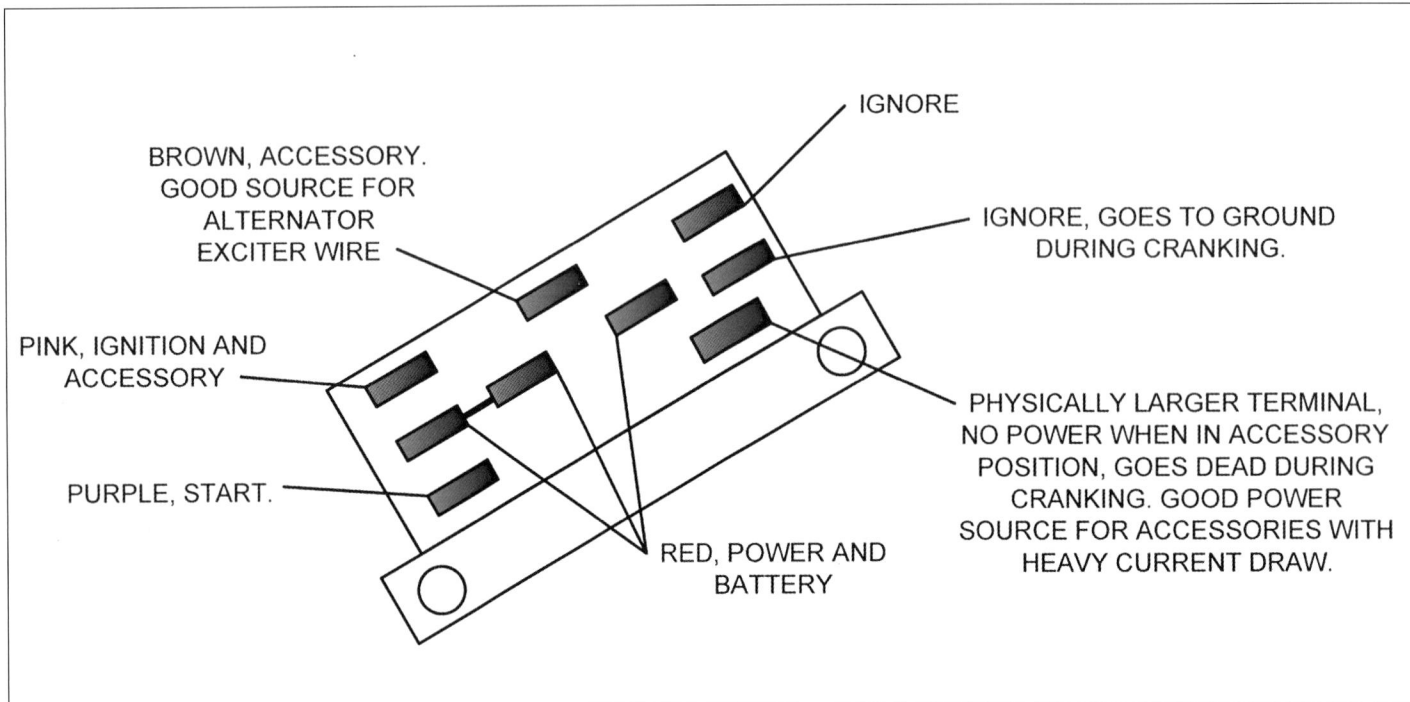

For a truck with a column-mounted ignition switch, there is typically a group of wires that are connected to the ignition switch that run down the steering column to a plug. The respective wires for the ignition circuit connect to the opposite half of the plug.

inder, verify that the ignition switch cannot rotate within the dash panel.

Newer dash-mounted ignition switches are a bit more complicated to remove, but they are not difficult. With the key in the ignition, push a paper clip (or a tiny Allen wrench) into the small round hole, rotate the key to the accessory position, and then pull. If you are attempting to remove the complete ignition switch and bezel, unthreading the bezel from the switch will allow the ignition switch to be removed from the dash.

Later vintage GM trucks (mid-1970s and later) came with the ignition switch mounted in the steering column. This may also be the case in earlier trucks that have been modified. When rewiring a truck with a column-mounted ignition switch, the wires typically connect to a plug on the column near the firewall, so

that is not a problem. However, when the column-mounted ignition switch requires replacement, first consult a vehicle-specific repair manual.

Batteries

Automotive batteries store electric power that is used to spin the starter motor as well as power the lights and any accessories in a truck. The two capacity ratings for an automotive battery are cold cranking amps (CCA) and reserve capacity.

The CCA rating is used to compare batteries between cold and warm climates. For most conventionally fueled vehicles, a CCA rating of between 500 and 750 is adequate. The higher the value, the more power is available to start the truck. For example, 500 CCA would likely be sufficient in the warmth of Florida, while 750 CCA may be required in Minnesota

due to colder winter temperatures.

Reserve capacity compares the ability of a battery in use if the charging system has failed. The reserve capacity measures the length of time that a fully charged battery can be discharged at a specified rate before doing irreparable damage to the battery.

As the engine speed or electrical demand increases or decreases, the voltage and current from the battery increase or decrease. This prevents power spikes in the system when a large-draw accessory, such as the air conditioning, is turned off.

In a similar fashion, when additional power is required, the battery provides it. With this in mind, it can be used to your advantage in certain situations, such as when operating a battery-powered winch on a trailer or to recover a stuck four-wheel-drive truck. If the engine is not running,

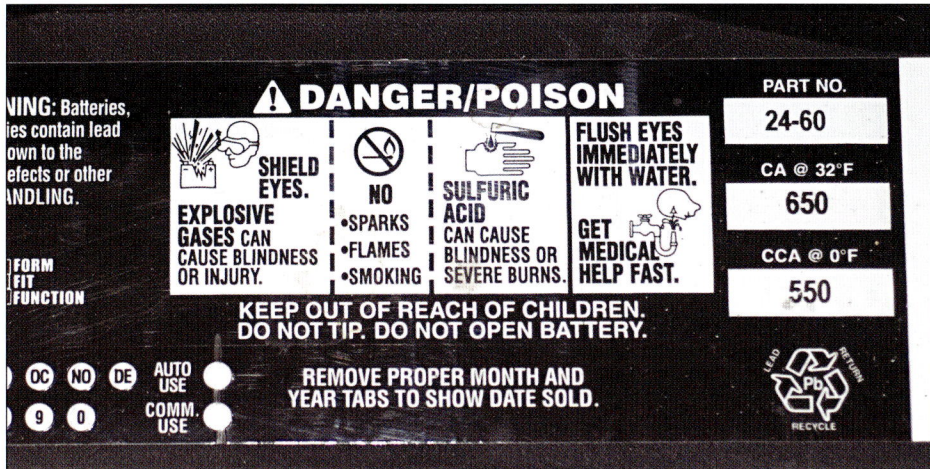

The reserve capacity for this battery is 650 amps at 32°F, and it has 550 cold cranking amps at 0°F, according to the right portion of the label. Safety warnings are shown near the middle of the label and are important.

This rotary type of master disconnect switch is designed to be mounted in the positive battery cable inline between the battery and the starter. Simply cut the battery cable at the desired location, crimp on two ring connectors, and secure each of them to the master disconnect. Remember to turn on the power before starting the truck and turn it off after shutting off the engine.

the winch would be draining the battery directly. If the engine is running at idle, the winch will operate, but it may be slow. If the engine is accelerated slightly, the winch will be provided with additional electric current, slightly speeding up the process.

The best maintenance for a battery is to ensure that both the positive and negative cable connections are kept tight and not allowed to corrode. The positive terminal of the battery should be connected to the starter with a minimum of 4-gauge wire. The negative terminal of the battery should be connected to a bolt that secures the transmission to the engine block to provide the best ground. Ensure that these battery cables do not touch the truck exhaust system or become entangled with anything that could cause damage.

Master Disconnect Switch

Installing a master disconnect switch (also known as a kill switch) is typically done for one reason: to shut down all electrical power to the vehicle. There are safety and security reasons for doing this.

In addition, regardless of how careful you try to be when rewiring your truck, you may run across a situation where an electrical draw from an unknown source drains the battery. Eventually, it can usually be found and corrected, but it may take a while. In the meantime, installing a master disconnect switch allows the power to be shut down when the vehicle is not being driven, saving the battery in the process.

A master disconnect switch can also serve as a theft deterrent. If a master disconnect switch is installed and you remember to switch it to the off position when you leave your truck, no one will be able to start it. That is, unless they know the location of the disconnect switch or they take the time to bypass it.

Most master disconnect switches are simply a two-position switch: on and off. For a master disconnect switch to work properly, install it inline between the starter and the battery. This will keep the engine from starting or running. With the stock location of the battery and the starter in these trucks being relatively close together, it may be necessary

to run some extra wire to be able to easily access and hide the master disconnect switch. Remember that this switch is going to be installed in a 2-gauge (or at least 4-gauge) battery cable, so the switch must be rated for that much current; otherwise, the switch will burn up.

Neutral Safety Switch

The purpose of a neutral safety switch is to prevent a vehicle from starting while in gear. For a standard (manual) transmission, this prevents the engine from starting unless the transmission is in neutral (out of gear) or the clutch is depressed. For an automatic transmission, the neutral safety switch requires the transmission to be in park or neutral.

Although designs may differ, the neutral safety switch activation is physically determined by the position

Most auto parts stores have battery cable in bulk, along with the appropriate terminals and a heavy-duty crimper for this larger wire in the back room. For a regular customer, they should be more than happy to cut and crimp custom-length battery cables for you. Just be sure to know the length needed for each cable. Use a ring terminal to connect to the battery terminal for accessory power or a ground connection.

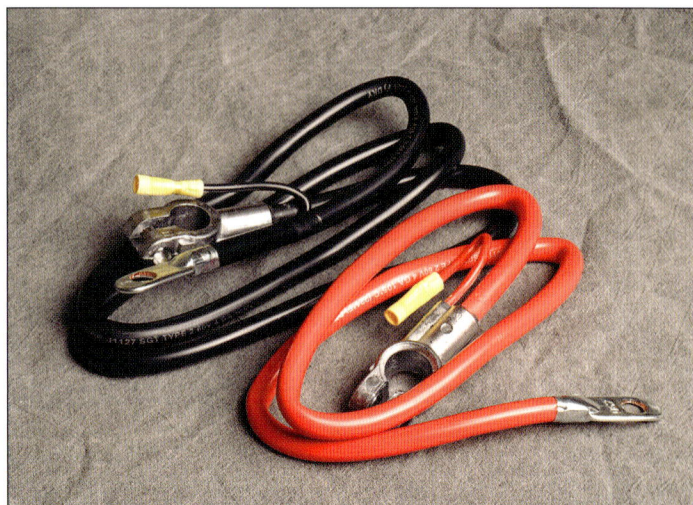

Most reputable auto parts stores and even most farm- and home-type retailers have automotive-grade battery cables that already have the appropriate terminals crimped onto them. Before purchasing, get a accurate measurements for the positive cable and the negative cable. Note that the cables also include an accessory lead for providing power or ground directly from the battery.

This is the electrical connection part of the neutral safety switch for an after-market floor-mounted shifter. Both neutral safety wires connect to the switch at these terminals (one wire to each terminal). Movement of the shifter lever combines with ball detents to open or close the switch electrically.

of the shifter linkage. Electrically, this switch is located in line between the ignition switch and the starter solenoid. The neutral safety switch has two electrical contacts: one for "park start" and one for "neutral start."

A common arrangement for the switch is with a ball detent as part of the switch. An eared tab on the shifter is positioned so that when the shifter is in park or in neutral, the tab presses the ball inward into the detent. This closes the electrical circuit, the starter solenoid receives power, and the engine starts.

Commercially available wiring kits show how to wire the neutral safety switch. However, designing your own wiring circuit requires you to know which terminals work with the neutral safety switch. This can be done with a test light.

Begin by attaching the ground lead of the test light to a known ground. Verify that the ignition

On a transmission-mounted neutral safety switch, an arm slips over the shifter input shaft that protrudes from the left side of the transmission. This arm has two tabs that push inward on the ball detent that operates the neutral safety switch. When adjusted properly, one tab pushes the ball inward when the vehicle is in park, while the other tab pushes the ball inward when the vehicle is in neutral. This neutral safety switch allows the vehicle to start only when the transmission is in park or neutral.

On a column-shift truck, the neutral safety switch is within the electrical connector that attaches to the lower portion of the steering column. It typically has four spade terminals. Two are for the neutral safety switch, while the other two are for the backup lights. The neutral safety switch and the backup lights are signaled by the location of the shifter.

switch is in the off position. With the power lead of the test light, probe terminals until the test light illuminates, indicating power (hot). Turn the ignition switch to the on position and place the shifter in the park position.

With the power lead, probe terminals until the test light illuminates, indicating "park start." Place the shifter in the neutral position. With the power lead, probe terminals until the test light illuminates, indicating "neutral start." If it is necessary to move the ignition switch to the start position to provide continuity between both terminals, have an assistant hold the key in the start position. When this is required, disconnect the ignition wire from the "S" terminal on the starter solenoid to verify that the engine does not start.

As far as vehicle manufacturers

GAUGES

are concerned, there are two basic schools of thought when it comes to monitoring a vehicle's health. One is by using analog or digital gauges in the dash panel to closely monitor the electrical voltage, oil pressure, coolant temperature, and vehicle speed. These properties could be considered to be the vehicle's vital signs.

The second school of thought is to simply provide a warning light, rather than to clutter the dash with informative gauges. The bad thing about a warning light is that it does not usu-

ally illuminate until there is already a problem that may possibly result in you waiting on a tow truck. Simply put, gauges allow the driver to be proactive, while warning lights require the driver to be reactive. When wiring a pickup truck, you can make the decision as to how much information will be available while driving.

Other properties that are good to know are the fuel level and engine speed. The fuel-level gauge is just for convenience, as its intention is to prevent you from running out of fuel.

Other than that, it does not measure any sort of engine or vehicle performance. Tachometers, which measure engine speed, are much more common on new vehicles now than they used to be. There was a time when a factory tachometer was available only on performance vehicles and, even then, were often an option that added to the price.

While the properties listed above are standard, other components can be measured and analyzed. Oil temperature and engine vacuum are a few that come to mind. Any additional properties depend greatly on the specific equipment on the pickup truck. If a turbocharger is installed on the engine, a gauge is needed to monitor turbo boost. For air suspension, a gauge is needed to monitor the amount of air pressure in the suspension system or reservoir.

Voltmeter/Ammeter

To monitor the electrical system, use a voltmeter or an ammeter. The one to use is dictated by your choice of an alternator or a generator. With an alternator, use a voltmeter. With a generator, use an ammeter.

A voltmeter measures electri-

This aftermarket gauge panel for 1955–1959 Chevrolet trucks consists of the panel itself that houses the electric gauges and a polished bezel. Three screws secure it in place in the dash. The gauges are (from left to right) for the fuel level, oil pressure, volts, and coolant temperature. The large gauge is the speedometer, and it includes an odometer and a trip odometer. The three small openings in the gauge panel are for turn-signal and high-beam-headlight indicator lights.

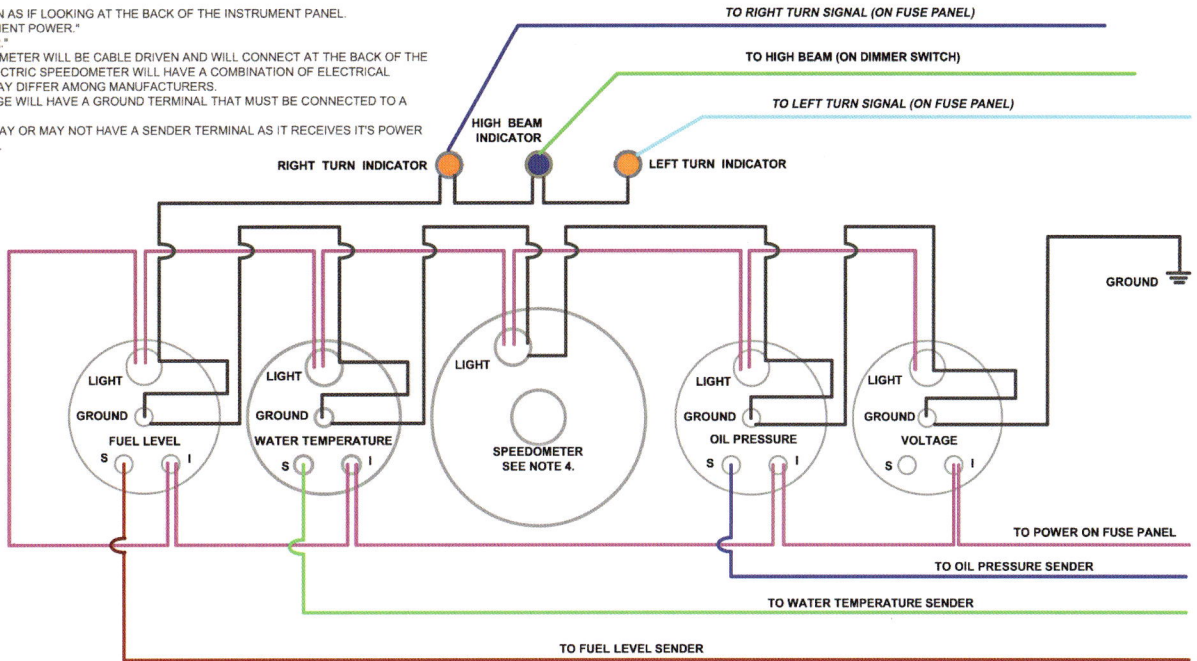

NOTES:
1. THIS DIAGRAM IS DRAWN AS IF LOOKING AT THE BACK OF THE INSTRUMENT PANEL.
2. "I" REFERS TO "INSTRUMENT POWER."
3. "S" REFERS TO "SENDER."
4. A MECHANICAL SPEEDOMETER WILL BE CABLE DRIVEN AND WILL CONNECT AT THE BACK OF THE SPEEDOMETER. AN ELECTRIC SPEEDOMETER WILL HAVE A COMBINATION OF ELECTRICAL CONNECTIONS THAT MAY DIFFER AMONG MANUFACTURERS.
5. EACH ELECTRICAL GAUGE WILL HAVE A GROUND TERMINAL THAT MUST BE CONNECTED TO A CHASSIS GROUND.
6. THE VOLTAGE GAUGE MAY OR MAY NOT HAVE A SENDER TERMINAL AS IT RECEIVES IT'S POWER FROM THE FUSE PANEL.

TO RIGHT TURN SIGNAL (ON FUSE PANEL)
TO HIGH BEAM (ON DIMMER SWITCH)
TO LEFT TURN SIGNAL (ON FUSE PANEL)

HIGH BEAM INDICATOR
RIGHT TURN INDICATOR
LEFT TURN INDICATOR

GROUND

LIGHT / GROUND / FUEL LEVEL / S / I
LIGHT / GROUND / WATER TEMPERATURE / S / I
LIGHT / SPEEDOMETER SEE NOTE 4.
LIGHT / GROUND / OIL PRESSURE / S / I
LIGHT / GROUND / VOLTAGE / S / I

TO POWER ON FUSE PANEL
TO OIL PRESSURE SENDER
TO WATER TEMPERATURE SENDER
TO FUEL LEVEL SENDER

This schematic provides the basic information for wiring electric gauges in a truck. While aftermarket gauges can be purchased separately, most gauge manufacturers offer their gauges in sets that typically include the senders as well.

cal pressure in voltage. In a standard 12-volt electrical system when the alternator is working as it should and the battery is in good condition, the voltmeter will typically read between 14.0 and 14.5 volts. Any failures in this system cause the display in the voltmeter to drop in direct proportion to the voltage drop.

When an ammeter is used, it will (ideally) read zero. A zero reading indicates that the battery is in good condition and the electrical system is working as intended. Any other reading indicates that the system is charging or discharging.

An advantage of the voltmeter is that the full voltage is not required to flow through it. The ignition sense and the battery sense wires that are

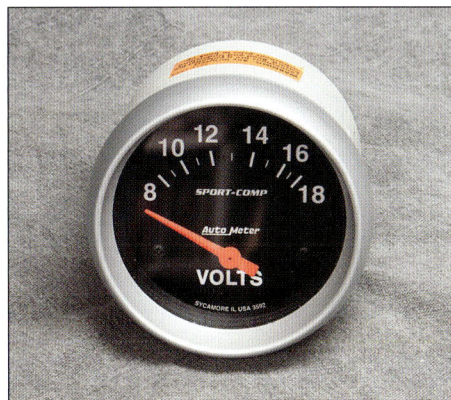

This is the Auto Meter Sport-Comp-series voltmeter. The voltmeter does not require any type of sender because it receives power directly from the fuse panel into the input terminal. This makes it easy to provide electrical power to each of the other gauges. A power wire from the fuse panel can be daisy-chained from the voltmeter to each of the other gauges.

connected to the alternator allow for this. This makes for a relatively easy and safer installation. For the voltmeter to operate properly, it simply requires a 14-gauge wire from the fuse panel.

An ammeter measures electrical current flow in amps. When the generator is working as it should and the battery is in good condition, the ammeter reads zero. The electrical current flow is from the ammeter to the battery, so when the battery is fully charged, the voltage regulator slows the flow of current. When the battery is low, the voltage regulator increases the flow of electrical current, therefore reading a higher number on the ammeter.

For the ammeter to measure and read correctly, the electrical current must all travel through the ammeter. This requires that the ammeter and related wiring that are sized appropriately for the possible amperage. A 12-volt electrical system will require heavier components than a 6-volt electrical system. If the gauge or wire fails, all electrical power will be lost. While there may be some exceptions, most Chevrolet and GM pickup trucks currently in use have a 12-volt electrical system, alternator, and voltmeter.

Oil Pressure

Perhaps the most vital gauge in a truck is the oil-pressure gauge. The oil-pressure gauge should read zero when the engine is not running. However, when the engine starts running, there must be oil pressure, and this gauge shows that. When there is no oil pressure in a running engine, it may not be running much longer. With electric gauges, the electric voltage output of the oil-pressure gauge reflects a direct proportion of the engine oil pressure.

It is easy to test an oil-pressure

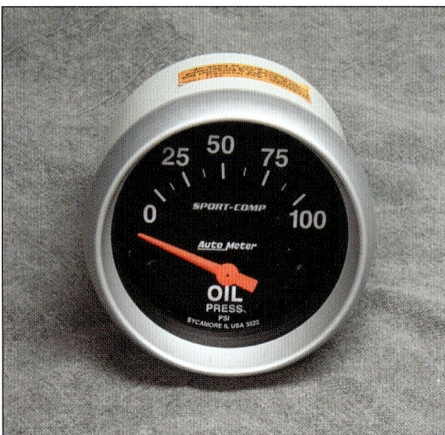

This is the Auto Meter Sport-Comp-series oil-pressure gauge. Being an electrical gauge, it requires power (often daisy-chained from the voltmeter) to the input terminal. It also requires a pressure signal from the oil-pressure sending unit to the sender terminal of the gauge. The gauge will also require a ground wire for the gauge itself, along with power and ground for the gauge lighting.

gauge. Disconnect the wire between the oil-pressure gauge and its sender from the sender and connect that wire to a known ground. When you turn the ignition to the on position, the oil-pressure gauge will immediately read at its highest reading. When the oil pressure does not respond as it should, the gauge may be faulty, or it may not be grounded properly.

Check for any Teflon tape or other sealant on the threads of the oil-pressure sending unit. Clean the threads, remove any Teflon, and retry the test. When the oil pressure does not work as it should at this time, the gauge is faulty and should be replaced. Since Teflon acts as an insulator, it should not be used on sending units for oil pressure or coolant temperature, as these senders are designed to be grounded to the engine block.

Coolant Temperature

The coolant-temperature gauge displays the temperature of the engine coolant at the location where

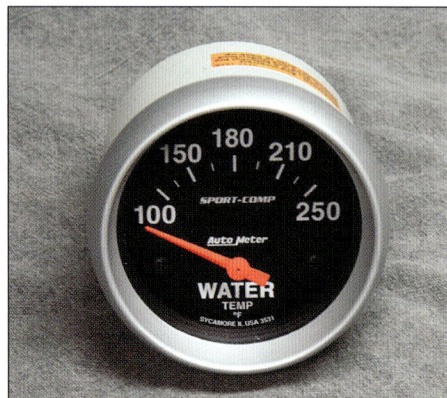

This is the Auto Meter Sport-Comp-series water/coolant temperature gauge. Much like the oil-pressure gauge, it requires electrical power to the input terminal and a temperature signal from the coolant-temperature sending unit to the sender terminal of the gauge.

the sender is located. The temperature will vary, depending on the location of the sender, such as in the engine block versus in the intake manifold.

The coolant temperature should never fall below 32°F or exceed 212°F. These extremes are the freezing and boiling points for water, respectively. Although boiling over is more common than freezing, neither one is good for an engine. Avoid using Teflon tape on the sender, as the sender must ground through its mounting location.

Speedometer

The speedometer displays the speed that the vehicle is moving in real time, which is useful to obey the posted speed limits. An odometer within the speedometer displays the total distance the vehicle has traveled, which is useful in maintaining that vehicle. Depending on the gauges used, the speedometer will display in miles per hour (MPH), kilometers per hour (Km/H), or both.

Connections vary from one manufacturer to another, but they typically require input from the transmission, a power source, and a ground. Conventional speedometers gather input from the transmission through an inductive sensor, an electronic control box, or a Hall-effect sensor. Speedometers that are based on global positioning systems (GPS) are relatively new. This GPS signal can be sent directly to a speedometer mounted in the truck or to a cell phone or other electronic devices.

When selecting aftermarket gauges for a truck, there is a choice to use a mechanical or electrical speedometer, even when the rest of the gauges are electric. For a mechanical speedometer, a change in rear-end gears or tire size typically requires changing a drive gear at the transmission connection to have a speedometer that provides an accurate reading. For an electrical speedometer, these same changes can be easily resolved through recalibration of the speedometer.

The actual step-by-step procedure

This Auto Meter Sport-Comp-series speedometer is available as part of a replacement gauge panel/gauges set specifically for the 1967–1972 Chevrolet trucks. The kit includes gauges for an electric speedometer, a tachometer, the fuel level, the oil pressure, the volts, and the coolant temperature.

The back of the speedometer includes two mounting studs, spaces for two dash lights, and spade connectors for a plug that works with the appropriate wiring for the speedometer-to-transmission connection.

for recalibration of a programmable speedometer varies. However, the process can be done anywhere along a highway that has mile markers or some method of driving exactly 1 mile (5,280 feet) apart. With the vehicle running but not moving, start the calibration procedure. Then, drive exactly 1 mile. Complete the ending calibration instructions. This will now provide a calibrated speedometer and odometer. If the rear-end gears or rear tire diameter are changed, repeat this process to continue having accurate measurements.

Fuel Level

Unlike the voltage, oil-pressure, and coolant-temperature gauges that measure and display specific values, the fuel-level gauge gives merely an approximation of the fuel level in the gas tank. It does not even provide how many gallons are left. It simply shows identifiers for being full, 3/4 of a tank,

A 1970 Chevrolet C10 that is used as an example in this book uses this Auto Meter Sport-Comp-series fuel-level gauge. The size and simple layout of the gauge make it easy to read. The electrical connection is as simple as a power wire (daisy-chained from the voltmeter), a wire from the fuel-level sender, and a ground wire.

1/2 of a tank, 1/4 of a tank, and empty.

For this reason, when replacing the gas tank, know its capacity. Knowing this and the average fuel economy of the truck will provide a rough idea of how far you can travel before running out of fuel. This can be especially helpful when traveling.

While you may not be really concerned about the performance of your truck's engine if it is running, you probably tend to keep an eye on the fuel-level gauge. After all, when you run out of gas, the engine will quit running. Most likely, you will not be at the most convenient location when that happens.

The fuel-level gauge has two distinct components: the fuel-level sending unit and the gauge itself. The fuel-level sending unit includes a float, an arm, and a variable resistor. The float is attached to one end of an arm that also connects to a variable resistor that is attached to the mounting bracket. This assembly attaches to a bracket that is inserted through an opening in the top of the tank.

As the float rides up or down with the level of the fuel, it moves a wiper along a strip of bimetallic metal that is grounded on one end. When the float moves so that the wiper is closer to the grounded end of the bimetallic strip, there is less resistance. When the float moves so that the wiper is farther away from the grounded end, there is more resistance. This amount of resistance (small or large) is what causes the fuel-level gauge to operate.

The gauge and sender must be compatible for the fuel-level sender to work correctly. Some gauges are designed so that a small amount of resistance indicates a full tank, and a large amount indicates an empty tank, while other gauges are designed in the opposite manner. When a new fuel gauge is purchased, the correct resistance (in Ohms) will be provided so that you can purchase a compatible fuel-level sender.

Some things to remember when installing a new fuel-level gauge are calibration and grounding. Most fuel-level senders are adjustable so that they can be used with fuel tanks of almost any dimension. Consult the instructions provided with the sender to adjust/calibrate for the tank that is being used, as the arm length must be adjusted during installation to compensate for the depth of the tank.

The fuel-level gauge and the sender must both be grounded. If the fuel-level gauge begins operating erratically, that is a sign that it has a faulty ground. While it is always a good idea to disconnect the negative battery cable from the battery when doing any wiring, it is especially important to do so to eliminate any sparks when working with the fuel-level sender or an electric fuel

pump because gasoline vapors may be present.

Most (if not all) of these vintage pickup trucks had the gas tank mounted in the cab behind the seat. Today, it seems difficult to imagine, but this location did allow for easy filling, simply due to gravity. It is now very common for the builders/restorers of these trucks to relocate the gas tank to under the bed. This is considered to be a much safer location, as the gas fumes are no longer inside the passenger compartment and the frame rails of the truck provide a bit more protection to the gas tank in the event of a collision.

When making this conversion, give some thought to the routing of the filler neck because this has a great impact on how easy or difficult it is to fill the tank. The filler neck must be higher than the tank. This may require a longer filler neck, but it will ultimately be better than one that does not flow well. The filler

neck does not have to be perfectly straight, but it should have no sharp bends that will slow down the flow when filling the tank. When there are sharp bends, the flow into the tank will slow down considerably and will often trip the automatic shut-off on the fuel pump.

Verify Fuel-Level Gauge and Sender Compatibility

Where people have issues with the fuel gauge is having a fuel-level sender that is compatible with their selected fuel gauge. Fuel-level gauges operate based on the amount of electrical resistance. This resistance is measured by a rheostat as the fuel level moves up and down. A common example of an incompatible sender/gauge is the gauge reading empty when the tank is actually full or vice versa.

The following table illustrates common empty/full resistance and general applications.

For example, when using an after-

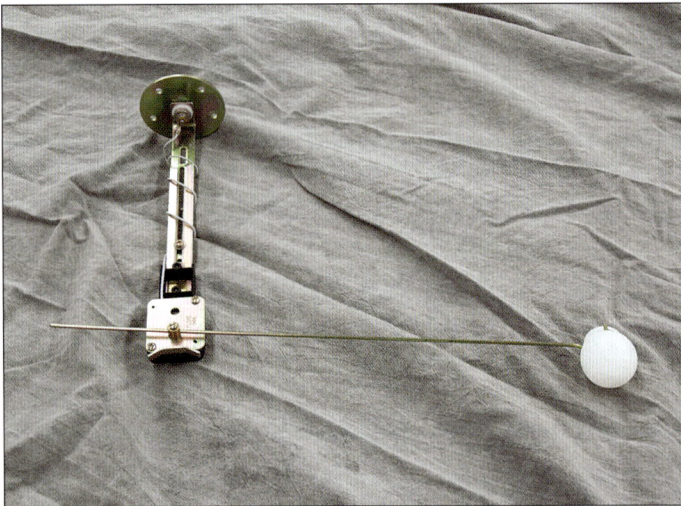

Unlike the oil-pressure and water-temperature senders, the fuel-level sender requires a float to determine the level of the fuel. The vertical portion of the sender is adjustable based upon the depth of the tank. The length of the float must also be adjusted based on the tank's depth. Electrical connections at the top of the sender are for the ground and to the fuel-level gauge.

The standard location for the gas tank in vintage GM pickup trucks is between the back of the seat and the back of the cab. New tanks are available if you choose to replace the tank in the stock location. The fuel-level float and sender are connected in the opening near the top of the tank. The sender wire can easily be run beneath the floor covering to go to the instrument panel.

Table 3-1: Fuel Gauge Resistance	
Empty/Full Resistance	**General Applications**
0/90 Ohms	Most GM vehicles from 1965 to 1996
0/30 Ohms	Most GM vehicles from 1950 to 1964
73/10 Ohms	Most Ford vehicles from 1950 to 1986; Most Chrysler vehicles from 1960 to the late 1980s
16/158 Ohms	Most Ford vehicles from 1987 to 2009
240/33 Ohms	Many aftermarket senders

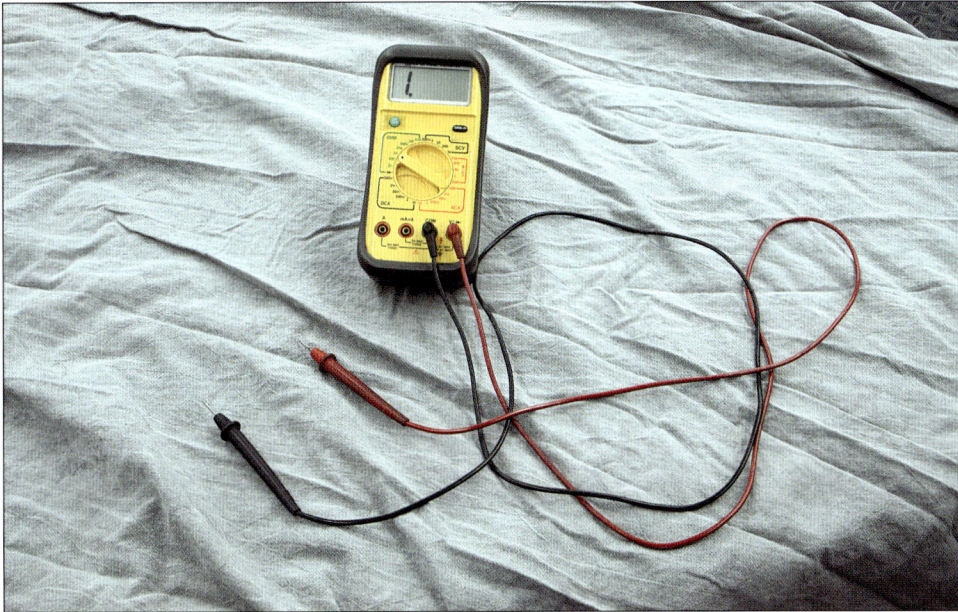

With the multimeter set to measure Ohms and no input, the multimeter will indicate an open circuit. With this unit, a "1" displays on the screen.

With the sensors touching each other, zeroes display on the screen, indicating that the multimeter is working correctly.

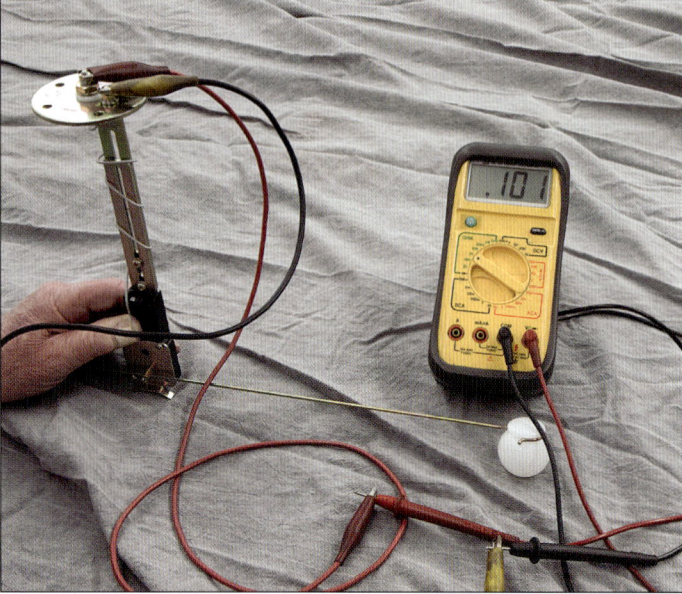

For the fuel gauge that is being used for this project, the sender must be designed for 240 Ohms when empty and 33 Ohms when full. With the positive lead of the multimeter connected to the sender, the negative lead to the ground, and the float at approximately mid-position, it should read approximately half of the range. At 101, it does.

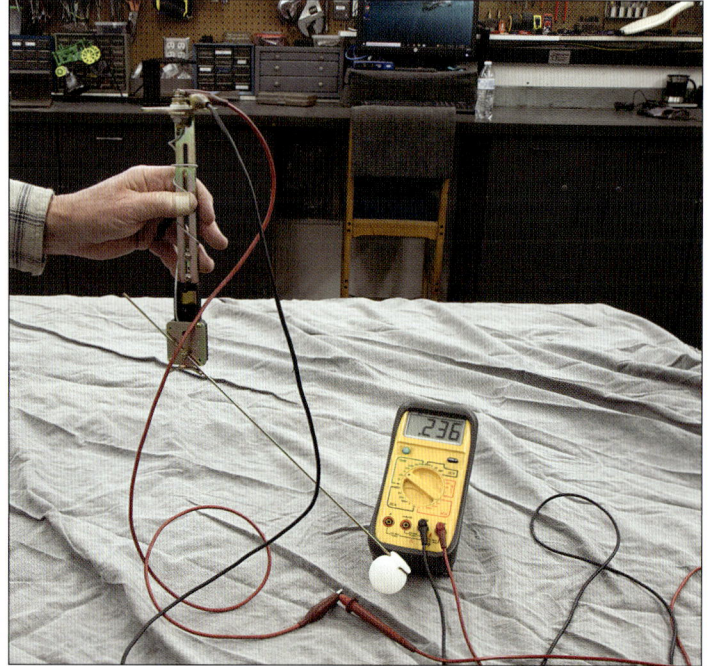

In this simulation of an empty tank, the reading is 236 Ohms. The advertised range is 233 for empty, but with meter readings, there is always the possibility of the numbers varying slightly, so do not expect the numbers to match exactly.

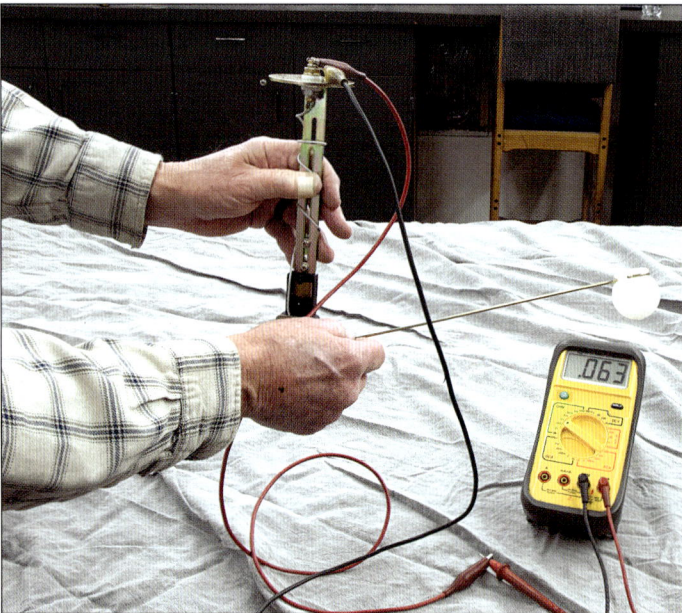

As the float rises to simulate more fuel in the tank, the number decreases, which is what is expected from this specific sender. Note that a high numerical reading indicates an empty tank for some senders while it indicates a full tank for other senders.

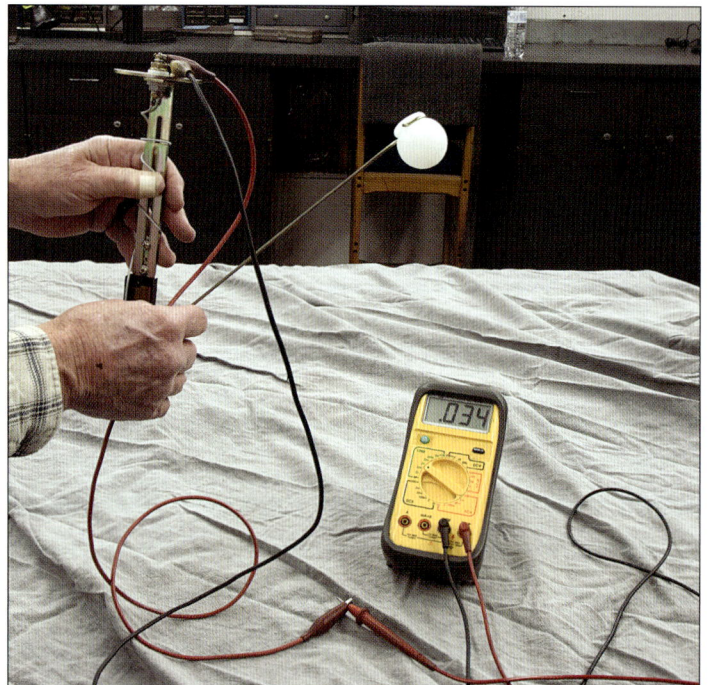

In this simulation of a full tank, the multimeter displays 34 Ohms, which is very close to the 33 Ohms that are expected for a full tank.

market gauge, it should read empty when it receives a 240-Ohm signal from the sender and should read full when it receives a 33-Ohm signal from the sender. In this example, the fuel level should read a half tank when 136.5 Ohms are received from the sender. Note that not all aftermarket fuel-level gauges use this same resistance, but the correct info should be provided with any new gauges that you purchase.

When you do not know what vehicle that your sender was originally installed in (such as one purchased at a swap meet), you can easily determine its resistance with a multimeter. First, test the multimeter to ensure that it is functioning correctly. With the multimeter turned on, set it to Ohms, and with the two leads not touching each other or anything else, the reading should represent an open circuit, such as "OL," "OR," or a flashing number "1." When the positive lead touches the negative lead, the multimeter should read approximately 0.00.

When the sender is still in the tank and you have a general idea of how much fuel is in the tank, disconnect the sender wire from the fuel gauge. Connect the positive lead of the multimeter to the sender wire that was just disconnected from the fuel gauge. Connect the negative lead of the multimeter to a ground. If you know that you have approximately a half tank of fuel, compare the reading to Table 3-1 to determine which sender you have. For example, if the reading is 45 Ohms, the sender is probably from a 1965–1996 GM product.

An open-circuit reading has three likely causes: no connection to the sender, no ground to the sender, or a faulty sender. When receiving a

reading near 0.00, there are three likely causes: the sender is shorted to ground, you have a 0/90- or 0/30-Ohm sender in an empty tank, or the sender float has sunk to the bottom of the tank.

When the sender can be removed from the tank, test the sender to determine its empty and full resistance readings. Connect the positive lead of the multimeter to the sender terminal and the negative lead to the sender ground. Starting at what would be the empty position of the float, record the reading of the multimeter. Slowly move the float to what would be the full position and record that reading. Note that these may not be precise numbers, but it will provide a good picture of what range the sender is designed for. Knowing this information allows you to purchase or find a fuel-level gauge that is compatible to the fuel-level sender that you have.

Besides incompatibility between the fuel-level sender and the fuel-level gauge, other sources of failure are bad electrical connections and no ground. With a metal fuel tank, the sender can usually be ground to the tank, but having a ground wire that goes directly to the negative side of the battery is often a better bet. With a plastic fuel tank, a ground wire to a chassis ground or the negative side of the battery is a must.

Tachometer

A tachometer displays the engine speed in revolutions per minute (RPM). There is no direct correlation between engine speed and vehicle speed. As the vehicle accelerates, the vehicle speed continues to increase. The engine speed, however, will increase to a point and then drop off

when the transmission shifts into a higher gear. Then, it repeats until reaching the highest gear.

Since the tachometer measures engine speed, it serves as a good diagnostic tool to determine possi-

The Auto Meter Sport-Comp-series tachometer is available as part of a replacement gauge panel/gauges set specifically for the 1967–1972 Chevrolet trucks. Aftermarket tachometers are commonly mounted on the steering column, but with the size of the gauge panel in the 1967–1972 Chevy trucks, the tachometer easily fits into the gauge panel.

Much like the speedometer, the back of the tachometer includes two mounting studs, spaces for two dash lights, and spade connectors for a plug that goes with the appropriate wiring for the tachometer to distributor connection.

ble problems or to measure performance improvements. To connect the tachometer, it requires input from the electronic ignition control box, the ignition coil, or from the tachometer signal from the alternator as well as a fused power source and a suitable ground.

A tachometer, which provides RPM, can very closely calculate vehicle speed when you know your rear tire diameter and your rear-end gear ratio. That equation is:

$$MPH = (RPM \times \text{tire diameter}) \div (\text{rear end gear ratio} \times 336)$$

For example, let's say that we are turning 2,500 rpm, have 30-inch tires in the back, and 3.08:1 rear-end gears. Plugging these numbers into the equation, the vehicle's speed is 72 mph.

What if you purchased a truck and you don't know the rear-end gear ratio? If the speedometer and tachometer work properly and you know the tire diameter, you can determine the rear-end gear ratio without pulling the rear end apart. You will need to rework the equation a bit. That equation is:

$$\text{rear end gear ratio} = (RPM \times \text{tire diameter}) \div MPH \div 336$$

Just in case you have an overdrive transmission or are considering installing one, the overdrive gear ratio fits into the equation as follows:

$$RPM = (MPH \times \text{rear-end gear ratio} \times \text{final-drive ratio} \times 336) \div \text{tire diameter}$$

With this information, you can see some of the advantages of having a tachometer.

Sending Units

For gauges to operate, they require a sending unit. For mechanical oil-pressure and water-temperature gauges, the sender connects to the gauge via a capillary tube. For all electrical gauges, the senders connect to the gauge via an electrical connection. Since you are potentially rewiring the entire vehicle anyway, wiring a few gauges should not be a difficult task.

On small-block Chevrolet engines, the oil-pressure sending unit is typically inserted into a threaded hole in the engine block relatively close to the distributor. On big-block Chevrolet engines, the oil-pressure sending unit is typically inserted into a threaded hole in the engine block relatively close to the oil filter.

If the engine is out of the truck for any reason, that would be the best time to install or replace the oil-pressure sending unit, as it is difficult to access while the engine is in the truck. Depending on the size of the sender, it may be necessary to use a reducer fitting for the sender to fit into the hole. Insert the sender into the hole, start it by hand, and firmly tighten it with a wrench. Since the sender is ground to the block, do not apply Teflon or any other sealant, as this would inhibit the grounding of the sender and cause the gauge to not operate correctly. Use a ring terminal to connect the wire from the oil-pressure gauge to the oil-pressure sending unit.

The coolant-temperature sending unit is typically inserted into a threaded hole in the intake manifold near the front of the engine. Most intake manifolds will have a variety of hole sizes, so it most likely will not require the use of a reducer fitting. Insert the sender into the hole, start it by hand, and firmly tighten it with a wrench.

Since the sender grounds to the intake manifold, do not apply Teflon or any other sealant. This would inhibit the grounding of the sender and cause the gauge to not operate correctly. Use a ring terminal to connect the wire from the coolant-temperature gauge to the coolant-temperature sending unit.

After installing the senders, plug all through holes in the intake manifold, cylinder heads, and engine block. Plugs for doing this are available with a recessed hex for use with an Allen wrench or with a square stud that can be used with an open-end wrench.

For a mechanical speedometer, a metal cable with a square end will slide into an opening on the left side of the transmission. It is secured by a threaded nut that threads onto a fitting on the transmission. On the gauge end, this same speedometer cable will be inserted directly into the back of the speedometer or into a control box that connects to the speedometer via wires.

For an electrical speedometer, a sensor threads into an opening on the left side of the transmission. This sensor has two wire pigtails connected to it: a positive and a ground. Wires connected to these pigtails are then connected to the appropriate terminals on the speedometer.

Remember that electric gauges and their senders must be grounded to work properly. This also applies to gauge lights.

A mechanically driven speedometer uses a cable that is square on both ends. One end slides into a square hole on the driver's side of the transmission and is secured by the hex nut that is shown. The opposite end is inserted into the back of the speedometer.

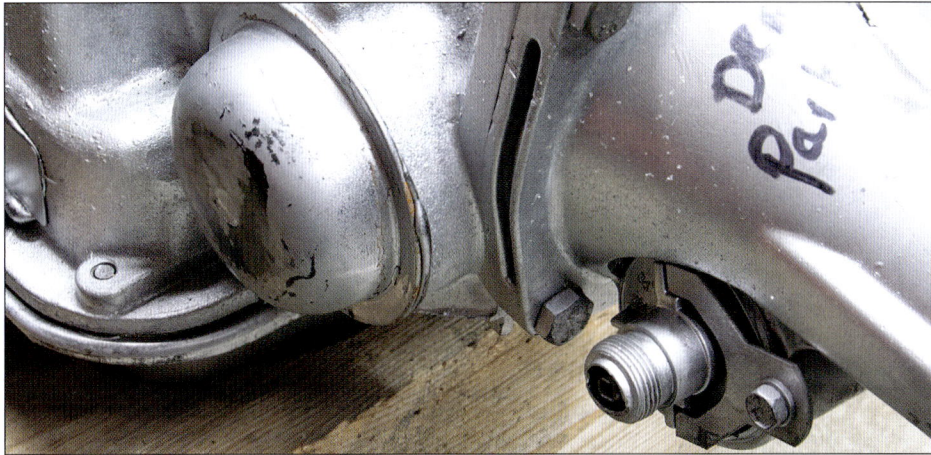

Regardless of the type of speedometer, the sender portion of it will thread onto this fitting on the left side of the transmission. It could be a square pin that drives a mechanical speedometer or a Hall-effect sensor that converts the revolutions to an electric signal.

At approximately 1½ inches in diameter, the oil-pressure sending unit is significantly larger than the sender for the coolant temperature.

For a completely electrical speedometer, a sensor threads into the opening on the driver's side of the transmission. The pigtail that is connected to this sensor allows for electrical connections to terminals on the back of the speedometer.

LIGHTING SYSTEMS

When compared to the ignition system or even some of the gauges, wiring the lighting system is easy to understand and complete. The only items that are required are a light bulb, a light socket, a power wire, a ground wire, and a switch mechanism. Failure of a lighting system is most commonly a result of an inadequate ground or a defective light bulb.

Exterior

Mandatory exterior lighting includes headlights, taillights, brake lights, and turn signals. In most cases on vintage GM trucks, the taillights and brake lights are addressed by the same wires, and the lighting is handled by a dual-filament bulb. Headlight wiring may seem a bit more complicated with a four-light system, but that is nothing to worry about. It simply requires a bit more wire and a few more connections.

Additional exterior wiring can include almost anything that you desire, but common examples are parking lights, side-marker and/or clearance lights, and cargo lights. These are all typically switched through the headlight switch, so

they should be included when wiring the headlights. Auxiliary fog lights and driving lights can be switched through the headlight switch but can also be switched through a separate circuit if desired. Note that auxiliary lights are a high-draw item and, therefore, require a relay to prevent overloading the switch.

Headlights

The headlights are controlled by the headlight switch that is mounted on the dash and a dimmer switch that is mounted on the floor. Newer GM trucks that use a rotary-style headlight switch or steering column–mounted dimmer switch are outside the scope of this book.

For the push-pull type headlight switch that is commonly found in these trucks, the headlights are turned on by pulling the switch knob all the way outward. Conversely, pushing the knob all the way inward turns the headlights off. An in-between

Chevrolet and GMC light-duty trucks did not have side-marker lights in the 1967 model year. The next year, side-marker lights (or headlights and taillights that wrap around) became a federal requirement. Using side-marker lights improves safety.

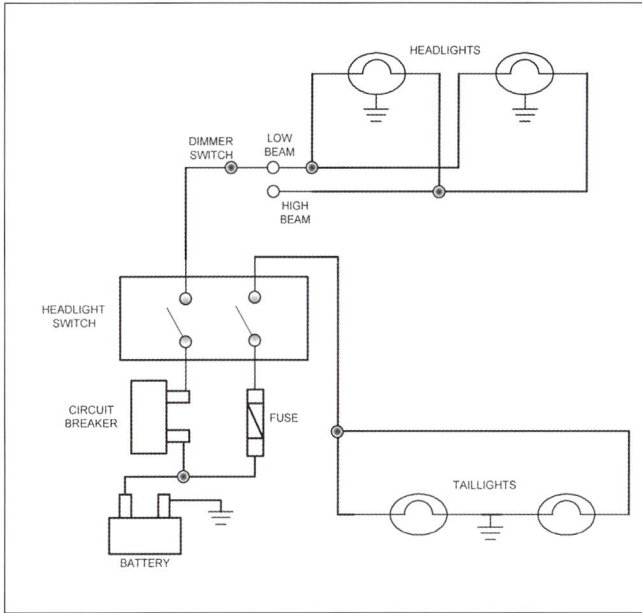

This schematic shows the basic layout for headlights and taillights and features all that you need to know when wiring them from scratch. Use a circuit breaker between the battery and the headlight switch because the headlights are a high-current-draw accessory. A fuse is sufficient for the taillights because they draw less current.

These vintage trucks can be fitted with light-emitting diode (LED) headlights, which provide a brighter light. The wiring for the headlights is the same, regardless of the bulb type.

Headlights in GM trucks are generally mounted to a bracket that is attached to the front fender or to the radiator core support. A bezel that covers the area immediately surrounding the headlamp must be removed to adjust the aim or remove the headlamp.

position turns on only the parking and/or side-marker lights, but these are also illuminated when the headlights are on.

The headlight switch has an input terminal along with separate terminals for headlights, taillights, courtesy lights, and parking lights. A power wire (12 gauge or larger) runs from the fuse panel to the input terminal on the headlight switch. Another wire runs between the headlight switch and the input terminal on the dimmer switch. A wire runs from the low-beam terminal of the dimmer switch to the power terminal of each low-beam bulb. A wire runs from the high-beam terminal of the dimmer switch to the power terminal of each high-beam bulb.

From the dimmer switch, these power wires can be routed to a physical location between each headlight and then split to run to each bulb or can be routed directly to one bulb and then to the other. A separate wire from the high-beam side of the dimmer switch connects to the high-beam

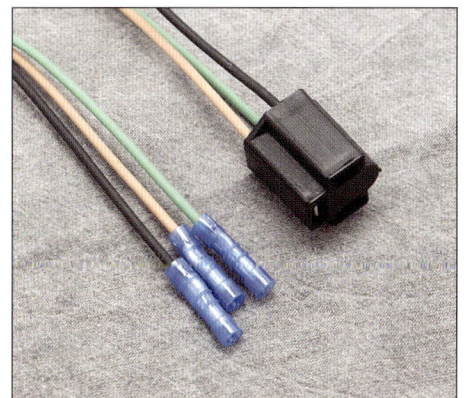

Most wiring kits include pigtails for a two-headlight system. The pigtails include a plug that matches the male connection of the headlights. The three wires are for low-beam, high-beam, and ground. Wires from the dimmer switch connect to the pigtails via a butt connector.

indicator light on the dash. The headlights and the high-beam indicator light must all be grounded to work properly.

Add Relays to the Headlight Circuit

Headlights draw a lot of current, so installing an electrical relay helps to prevent overloading the headlight wiring. In addition, an electrical relay can minimize the resistance in the circuit and provide more power to the headlamps, enabling them to burn brighter.

Install one 20-amp relay between the dimmer switch and the low-beam terminals of the headlights and another 20-amp relay between the dimmer switch and the high-beam terminals of the headlights. Electrical relays are available with a mounting tab, which makes mounting these two relays to the inner fender or the radiator core support near the headlights very convenient. Ensure that heat-shrink tubing is used in all electrical connections that are exposed to weather, even if it is under the hood. The engine compartment does get wet.

Each relay requires a fused power source that is connected to terminal 30 of the relay. This power source can be from an ignition "on" circuit in the fuse panel, the starter solenoid connection, or directly from the battery. This power source must have a 30-amp fuse or a circuit breaker installed close to the battery. One power wire can run to the general vicinity of the relays and then split to connect to each relay. In addition, each relay requires a ground wire connected to terminal 86 on the relay. This ground wire must also connect to the ground terminal on each headlight and finally to an adequate ground.

These 30-amp electrical relays with a mounting tab are available from NAPA with a plug and pigtail. Whether or not you use the pigtail is up to you. You can use a spade connector for each connection, which helps to minimize the rainbow of colors. Verify that the wire connections are correct (whether they are going directly to the terminals or to the pigtail).

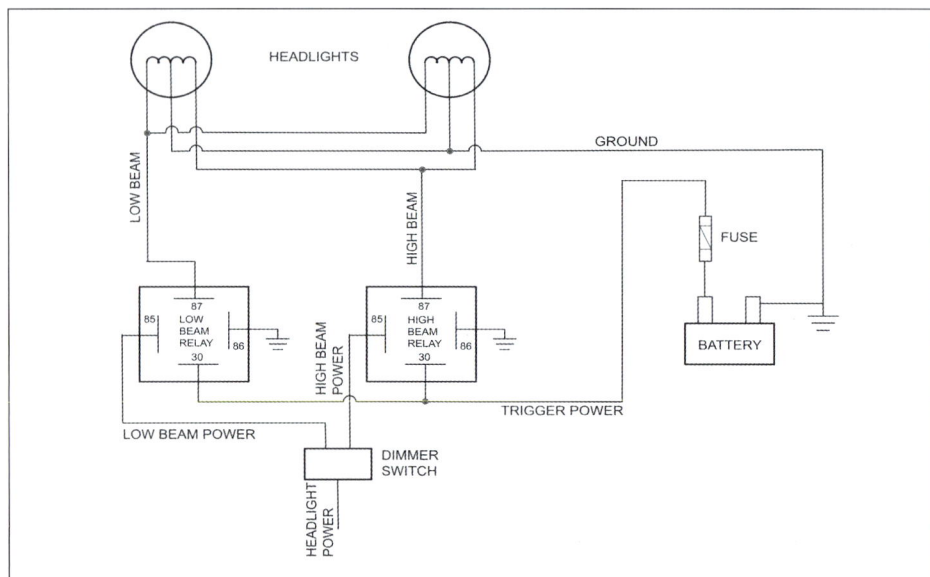

Headlight power goes to the dimmer switch from the headlight switch. From the dimmer switch, connect the low-beam wire to the low-beam relay and the high-beam wire to the high-beam relay at terminal 85. Connect a fused power wire to terminal 30 of each relay. Connect a power wire from terminal 87 of the low-beam relay to the low-beam terminal of each headlight. Connect a power wire from terminal 87 of the high-beam relay to the high-beam terminal of each headlight. Connect a ground wire to terminal 86 of each relay and to the ground terminal of each headlight.

The low-beam headlight power wire from the dimmer switch connects to terminal 85 on the low-beam relay. A power wire connects to terminal 87 on the low-beam relay and to each low-beam terminal on the headlights. The high-beam headlight power wire from the dimmer switch connects to terminal 85 on the high-beam relay. A power wire connects to terminal 87 on the high-beam relay and to each high-beam terminal on the headlights.

Note that some wiring kits provide two low-beam power wires and two high-beam power wires (one of each for each side of the vehicle), while other kits simply provide one low-beam power wire and one high-beam power wire. Whether it is one or two, all low-beam power wires must connect to terminal 85 of the low-beam relay, and all high-beam trigger wires must connect to terminal 85 of the high-beam relay. Likewise, a wire from terminal 87 of the low-beam relay must connect to the low-beam terminal of all headlights, and a wire from terminal 87 of the high-beam relay must connect to the high-beam terminal of all headlights.

Turn-Signal Lights

Presuming that a steering column that includes a turn-signal lever (switch) is being used, wires from the turn-signal lever run along the inside of the steering column to a point and then connect to half of a plug. The other half of the plug connects to wires that run to the horn, each front turn signal, hazard lights, turn-signal power, and the rear turn signals. Even if an aftermarket turn-signal switch that clamps onto the steering column is used, the same electrical connections need to be made.

Using a plug to make these connections allows for the steering column to be removed (if necessary) without damaging any wiring. The plug also ensures that no wires get crossed (as long as they are installed correctly initially). During the initial wiring, it is easy to match up the various colors of the wires, but after a few years, those colors may begin to fade and not be so different from one another.

Parking/Side-Marker Lights

Parking or side-marker lights are powered by a wire from the parking-light terminal on the headlight switch. Pulling the headlight-switch knob to the first detent turns on the parking lights, while pulling it outward all of the way also turns on the headlights. The wire from the headlight switch runs to

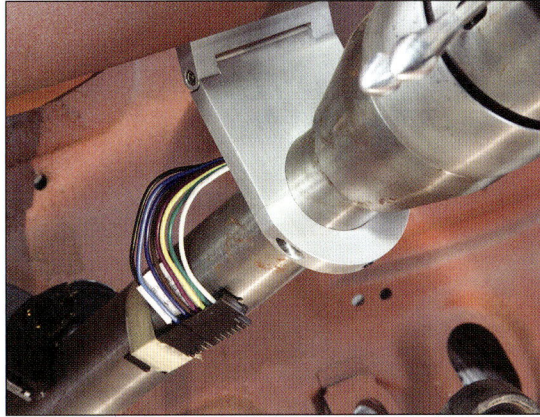

Most aftermarket steering columns include wiring for the horn, each front turn signal, hazard lights, turn-signal power, and the rear turn signals terminated in a plug toward the lower end of the steering column. The wires from those components are terminated at the other end of the plug. This makes for easy disassembly for servicing.

Aftermarket turn signals mounted atop the front fenders are common on earlier vintage trucks and especially the larger trucks. This 1954 or first-series 1955 model is equipped with factory front parking lights between the grille and the bumper.

This GMC Stepside is very nice overall and is a nice, clean example of contemporary styling. From this vantage point, it is evident that the front grille and lighting would be very difficult to see from the side, which makes side-marker lights a safety benefit.

one terminal on the left parking-light socket and then over to one terminal on the right parking-light socket.

When the parking-light sockets have a second terminal, they require a ground wire to be connected to the socket and to an adequate ground. If there is no second terminal, the socket is intended to ground through its housing. A ground wire will typically provide a more consistent ground.

When a truck has side-marker lights, these can be wired to operate as turn signals rather than merely parking lights. To do this, connect the turn-signal wire to one terminal of the side-marker light and to the front turn signal. Connect the parking-light wire to the other terminal of the side-marker light and to the front turn signal. When wired in this manner, there is no need for a ground wire, as the two lights will ground through the front turn signal.

Taillights

Taillights are powered by a wire from the taillight terminal on the headlight switch. Pulling the headlight-switch knob to the first detent turns on the taillights as well as the parking lights, while pulling it out all of the way also turns on the headlights. The wire from the headlight switch ultimately powers multiple lights on the back end of the truck.

The left taillight wire connects to the left rear side-marker light (if used), to the taillight, and finally to the license-plate light. In similar fashion, the right taillight wire connects to the right rear side-marker light (if used) and then to the taillight. If the license-plate light has two lamps, you can connect either the left or the right taillight wire to the second license-plate light.

Brake Lights

The brake-light circuit requires two major items: power to the lights and a switch to control that power. However, unlike headlights that require direct input (manually pulling the headlight-switch knob to the on position), the brake lights illuminate due to the indirect input of applying pressure to the brake pedal. In very simple terms, when all is working as it should, simply pressing the brake pedal will apply the brake and illuminate the brake lights.

On most vintage GM trucks, the brake lights and turn signals are integrated, meaning that one wire provides the necessary power for the two functions. One dual-filament bulb allows for the taillights and the brake lights/turn signal to be contained in one socket. While both taillights are powered by one wire, the integrated brake light/turn signals require one specific wire for the left side and another specific wire for the right side.

Brake-Light Switch

Electrical power is provided to the brake-light switch when the ignition is in the run or accessory position. A wire from the brake-light switch connects to the turn-signal switch, splitting the circuit when the turn-signal indicator is activated. This allows for one taillight to work as a brake light while the other works as a turn signal. When pressure is applied to the brake pedal, it activates the brake-light switch, which closes the circuit and illuminates the brake lights.

On most GM light-duty trucks, the parking (or side-marker) lights are secured in place with just two or three screws, depending on vintage.

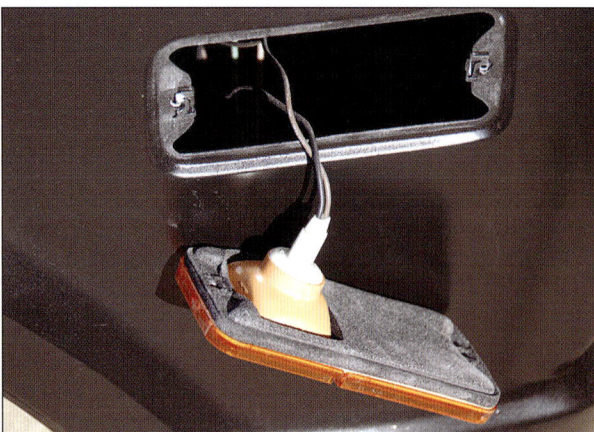

To access the light bulb and the wiring connection, remove the two or three screws that secure the lens to the body. With a simple twist, the light socket can be removed from the lens.

The wires that provide power to taillights on Stepside trucks are exposed in their stock form because the lights are not recessed into the body's sheet metal. These wires can be protected by braided stainless conduit, wrapped with shrink wrap, or wrapped in electrician tape. It is not recommended to leave the wires unprotected.

Taillights on Stepside trucks typically mount on a bracket that is attached to the truck bed, providing a very utilitarian look. However, this also allows for some customization by using different taillights and/or custom brackets. The mounting studs for the taillight assembly to the mounting bracket provide the ground.

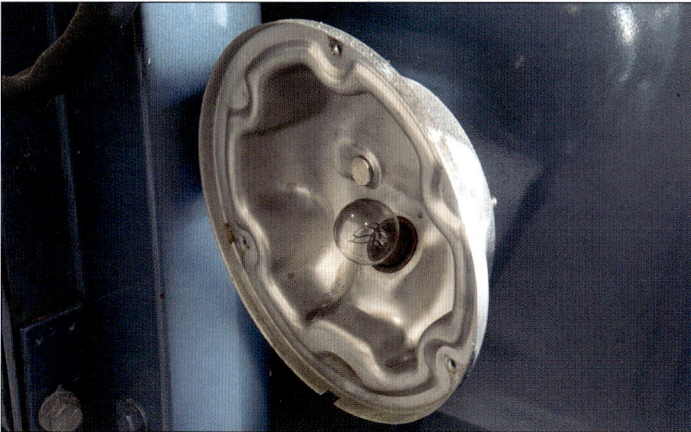

A single 1157 bulb inside of a clean housing provides taillights, turn signals, and brake lights on many vintage GM trucks.

To provide taillights, turn signals, and brake lights all in one bulb, that bulb must be the dual-filament type.

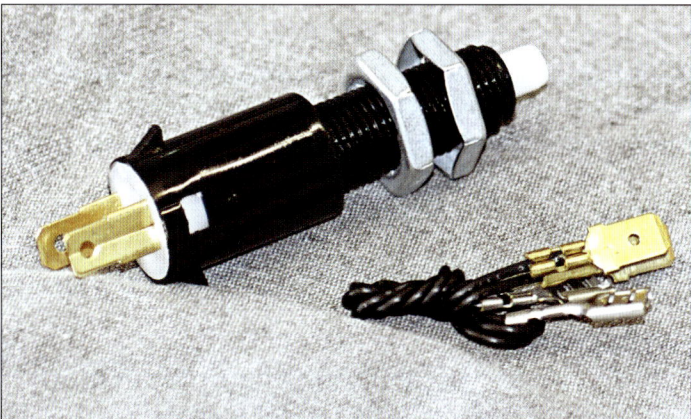

Most vintage GM trucks used a button-type brake-light switch from the factory. This type of switch must be positioned so that the brake-pedal arm pushes the button in when the brakes are applied. This closes the electrical circuit, and the brakes lights illuminate. The two spade connectors are for power and ground wire connections. The two nuts on the threaded shaft allow for mounting the brake-light switch. A lever-type brake-light switch works in the same way.

The brake-light switch is one of three general types of switches: button, lever, and pressure. The button and lever types are very similar, as they physically interact with the brake-pedal arm. The brake-light switch is mounted so that the brake-pedal arm presses the button or pushes the lever to electrically close the brake-light circuit, switching the brake lights on in the process.

Some vehicles are wired just the opposite: the circuit is open until the brake-pedal arm is pushed away from the spring-loaded brake button or lever. When positioned correctly, either of these mechanical-type switches work quite well and do not require any maintenance. This makes them common in OEM applications.

The pressure-activated brake-light switch is mounted inline as part of the brake line. When the brake pedal is applied, pressure in the brake line increases, activating the switch and powering the brake lights. Since the brake lights are a high electric draw, an electric relay should be used with the pressure-type brake-light switch to prevent switch failure. Note that this type of switch operates on fluid pressure, so low brake fluid and/or a brake-line leak could result in no brake lights.

Auxiliary Lights

Although auxiliary lighting is not as common on vintage pickup trucks as it may be on some other types of vehicles, it is not uncommon to add fog lights or driving lights. Of course, as long as you are well versed in the basics of automotive electronics, you are capable of adding any lights that you want.

Most aftermarket lighting includes at least a schematic of how it should be wired. Whether or not instructions are included, the minimum requirements for lighting are power, ground, and an on/off switch. For any electrical accessories that are not included in the vehicle's stock wiring, include an electrical relay to prevent burning up the accessory switch. In addition, ensure that the equipment is adequately grounded, whether that is through the fixture mounting or via a wire to a ground stud.

This restored tow truck is a good example of the use of auxiliary lighting, as it has an emergency beacon and clearance lights mounted atop the cab. The hazard flashers that are mounted atop the front fenders provide additional safety lighting.

A pressure-activated brake-light switch threads into a T-fitting that is mounted in the brake line. Use bullet-type connectors to connect positive and ground wires to the brake-light switch. When the brakes are applied, the pressure of the brake fluid closes the circuit to illuminate the brake lights. Using an electrical relay with this type of switch is recommended.

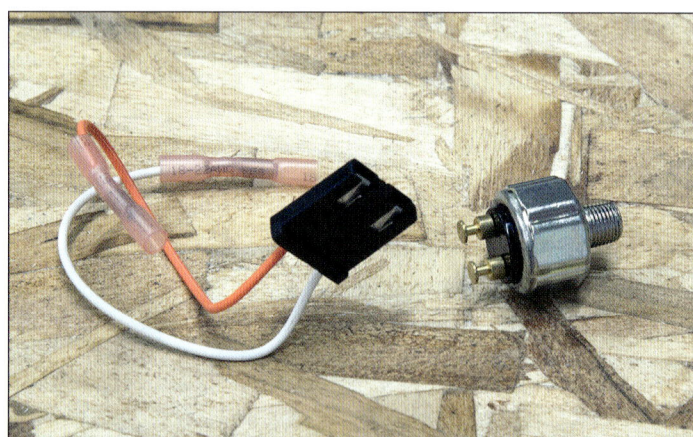

This is a pressure-activated brake switch that has the same characteristics (other than the electrical connection). These button-type connections require the pigtail (as shown) that slides on across the top of the connection buttons.

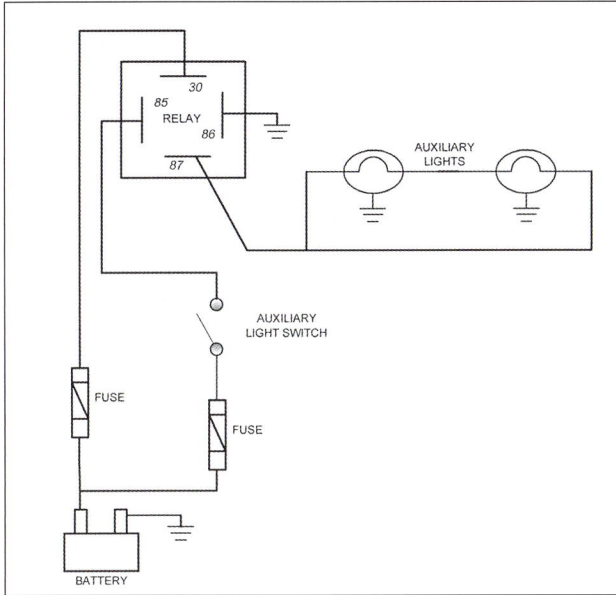

The relay trigger wire connects to terminal 30, and the ground wire connects to terminal 86.

Fog lights, as well as most auxiliary driving lights, draw lots of current. Therefore, they typically burn out the switches that are normally included with the lights. To protect the wiring and prevent the switch from burning out, install an electrical relay between the switch and the lights. Power in from the switch connects to terminal 85, and the power wire to the lights connects to terminal 87.

specifically lights, power outlets in a truck are a welcome convenience with all of today's electrical devices that require charging on occasion. These power outlets are available in at least three different configurations: as a cigar lighter type, a 110-volt outlet, or a USB port. These are easy to install, and with all of the accessories that are available, it might make sense to install one of each of them in your truck.

Indicator

By definition, indicator lights must indicate something, which means that they must have some sort of sender to make them illuminate. This must be something other than an on/off switch and must be tied into the system that it is monitoring.

For all intents and purposes, all trucks will have a high-beam light indicator and lights that indicate when the turn signals are on. These are all included in the truck's wiring system, whether it is stock wiring or an aftermarket wiring kit.

This type of fog light includes a power wire, but it does not include a ground wire because it is intended to ground through the mounting bolt. When this does not suffice, it is possible to use a ring terminal placed over the mounting shaft to run to a known ground source.

Interior

Vintage trucks had little more than dash lights and a dome light from the factory. With the 1967 model year, additional lighting began appearing on the options list. However, that is not to say that interior

lighting cannot be added to meet your needs.

Courtesy lights that illuminate when a door opens are a nice convenience. Depending on the wiring, these can be included with map or reading lights. Although they are not

The interior of this Task Force truck features many cool details and hints of many electrical accessories. A switch in the door indicates power windows, and vents in the dash and the center console as well as the Vintage Air panel indicate that it has air conditioning. The courtesy light in the console looks good, and I'm not sure what the square push-buttons control.

However, there are other components that could benefit from an indicator light. If there are no running gauges, add an indicator for low engine oil pressure and high engine coolant temperature. These warning lights (also known as idiot lights) were common when these trucks were new. Additional items where an indicator or warning buzzer might be handy include one for leaving the lights on when the engine is shut off or when the emergency/parking brake is still engaged.

To wire almost any indicator light or audible warning device, run a wire from the power supply of the device being monitored to the indicator. The indicator will also require a ground. With a good knowledge of automotive electrical systems, the only limit is your imagination when it comes to vehicle lighting. One would hope that good taste comes into play as well.

Indicator lights are available in various colors. Red, blue, green, and amber are the most common. They are available in various sizes as well. Aftermarket dash panels often have indicator-light holes that have been pre-drilled, so verify the size that is needed before purchasing. In addition, remember that dash-mounted indicator lights should not be so large that they are overwhelming when driving.

Dome/Courtesy Lights

The stock dome light in these vintage GM trucks has not varied much in operation and very little in appearance over the years. Typically, the dome light can be manually turned on through the headlight switch. With the addition of a doorjamb switch, the dome light can be wired to automatically illuminate when one or both doors are opened.

A doorjamb switch is a plunger that slides in and out. It is usually wired to a ground wire so that when the door is closed, a plunger slides inward in the mounting, creating an open circuit (no dome light). When the door is opened, the plunger slides outward in the mounting, creating a closed circuit and thereby turning the dome light on.

Courtesy lights can be installed in addition to the standard dome-light location. Common locations are in a center console to illuminate the floor, in an overhead console for use as a map light, or in the doors as a caution light when entering and exiting the vehicle.

Today's salvage yards are full of vehicles that have all sorts of creature comforts, so that might be a good place to search for additional (and affordable) interior lighting for a truck. If you are willing to spend a bit more money, the automotive aftermarket has a wide variety of configurations, sizes, and shapes of interior lighting.

Regardless of the interior lighting used, give the placement some thought. It is senseless to install additional lighting that does not illuminate the area that you want it to. If you want a light that will enable you to read a map, make sure that the light is placed high and in front, where the map would be. If you want a light to see inside a storage compartment located between the bucket seats, mount the light there.

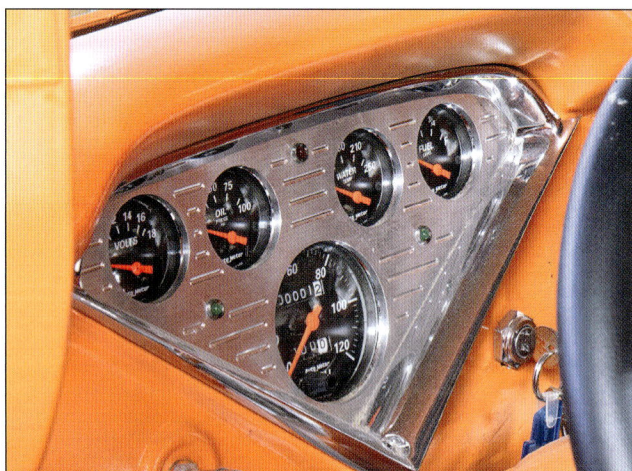

The dash panel of this 1955 pickup includes three indicator lights. The two green lights on each side of the speedometer are the left and right turn-signal indicators. The red light toward the top of the dash panel is the high-beam-indicator light.

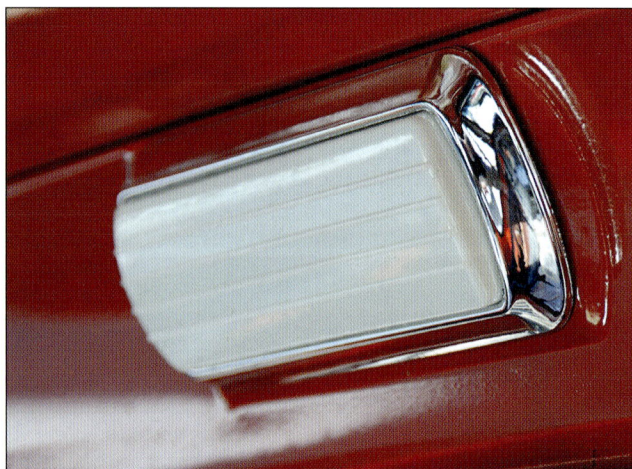

There is nothing wrong with the stock-style dome light that has not changed much through the life of these vintage trucks. In its stock location, it is above and behind the driver and passenger, providing ample light for reading a map.

LEDs

Light-emitting diodes (LEDs) are very bright and are less likely to burn out than filament-type bulbs, making them very popular as a lighting source. They also require very little power, which makes them efficient.

While LEDs are very bright when viewed head on, they are directional. This means that they are perfect for use on the back of a truck, as they provide very bright taillights, brake lights, and turn signals for anyone driving a vehicle right behind you. To disperse the light over a larger area, a prismatic lens is required, as the LED would not be easily seen from even a slight angle.

LEDs are great for use in an internal map light or any other situation where a bright light is required in a relatively small area. LEDs for headlights are suitable for high beams and high-speed driving because they can illuminate a small circle of light for a long range. However, LEDs are not really suitable for low-beam headlights when you want to see anything that is alongside the road right in front of you.

Potential Concerns

One area of concern with LEDs is when using them as a turn signal. A standard bimetallic-type flasher that operates based on continuity (heat) switches the flashing lights of a filament-type bulb on and off quite well. However, LEDs do not create heat. Therefore, the LEDs may not flash.

LED turn signals require a no-load flasher to work properly. When using filament bulbs in the front turn signals and LEDs in the rear turn signals, it may require two separate flashers or a dummy load so that the LED portion of the circuit will flash.

Light Switches

Most standard lighting on vintage GM trucks is controlled in one form or fashion by the headlight switch. This standard lighting includes the headlights, taillights, parking lights, dash lights, dome light, and cargo lights. The position of the knob within the switch is what determines which lights are on and how bright they are. Of course, this depends on how the headlight switch is wired.

Newer GM trucks use a rotary switch, but the vintage trucks discussed in this book all used a push-pull headlight switch when they rolled out of the factory. Optional lighting, such as fog lights, driving lights, or any emergency lights, are typically operated by a separate dedicated switch.

Headlight Switch

In the automotive world, there are several variations of headlight switches, ranging from very basic to very complicated. A typical auto parts store will usually sell a headlight switch that has only three terminals: incoming power to the switch, power to the high-beam circuit, and power to the low-beam circuit. For a contemporary Silverado, the headlight switch is more complex, as it will also control dome/courtesy lights, daytime running lights, parking lights, and dash lights. For our vintage GM trucks, the headlight switch is somewhere between these two extremes.

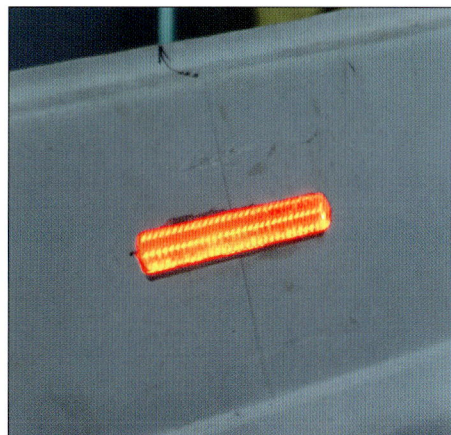

LEDs are a very common light source these days. They are very bright, which makes them a great upgrade for things such as taillights and brake lights. A third brake light is shown that mounts from inside the vehicle and protrudes through the sheet metal. After installation, the lens can be sanded flush with the surface, making for a very smooth surface with plenty of light when needed.

This is an aftermarket light switch that is available at a local auto parts store. It includes a plug and connectors that allow you to simply remove the plug from the switch to do the wiring and then plug it back in. This eliminates connecting wires to the wrong terminal, which would be possible if the wires were connected separately.

Some headlight switches use ring connectors, but most stock GM headlight switches use push-on connectors. The type of connector used does not matter. The critical aspect is whether or not the switch is wired correctly.

Some switches are labeled, while others are not. Having a wiring schematic for the specific switch is handy but not always available. Many schematics are available on the Internet, but some of those are questionable at best. In some cases, they are downright confusing.

If the headlight switch is an aftermarket universal unit, it may look similar to another switch but may be wired differently internally. For this reason, using a continuity tester or a test light to verify which terminals have power at each knob position will make electrical chores easier.

Taking notes of the following process is important. First, determine how many positions the headlight switch has and then make a sketch of the electrical terminals. Sketch for each position of the switch or make your notes accordingly. While there may be exceptions, headlight switches typically have two positions that have power. One is pulled out partially (there is a distinct detent at this position), and the other is pulled out completely.

Begin by connecting a power source, such as a battery charger, to the power input terminal of the headlight switch. Connect a continuity tester or test light to a known ground and probe each terminal of the headlight switch while the switch is in each of its various positions. With the headlight-switch knob in the first position, check each terminal and make notes regarding which terminals have power and which terminals

Table 4-1: Headlight Switch Current		
Terminal	First Detent	Full Out
Headlights (to Dimmer Switch)	No Power	Power
Front Parking Lights	Power	Power
Rear Taillights	No Power	Power
Dash Lights	No Power	Power

This headlight switch is common to the vintage GM trucks that are covered in this book. There are two designs: the early design and the late design. For all intents and purposes, the only change is the placement of the terminal used for the parking lights.

On many GM trucks, when removing or installing the headlight switch, the knob must be removed before removing the switch from the dash. The knob can be removed by pressing the spring-loaded button located near the middle of the switch on the flat side. Push the button in while pulling the knob outward. The knob may need to be rotated slightly, but it will come out if you are pressing the spring-loaded button.

do not have power. When this is completed, move the headlight-switch knob to the second position and repeat the process.

On a push-pull headlight switch, the headlights should be on only when the switch is pulled to the full out position. Note that there is only one terminal for the headlights at

the headlight switch. A wire from this terminal runs to the dimmer switch, where headlight power is toggled between the high beam and low beam.

The front parking lights should turn on when the headlight switch is pulled to the first detent and remain on when the switch is pulled to the full out position. The rear taillights and dash lights should turn on when the switch is pulled to the full out position. A rheostat on the headlight switch brightens or dims the dash lights by turning the knob clockwise or counterclockwise, respectively.

Doorjamb Switch

For the dome light and/or courtesy lights to illuminate when one of the doors is opened, a doorjamb switch is used. One doorjamb switch is required for each door that you want to use to operate the light. The switch is installed in an appropriately sized hole in the stationary side of the doorjamb and positioned so that the plunger will push in when the door closes against it.

Note that with the somewhat-loose tolerances of some of these truck doors, proper positioning of the switch is critical (so that closing the door pushes the plunger inward). The switch itself is connected electrically by using a bullet connector to con-

nect a ground wire. When the door is closed, the switch is in an open circuit and there is no light. When the door is opened, the doorjamb switch closes the circuit and the dome light illuminates.

A magnetic doorjamb switch is a variation of the manual push-button-style doorjamb switch. As the name implies, this type of switch uses a magnet. A magnet is mounted in the opening edge of the door, while a reed switch is mounted on the stationary side of the doorjamb. The reed switch allows for the contacts to be normally open or normally closed. When the magnetic switch is normally open, the electrical circuit will close and turn the lights on when a magnetic field is present. Conversely, when the magnetic switch is normally closed, the electrical circuit opens and turns off the lights when there is no magnetic field present. Therefore, the wiring must be correct; otherwise, there will be lights on when the door is closed and no lights when the door is open.

Dimmer Switches

The dimmer switch is electrically mounted inline between the headlight switch and the headlights. This switch has three terminals and receives power directly from the headlight switch through one wire. The other two terminals are connections for wires to send power to the high-beam headlights or the low-beam headlights. It is a single-pole, double-throw switch that sends power to the high-beam lights or the low-beam lights. In a two-headlight system, you cannot have low-beam and high-beam lights on at the same time.

However, we all know that the

1958 and 1959 Chevrolet/GMC pickups had a four-headlight system, as did the GMC pickups during the 1967–1972 model years. From the factory, these systems had a standard headlamp (high beam and low beam) at the outward-most position and a high-beam-only headlamp at the inward-most position on each side.

From the dimmer switch, a power wire would connect to the low-beam terminal on each of the outermost headlamps. From the dimmer switch, a power wire would connect to the high-beam terminal on all four headlamps. So, yes, on a four-headlight system, lighting went from two low beams to four high beams with just a click of the dimmer switch.

Floor Mounted

To replace a floor-mounted dimmer switch, unplug the wiring connections and then remove the one

Each push of the plunger on a floor-mount dimmer switch toggles the headlights between high beam and low beam. The power wire from the fuse panel connects to the terminal in the middle. The low-beam power wire connects to one of the two lower terminals, while the high-beam power wires connect to the remaining terminal. The ears on the side of the dimmer switch allow it to be secured to two threaded holes in the floorboard.

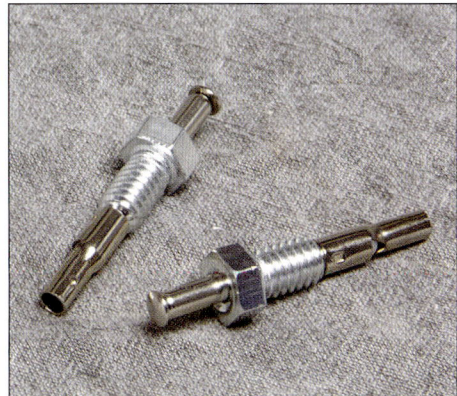

The doorjamb switch operates when the plunger is pressed inward as the door is closed. Ensure that the switch is located so that the door will make contact with and push the plunger inward. In addition, the wiring must be correct so that the courtesy lights are on when the door is open.

If your truck has dual headlights and you want to run a set of fog lights but don't want to mount them in the bumper, they can be mounted in the inner head-light location. Wire the headlights as a standard two-light system, and then wire the fog lights as an auxiliary light application.

or two bolts that secure the dimmer switch to the floor. Secure the replacement dimmer switch to the floor with the previously mentioned hardware. Then, plug the wiring back into the dimmer switch.

To save a possible second trip to the auto parts store, take the original dimmer switch along when purchasing a new one. Floor dimmer switches all look alike, but the spacing on the connectors is different on some of them. If you connect each wire separately rather than using a plug, it does not matter which one is used.

Column Mounted

The vintage GM trucks that this book is written about never had a dimmer switch mounted on the column from the factory. However, one of these newer steering columns could have been swapped in at one time or can be in the future. If the vehicle has one of these newer columns, consult with a vehicle-appropriate service manual for service information.

Finding an appropriate manual requires knowing what type of vehicle that the column was originally installed in. So, if you are considering the purchase of a steering column at a swap meet or other source, try to determine the source of the steering column. In addition, do yourself a favor and ensure that the steering column has an ignition key with it.

Accessory Switches

Switches are a means to control the flow of electricity through a circuit. By opening or closing an electrical circuit, an electrical device can be energized or shut down, sped up or slowed down, or movement changed from one direction to another. Switches can be controlled manually or electromagnetically.

Before purchasing a switch, verify that it will serve the desired purpose: does it have enough circuits, does it have the required terminals, and will it fit where it needs to be located? A headlight switch controls not only the headlights but also the taillights, parking lights, and potentially others. A wiper-motor switch must turn the wipers on and off, but it may be desired to control the speed of the wipers as well.

Toggle Switches

Unlike a headlight switch that controls multiple circuits, a toggle switch is very simple, as it merely turns an electrical device on or off. For automotive wiring, common configurations are single pole, single throw (SPST); single pole, double throw (SPDT); and center off. The physical arrangement may require sliding a button, flipping a lever, or turning a knob.

SPST

An SPST is the simplest of toggle switches because it is simply on or off. While in the on position, the circuit is closed and electrical current flows to the accessory being powered. While in the off position, the circuit is open and no electrical current flows to the accessory being powered. This type of switch is installed inline between the power source and the accessory and has only two terminals.

The accessory must be grounded either through its housing or via a separate wire to a known ground. When the switch includes an indicator light, it will also have a third terminal. This terminal is for connecting a ground wire for the light. The indicator light is powered by the same power that feeds the accessory.

SPDT

With an SPDT switch, the electrical circuit is closed all of the time. It has three terminals: common, normally closed, and normally open. A wire from the power source connects to the common terminal. Another wire runs from the normally closed terminal to the first accessory, and another wire runs from the normally open terminal to a second accessory. The position of the switch dictates which accessory is energized when power is applied.

When the switch is in the normally closed position, the first accessory is powered. When the switch is in the normally open position, the second accessory is powered. A common example of this type of switch is a dimmer switch, which allows low-beam or high-beam headlights but not both simultaneously.

Center Off

A center-off switch is a variation of an SPDT switch. It has three terminals: normally open, common, and normally open. A wire from the power source connects to the common terminal. Another wire runs from the normally open terminal to the first accessory and another wire runs from the other normally open terminal to the second accessory. When the switch is in the center (neutral) position, the circuit is open, and no electric current is passing through the circuit. The most common example of this type of switch is a turn signal.

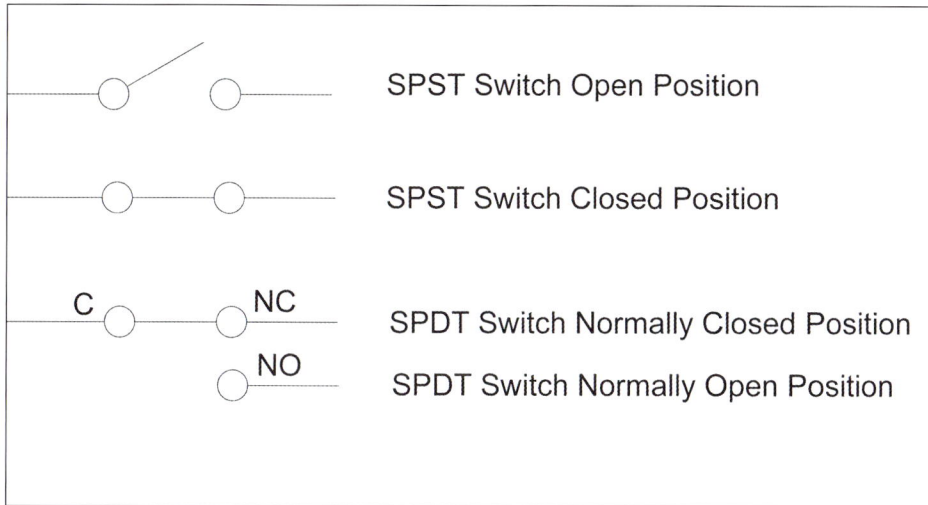

SPST Switch Open Position

SPST Switch Closed Position

C — NC — SPDT Switch Normally Closed Position

NO — SPDT Switch Normally Open Position

For an accessory that is either on or off, a single-pole, double-throw (SPDT) switch with just two terminals is required. The switch is simply installed inline of the power wire, with the power wire connecting to both terminals. Switches are available in various configurations, including toggle, rotary, slide, and rocker. Most of these are also available with some form of light that illuminates when the switch is in the on position.

A SPDT switch is commonly used as a dimmer switch for the headlights, but one could be used to switch between a main and auxiliary fuel tank. The electrical aspect of that application is to switch from one electric fuel pump to the other and requires an electrical connection for each fuel pump.

In addition to use as a turn signal, a center-off switch is useful for vehicles with various sets of auxiliary lights. For example, during off-roading, one position could turn on driving lights mounted on a roll bar, while the other position could turn on fog lights that are mounted on a grille guard. The physical wiring is the same as for any other SPDT switch but offers an off position.

When wiring an SPDT switch, the power-supply wire connects to the central (common) terminal. The wire that sends power to the first accessory connects to the terminal closest to that position of the switch, while the wire that sends power to accessory #2 connects to the terminal closest to the opposite position of the switch.

CIRCUITS FOR ACCESSORIES

While the ignition and lighting circuits are mandatory to operate these trucks, other electrical circuits are commonly found in them as well. These additional circuits can range from those that are required, such as an electrical fuel pump or an electric cooling fan, to comfort-based options, such as HVAC or audio/video systems.

When completely rewiring a truck, these optional accessory circuits can be wired as part of that process. However, they can also be added as a retrofit to the existing wiring systems. Quite often, these extra circuits simply require a power source, a suitable ground, and the addition of a relay or two.

Most of the contemporary GM automatic overdrive transmissions are electronically operated. For them to shift properly, they must be wired properly. If you use a high-performance engine and/or one that is using electronic fuel injection, an electric fuel pump is a requirement. That same high-performance engine will also benefit from an electric fan, rather than an inefficient mechanical fan that runs only while the engine is running.

We already know that driving a truck is cool, but having a complete HVAC unit that provides cool air, warm air, and can defrost the windshield when needed is a bonus. In many parts of the country, only one of those features may be necessary, but in other parts of the country, needing all three in the same day may occur.

Prior to installing electrical components, consider the fact that they may require maintenance down the road, so plan accordingly. Most electrical service issues are relatively simple as long as the necessary components can be accessed.

Electric Fuel Pumps

While an electric fuel pump may be installed inside or outside of the fuel tank (depending on the design), electrically it merely requires power and ground. However, since a fuel pump draws a large amperage, the fuel-pump circuit should include an electrical relay. Decide before purchasing the fuel pump whether you want to mount it in the tank or inside one of the frame rails because the pumps are different.

Mounting the electric fuel pump within the fuel tank allows the fuel to keep the pump cool. Mechanical fuel

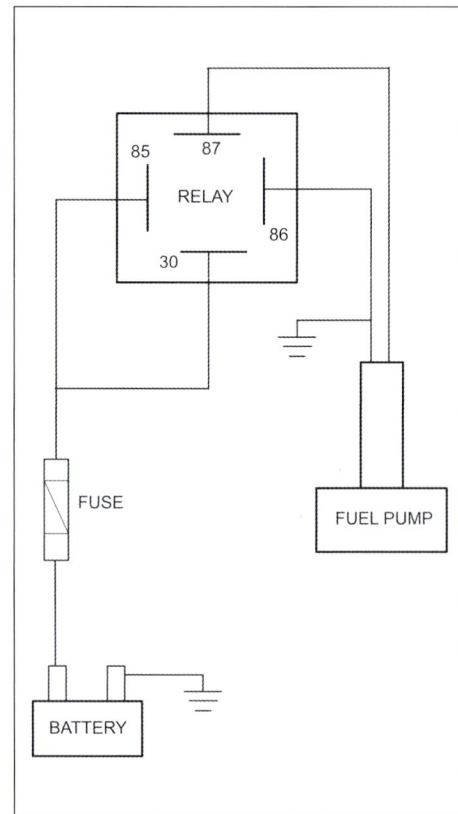

When using an electric fuel pump, an electrical relay is required to prevent system failure. Connect a 12-volt power wire to terminal 85 and to terminal 30. Connect a wire from terminal 87 to the positive side of the fuel pump to provide power. Connect a ground wire from terminal 86 to the negative side of the fuel pump and to chassis ground.

Installing an Electric Fuel Pump

1 This electric fuel pump is intended to be mounted outside of the fuel tank. The body of the pump has an engraved arrow showing the direction of flow. On the inlet side of the pump is an inline fuel filter. On the outlet side of the pump is a barbed fitting for use with rubber fuel-line hose. The electrical connections are a red wire for power and a black wire for ground. However, the electric fuel pump should always be wired using an electrical relay.

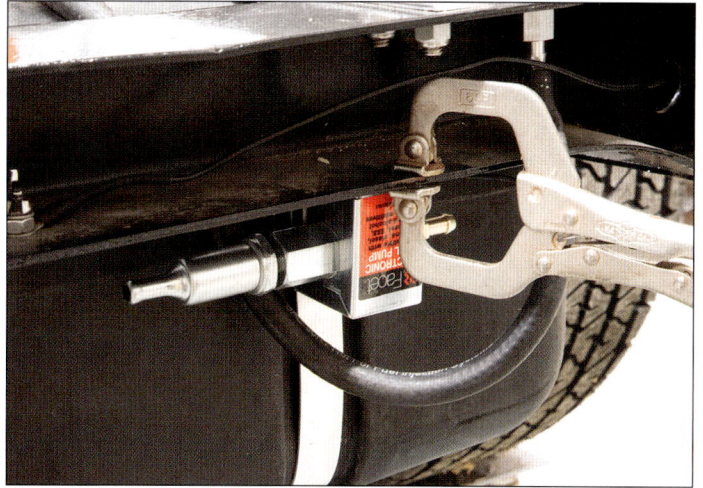

2 Determine a suitable location for the pump. The pump should be located no more than 12 inches higher than the bottom of the fuel tank. Clamp the pump in position. Then, mark and drill the necessary mounting holes.

3 Mount the fuel pump in place and secure with the necessary hardware. Note that the fuel line shown in this photo is actually running to a rollover vent valve, which will cause the fuel to stop flowing if the tank is turned upside down.

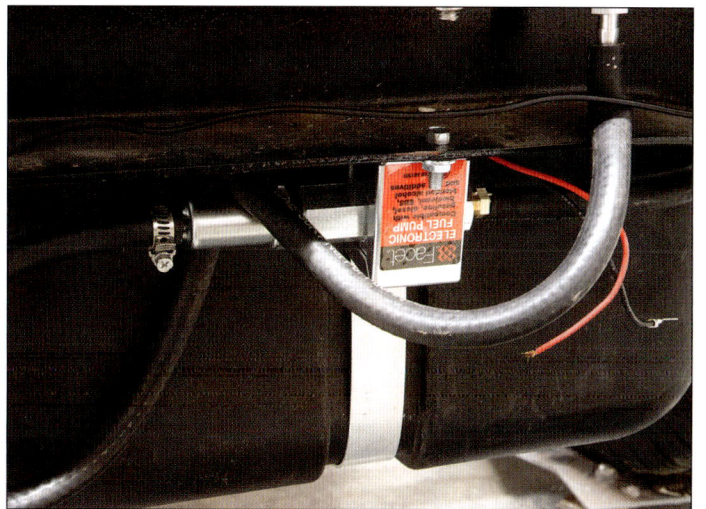

4 The fuel line connects to the pickup tube on the top of the tank, runs down between the fuel tank and crossmember, and then connects to the inlet side of the fuel pump. Connect a fuel line to the outlet side of the pump and route it to the induction system. Be sure to use appropriately sized hose clamps on all fuel-hose connections.

Installing an Electric Fuel Pump *continued*

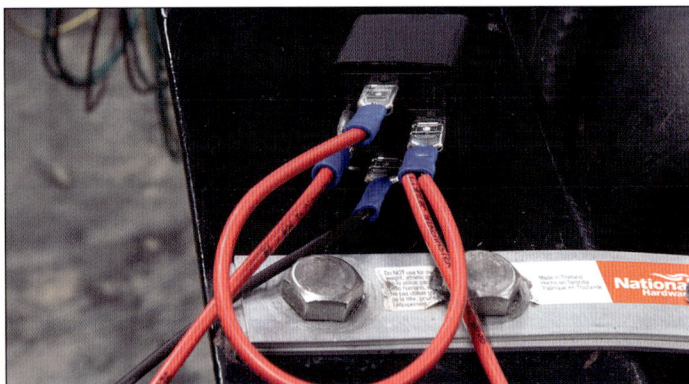

5 *Run a 16-gauge wire from the fuse panel to terminal 30 of the electrical relay with a jumper to terminal 85 of the electrical relay. These will provide power to the relay. Connect a 16-gauge wire from terminal 87 of the electrical relay to the power wire of the fuel pump. Connect a 16-gauge wire from terminal 86 of the electrical relay and the ground wire of the fuel pump to a suitable ground.*

6 *A ground stud in the rear crossmember is a convenient ground for taillights, a fuel-gauge sender, and a fuel pump.*

pumps are good at siphoning fuel, but electric fuel pumps work better and more efficiently when they are pushing the fuel. Therefore, if the fuel pump does not mount inside the tank, mount the electric fuel pump close to and within 12 inches (vertically) of the bottom of the tank.

Begin by mounting the fuel tank in its desired location. Then, connect the fuel line from the tank to the inlet side of the fuel pump. Whether a fuel filter comes with the fuel pump or not, install an inline fuel filter between the fuel tank and the fuel pump. Run another fuel line from the outlet side of the fuel pump to the induction system of the engine, whether it is carbureted or fuel injected. Note that some induction systems require a return line back to the fuel tank.

A SPST relay can be mounted in a convenient location and should be labeled as "fuel pump" if it is located near other relays. Verify that the relay is positioned somewhere safe from the elements and not too close to any source of excessive heat. Connect a wire from a fused power source to terminal 85 and to terminal 30 of the relay. Connect a wire from terminal 87 of the relay to the positive (power) terminal of the fuel pump. Connect terminal 86 and the negative terminal of the fuel pump to a known ground.

Transmission Lockup

The torque converter in most GM automatic transmissions uses a lockup clutch. When the clutch locks the turbine and pump together at highway speed, the fluid-flow interference and turbulence-related inefficiencies are eliminated. This increases the efficiency of the transmission, allowing it to effectively work as an overdrive, which increases gas mileage. In addition, this reduces heat within the transmission. Overheating is one of the main causes of failure in any automatic transmission.

For more information on servicing the transmission-lockup solenoid on your vehicle, refer to a model-specific repair manual.

TH350

When using an automatic transmission that incorporates a vacuum modulator, such as a TH350 or a Powerglide, a kickdown cable is required for proper operation. This kickdown cable works in unison with the throttle cable to cause the transmission to shift into a lower gear when the engine is under load, such as when climbing a hill or when passing another vehicle at highway speed. This is where the term "passing gear" originated.

The transmission can work without a kickdown cable but would require the driver to manually downshift when under a load. This simply defeats the purpose of having an automatic transmission. However, it is good to know when on a road trip and having issues with the kickdown cable.

TH400

When using an automatic transmission that incorporates a throttle switch, such as a TH400, the throttle switch must work with the electric choke for proper operation. This throttle switch requires 12 volts of electrical power to downshift the transmission. It is commonly located on the throttle pedal inside the cab or on the throttle linkage atop the engine.

To wire the throttle switch, run a 12-volt power wire from the fuse panel to the positive side of the electric choke on the carburetor. Before crimping the connector in place, add another wire that will connect to the input side of the throttle switch. This will result in having two wires connected to the positive side of the electric choke.

Now, run a wire from the output side of the throttle switch to the kickdown detent located on the transmission. A cable on the throttle switch must then be connected to the carburetor.

700R4

When using an automatic transmission that incorporates a throttle valve, such as a 700R4 or 2004R, a throttle valve (TV) cable is required for proper operation. One end of the TV cable is inserted into the transmission, where it connects mechanically. The other end of the TV cable connects the carburetor or throttle body.

This TV cable must be adjusted properly, as it controls partial-throttle downshifts, detent downshifts, and line pressure. The incorrect adjustment of this cable is the typical cause of failure for these transmissions. Therefore, refer to the instructions provided with the TV cable.

A/C, Heat, and Defrost

Whether the truck has only a heater (which typically includes a defroster) or includes air conditioning as well, all of this comes from one system. As a side note, on some of the Chevrolet trucks, the heater was an extra-cost option.

Air-conditioning systems have evolved considerably over the years. At one time, most of the controls were operated by cables, whereas they are now controlled and activated with relays and switches. As the OEMs evolve, so do the aftermarket manufacturers.

Depending on the manufacturer and the vehicle, some A/C systems have relatively few electrical connections to make, while other systems have several. For these reasons, refer to the specific instructions for whatever kit is being used when installing an HVAC system in the truck. There are typically many wires but not a whole lot of electrical connections for the installer to make. The best advice is to carefully read and reread the provided instructions, become familiar with the products components, and take your time when installing the HVAC system.

Regardless of the installation process, the basic operation of the A/C system is as follows: When the A/C is turned on via the A/C thermostatic

The upper cable in this photo simply connects the throttle pedal to the carburetor. The lower cable is the TV cable for a 700R4 automatic overdrive transmission. It is merely mocked up at this time but will require some trimming. When properly adjusted, this cable will be tight.

The opposite end of the TV cable has a loop, into which a hook inside the transmission connects. The TV cable housing then slides into the hole in the transmission and is secured in place.

Table 5-1: A/C Terms in Layman's Terms

Term	Description
A/C Compressor	The A/C compressor is the component that squeezes the refrigerant that is contained within the A/C system to begin the heat transfer cycle. This process turns the refrigerant into a warm liquid that is under high pressure. As the warm liquid passes an expansion valve, the refrigerant turns into a cool, low-pressure liquid. Since this is a pressurized component, it should be protected by a safety switch.
A/C Thermostatic Switch	This is simply the HVAC control panel that is typically mounted in the dash.
Condenser	This is where the gaseous refrigerant is converted to a liquid as it cools. The condenser is usually mounted in front of the radiator to be cooled by air flowing over the condenser's cooling fins.
Drier	The drier serves as a temporary storage location for refrigerant that is not being used. The drier typically contains a filter and/or desiccant.
Evaporator	The evaporator facilitates the expansion and evaporation of the refrigerant.
Fan (Blower Motor)	This is the fan contained within the HVAC that pushes air through the A/C, heat, and defrost ducts.
Fan (Electric Driven)	This is a standalone fan that is electric and needs a temperature switch to turn on and off based on temperature within the system, whether the engine is running or not. A pusher fan is placed in front of the radiator. A puller fan is placed behind the radiator. In either placement, the fan is used to cool the fluid inside the radiator.
Fan (Mechanical Driven)	This is the fan that is driven by the engine that pulls air through the radiator to cool the engine.
Safety Switch (Binary)	A binary safety switch should be used when a mechanically driven fan is used. When pressure is too high or too low in the A/C system, the binary switch simply shuts down the A/C compressor.
Safety Switch (Trinary)	A trinary safety switch should be used when an electric fan is used. The four wires of the trinary switch allow for implementing a temperature switch, which will turn the electric fan on when needed and/or shut the fan off when it is not required.

switch, the safety switch verifies that the pressure within the system is within specification. When it is, the compressor begins pumping refrigerant through the low pressure of the evaporator. The evaporator turns cool, and cool air is moved through the ductwork via the blower-motor fan. The hot air in your truck evap- orates into the evaporator coil fins under high pressure and is returned to the condenser to be cooled. When the pressure within the system is too high or too low, the safety switch will be triggered. When running a binary safety switch, it will shut down the A/C compressor until the ambient air cools down the system. When run- ning a trinary safety switch, the temperature switch will cause the electric fan to turn on.

Aside from the control panel, which serves as the interface to control the movement of warm or cool air within the truck cab, the HVAC system is typically controlled by a series of multiple electrical relays. Overall unit power is provided to the power relay from the fuse panel. So that the HVAC system will operate only when the truck engine is running, switched power is also connected to this same power relay. Of course, this power relay must also be grounded. This power relay provides power to the fan relay and is controlled by the fan switch located in the control panel.

Evaporator

Microswitches for A/C, heat, and defrost are all directly or indirectly switched on or off by the control panel. These switches control the doors within the duct system, directing air to the correct outlets. The A/C compressor is controlled by an A/C thermostat that is connected to the compressor safety switch (binary or trinary) and then to a compressor clutch. The A/C compressor is also connected internally to the A/C and defrost microswitches.

The heater microswitch is connected to a heater-valve vacuum solenoid. This heater-valve vacuum switch, the fan motor, and all relays must be grounded. However, depending on the kit being installed, this may be done internally. Again, it is extremely important to read and fully understand the instructions that are provided with any HVAC kit that is being installed. It is not overly complicated, but it is important to understand what has already been done by the manufacturer and what is still required for the installer to do.

Whether you are servicing an existing air-conditioning system or installing a new system, most of the wiring should already be intact. Other than replacing a damaged wire, faulty connections, or a failed relay, most of the wiring within the system should be left as is. Consult a vehicle-specific service manual for service on an existing system or the installation manual for the specific A/C system for instructions.

Power and ground need to be provided to the system. A 14-gauge wire from the HVAC fuse serves as the switched ignition power source for the HVAC system. In addition, there are a few electrical connections that must be made as part of the HVAC (or specifically air conditioning) installation. These are the A/C compressor clutch, an A/C system binary or trinary safety switch, and the fan relay activation.

A/C Compressor Clutch

A 14-gauge wire connects the A/C thermostatic switch (HVAC control panel) to the safety switch (binary or trinary) to ultimately provide power to the A/C system's compressor clutch. Simply put, when the safety switch indicates that it is safe to do so, the air-conditioning system will begin running when the A/C switch is turned to the on position.

A/C System Binary or Trinary Safety Switch

Since the coolant within an A/C system uses a compressor, that coolant is pressurized. Therefore, it must be kept in check. This can be done with a binary or a trinary safety switch. For automotive air-conditioning systems, the high-pressure limit is approximately 406 psi, while the low-pressure

A stock replacement HVAC control panel for a 1967–1972 Chevy/GMC is available from Vintage Air. This one will be going into the work truck when the new A/C system is installed.

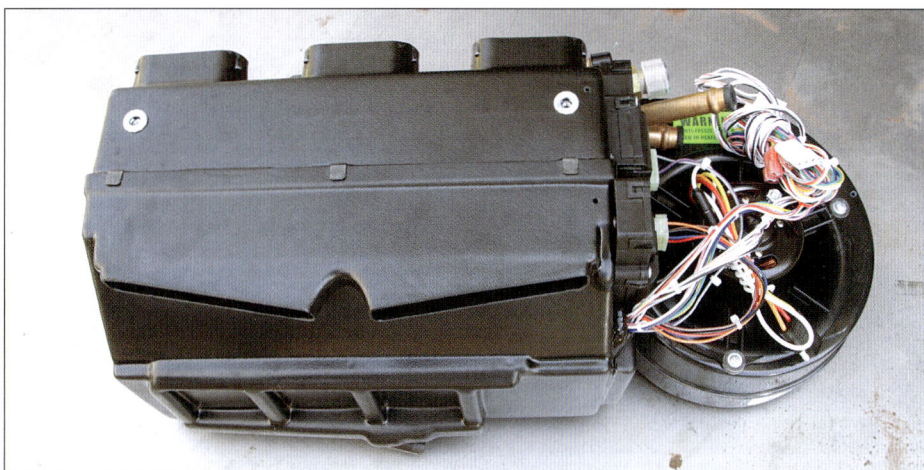

Many wires and other electrical components, such as relays and switches, are included in most aftermarket air-conditioning units. However, do not let that scare you away from installing a new HVAC unit, as most of those wires are already connected.

This shows the evaporator in place in my 1955 Chevy truck before anything else is connected to it. Mount the evaporator high enough that passengers are not kicking it but low enough that there is still room to route all the vents.

Electrically, there is one connection to the A/C-compressor clutch. This one wire on the A/C compressor connects to a terminal on the binary or trinary safety switch. This connection is commonly made with a bullet connector, which allows for an easy electrical disconnect during service.

The drier mounts inline between the condenser and the evaporator. Although a safety switch (binary or trinary) can be mounted somewhere other than at the drier, the drier provides a good mounting location.

The binary safety switch (shown with green over the threads) threads into the drier. The plug with two wires fits over the switch. One wire connects to the compressor clutch and the other to the A/C thermostat.

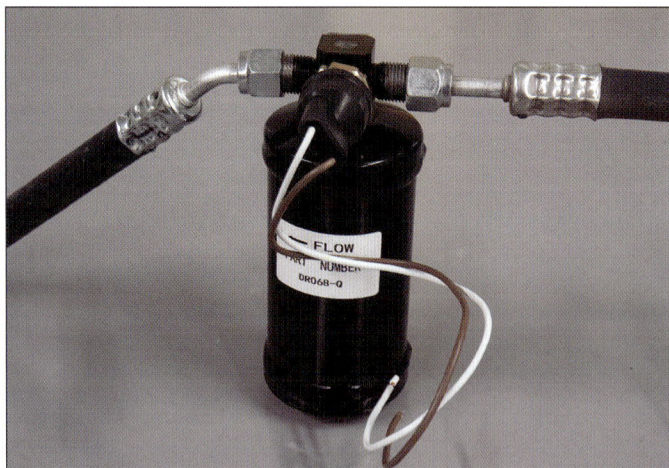

With the "flow" arrow pointing to the left in this photo, the line from the right is a 6-gauge line coming off the condenser into the drier. Moving from the drier and to the left is a 6-gauge line running to the evaporator. One wire from the binary switch connects to the compressor clutch, while the remaining wire connects to the A/C thermostat.

limit is approximately 30 psi. For a trinary switch, these pressures are similar, with fan activation occurring between 245 and 254 psi.

Binary Safety Switch

When using a binary safety switch, it is placed electrically in line between the evaporator's main wiring and the A/C compressor clutch (often as part of the drier). Physically, the safety switch is placed between the condenser and the evaporator. When the pressure in the system is too high or too low, the safety switch prevents the compressor clutch from engaging, effectively shutting down the A/C system.

Trinary Safety Switch

A trinary safety switch is situated and works in the same fashion as a binary switch; however, a trinary safety switch has four wires connected to it. Refer to the instructions included with the components to ensure that they are connected properly because colors may vary.

One of the wires connects to the A/C thermostat switch and can be considered a power wire. Note that in some circles, this is referred to as a temperature switch. Another wire connects the trinary switch and terminal 86 of the fan relay to provide power to the electric fan. Another wire from the trinary switch connects to the A/C compressor, and the final wire from the trinary switch is a ground wire.

The pressure/temperature switch turns the electric fan on when the system pressure/temperature is above a specified pressure/temperature. It turns the electric fan off when the system pressure/temperature is below a specified pressure/temperature.

Electric Fans

The engine must have a fan to push air through or pull air into the truck's radiator to keep it cool. An electric fan has an advantage over a mechanical fan, as the mechanical fan runs only when the engine is running. With an electric fan, it can be set up to continue running even after the engine is shut off to cool the engine.

In addition to an electric fan, a shroud should be used to direct the airflow over the entire radiator. Electric fans are available in various sizes, and the largest fan moves the largest amount of air. Trucks generally have relatively large radiators, so install the largest fan that will fit for maximum efficiency.

Electrically, the fan requires a fuse, a thermostat, a relay, and a circuit breaker. Except for the thermostat, these components are commonly included with an aftermarket wiring kit. However, if you are simply upgrading the existing wiring, ensure that all of these components are in place. A 3-amp fuse must be installed between the fuse panel and the electrical relay.

For the best results, a thermostat should be installed to control the fan. This thermostat sets the temperature that the electric fan starts and shuts off, providing consistency for cooling the engine's coolant temperature.

Remember that an electric fan draws lots of electrical current, making an electrical relay an essential part of the installation. When a relay is not used, the fan switch will most likely fail, causing the fan to fail, which will result in an overheated engine. None of those things are good.

Fan Relay Activation

An 18-gauge wire provides switched ignition power to the temperature switch via the electric fan relay. The power wire for the electric fan connects to terminal 87 on the fan relay, and the ground wire connects to a suitable ground.

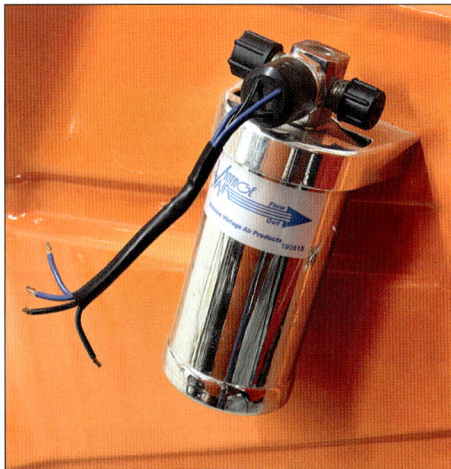

The drier must be mounted somewhere that is convenient for connecting both hoses and electrical wires. This drier is mounted on the passenger-side inner fender of the 1955 Chevy truck. The stud with a wing nut will be used as an engine-compartment ground stud.

Electric fans are available in a variety of sizes, but, more importantly, they are available as pushers or pullers. Pusher fans are designed to be mounted in front of the radiator to push airflow into the radiator. Puller fans are designed to be mounted behind the radiator to pull airflow through the radiator.

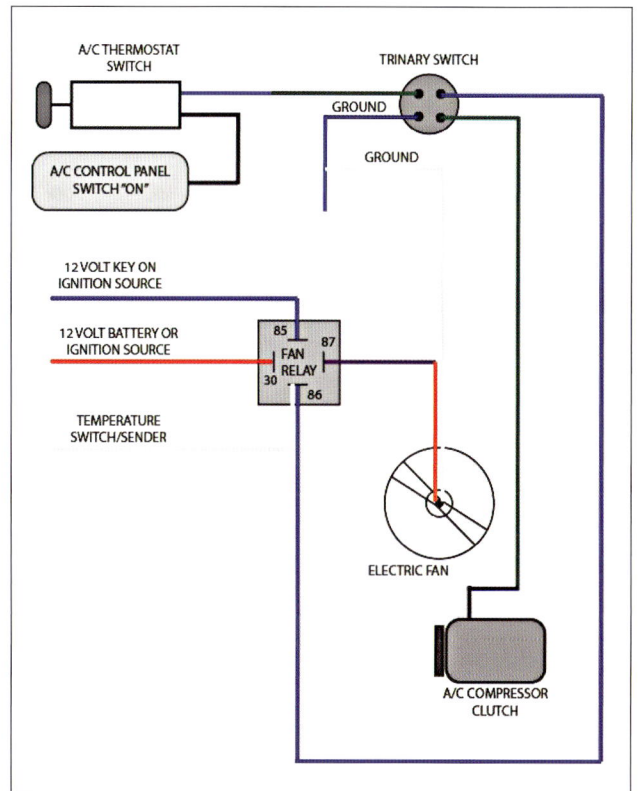

When using a trinary safety switch in the HVAC system, a wire connects the A/C thermostat switch and one terminal of the trinary switch. Another wire connects the trinary switch and terminal 86 of the fan relay. Another wire from the trinary switch connects to the A/C compressor, with the final wire from the trinary switch being a ground wire.

A 12-volt battery or ignition source should connect to a 40-amp circuit breaker before connecting to terminal 30 of the fan relay. A wire from the temperature sender in the engine should connect to terminal 86 of the fan relay. Finally, a 12-volt ignition-on source should connect to terminal 85 of the fan relay.

This cannot be stressed enough: Do not use this wire to directly provide power to the electric fan. An electrical relay must be used to provide power to an electric fan.

Two wires (both 18 gauge) can be used to activate an electric cooling fan. The first comes from the fuse panel to provide switched ignition power to a temperature switch (if used) or directly to the fan relay as an activation source. The second wire is used only when a temperature switch is used and provides an activation source to the fan relay. Neither of these wires should be connected directly to the cooling fan. An electrical relay must be used when powering an electric cooling fan.

Two wires (both 14 gauge) can be used to power the HVAC system. The first comes from the AC/heat fuse on the fuse panel to provide switched ignition power to the factory or aftermarket A/C system. This is the wire that connects to the thermostatic switch (A/C and heater controls) in the dash. When an inline circuit breaker has been provided for installation between the 12-volt power source and the fan relay, it can be omitted because the power wire originates from the fuse panel.

The second wire runs from the A/C thermostatic switch to a binary safety switch and then onward to the A/C compressor clutch.

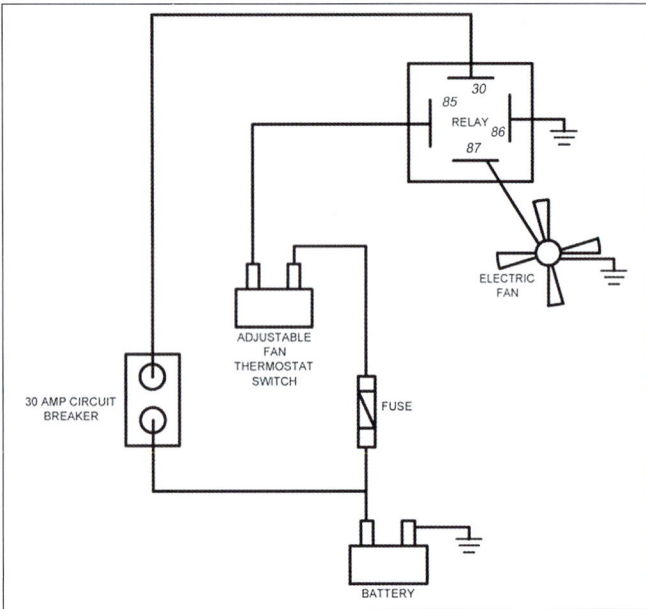

When wiring an electric fan, connect the power wire from the fan's thermostat switch to terminal 85 on the fan relay. Connect a wire from the 30-amp circuit breaker to terminal 30 on the relay. Connect a wire to terminal 87 to power the fan and a ground wire to terminal 86.

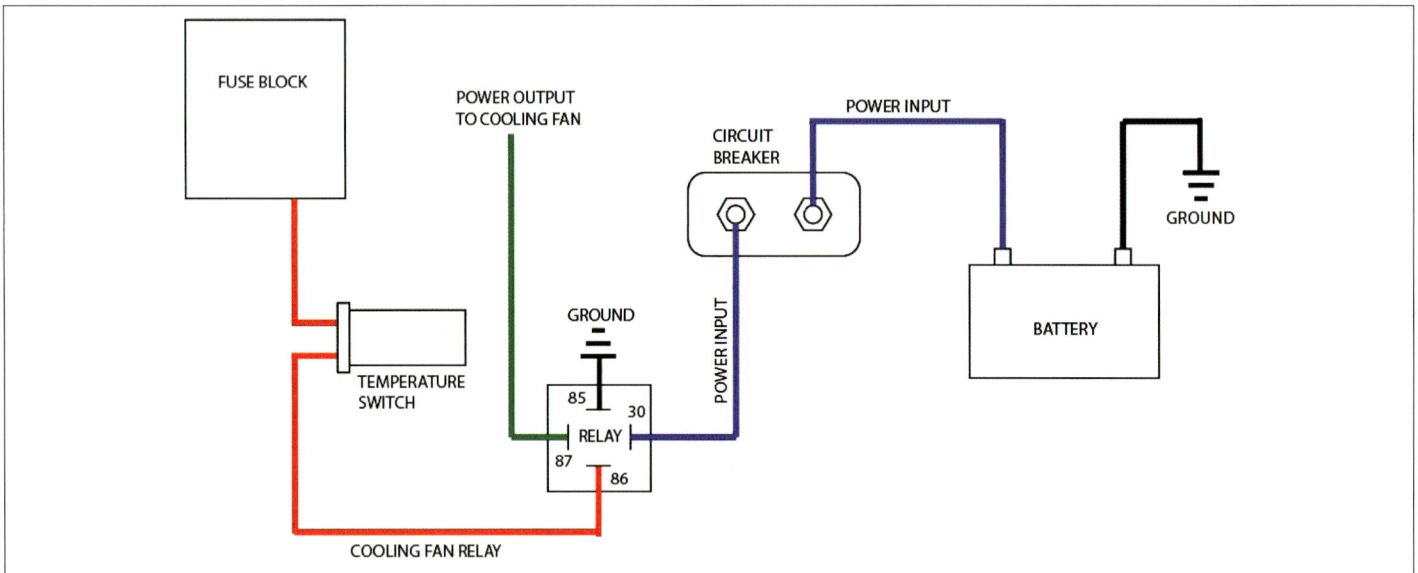

To wire the cooling-fan relay, connect a fused constant battery power source to terminal 30 of the relay. Connect the temperature switch to terminal 86. The first of these will provide power to the relay, while the second will serve as a signal when to apply that power. Connect a ground wire to terminal 85. Terminal 87 should connect to the cooling fan.

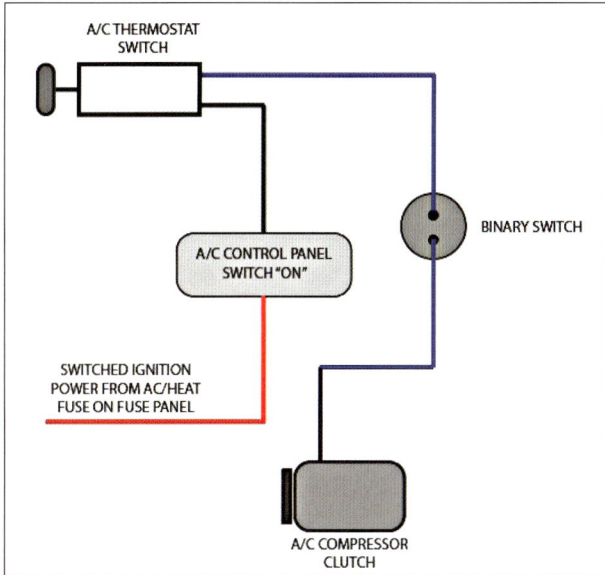

A/C THERMOSTAT SWITCH

BINARY SWITCH

A/C CONTROL PANEL SWITCH "ON"

SWITCHED IGNITION POWER FROM AC/HEAT FUSE ON FUSE PANEL

A/C COMPRESSOR CLUTCH

When using a binary safety switch, a switched ignition power wire from the fuse panel connects to the A/C control panel and then continues to the A/C thermostat switch. From the A/C thermostat switch, a wire runs to one terminal of the binary switch and then goes on to the A/C compressor.

Windshield-Wiper Motor

Admittedly, I am not sure when General Motors stopped using vacuum-powered windshield wiper motors in their trucks, but it was not too soon. The stock vacuum-powered wipers worked sufficiently when the engine was creating enough vacuum. However, when the engine is under load, such as passing or going up a grade, there is little-to-no vacuum and the wipers stop moving back and forth. A very simple cure to this is to install an electric-powered wiper motor. Typically, the only electrical connections to make are power, ground, and to the switch.

Depending on the truck's vintage, the wiper motor is secured in place behind the dash and below the windshield with two or three bolts. The wires on the wiper motor may not be very long, which makes connecting them to the electrical circuit difficult.

Rather than attempting to connect power and ground wires to the short wires of the motor while the motor is in a difficult position to get to, connect longer wires to those short wires by using butt connectors and heat-shrink tubing. Mount the wiper motor in place, trim the lengthened wires to the correct length, and connect them to the wiper motor switch, power, and ground.

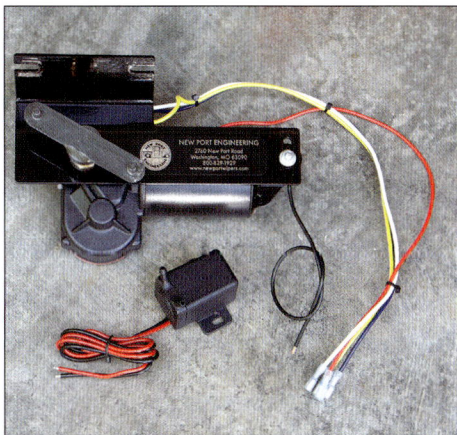

Regardless of the year of the truck, these electric wiper motors from New Port Engineering are easy to install and work well. They are not a universal fit, so order one specifically for the make and model of vehicle that you have.

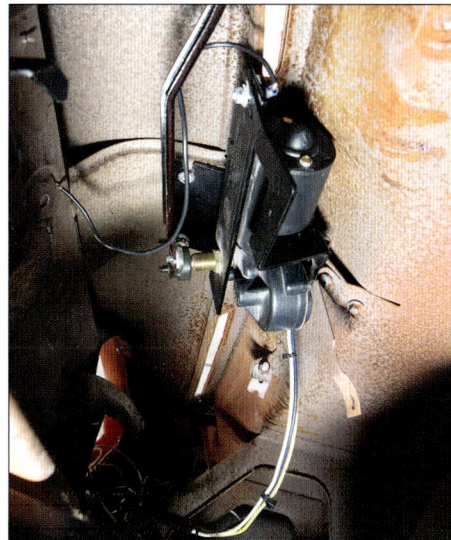

On the 1955 Chevy truck, the wiper motor is secured beneath the dash with two screws that fit into the notches of the flat mounting plate that abuts the center dash support. The yellow, white, and blue wires connect to the wiper-motor switch. The ground wire shown in this photo still needs to be connected to a ground stud.

Power Windows

There are three common switching methods for power windows: 1) voltage reversal rest at ground, 2) voltage reversal rest at 12 volts switched, and 3) voltage reversal rest open. These are all similar with subtle differences.

Aftermarket manufacturers may use any of these methods across their product lines. Follow the instructions and wiring schematics for the specific kit that is being used. Unlike power-door circuits that typically lock or unlock all doors, power windows can be operated independently.

When the power-window switch is in a central location, only one switch is required for each window. When the switches are in each door, one switch is required for the driver-side window and two switches are required for the passenger-side window (or any additional windows, such as in a crew cab).

Whenever wiring must be run into the doors, a flexible conduit must be used to protect the wires. This applies to power windows, power door locks, and interior courtesy lights.

Rocker switches are typically used to operate power windows. These are the switches required to operate the power windows for both sides of the truck from the driver's side. An additional single switch will still be required on the passenger side to allow the passenger to operate his or her window. If the switches were in a central location, only two single switches would be required.

Just below the interior door handle is the switch for the power window for the passenger's side. Since the window switches are mounted on the doors of this truck, the driver's side requires two switches (one for each door).

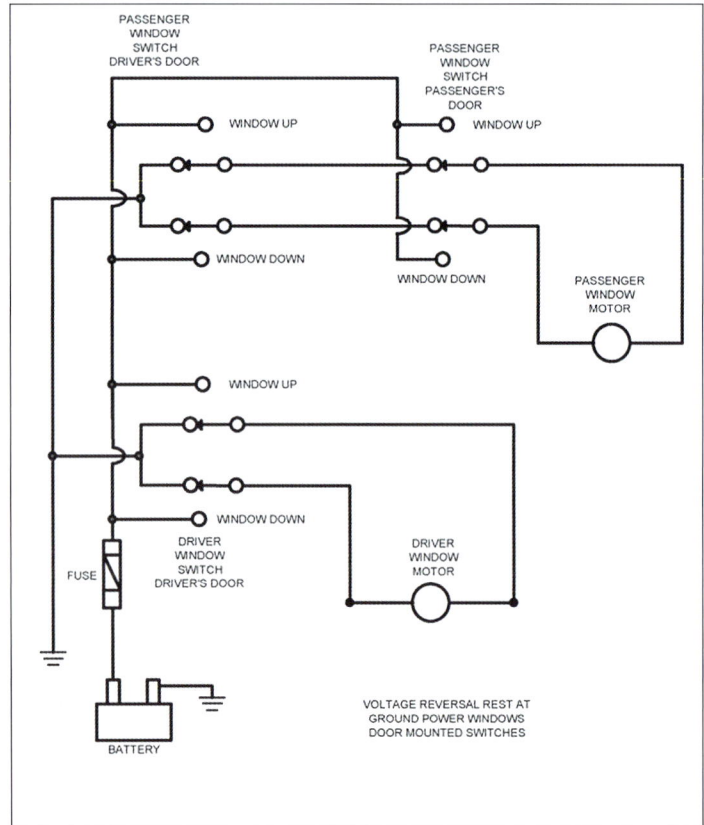

In this voltage reversal rest at ground configuration, the windows move when the switch receives power. Schematics for power windows can be intimidating. However, most wiring for aftermarket kits is already completed, leaving merely the connection of power and ground to the installer. Still, this schematic is handy when troubleshooting.

The switching process varies from each manufacturer, and even from one vehicle to another. For this simple reason, it is recommended to consult with a vehicle-specific service or repair manual prior to attempting service to power-window circuits.

Voltage Reversal Rest at Ground Type Circuit

In this type of a circuit, the window moves up or down when power is applied to the window actuator. With centrally located switches, one double-pole, double-throw (DPDT) switch controls movement for each window. One pole on the switch controls upward movement, while another pole controls downward movement.

With door-mounted switches, one DPDT controls movement for the driver-side door. A second DPDT switch in the driver-side door and a DPDT switch in the passenger-side door control movement for the passenger-side window.

One of these switches will be considered as the master switch and will have four wires connected to it. The opposite switch will be considered as the slave switch and will have five wires connected to it. It does not matter which side of the truck on which the master switch is located. No electrical relays are used in this system, so all wires used should be 14 gauge (if not 12 gauge), as there is a high current flowing through the circuit.

Voltage Reversal Rest at 12 Volts Switched Circuit

This type of circuit is the same as the voltage reversal rest at ground circuit, except that window movement occurs when the switch receives ground. This type of circuitry is common when switches are mounted in the doors.

Voltage Reverse Rest Open Circuitry

This type of circuit is also very similar to a voltage reversal rest at ground–type circuit. The notable difference is that when the switch is activated, both power and ground are sent to the actuator to raise or lower the window.

Power Door Locks

Power door locks simply lock or unlock the door remotely, rather than mechanically using a key to turn the lock cylinder. When manually operating the remote switch, electric current causes the lock actuator to move. When the correct button on the key fob is pressed, the doors lock when they are unlocked (or unlock when are locked).

When the lock button is pressed when the door is already locked, nothing happens. Power door locks usually incorporate a two-position toggle or a rocker switch to operate a two-wire design. When power is applied to one wire and the second wire is grounded, the actuator will move the door lock. Typical switching methods are negative pulse, positive pulse, and positive pulse without relays.

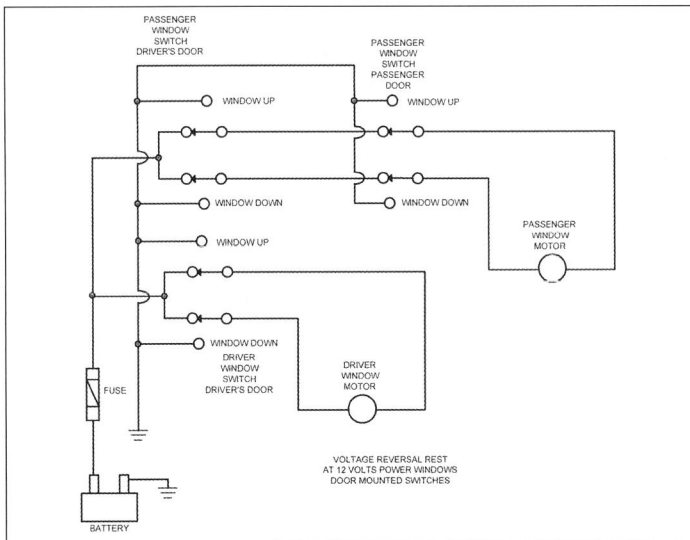

In this voltage reversal rest at 12 volts configuration, the windows move when the switch receives ground. Otherwise, wiring is the same as the voltage reversal rest at ground configuration.

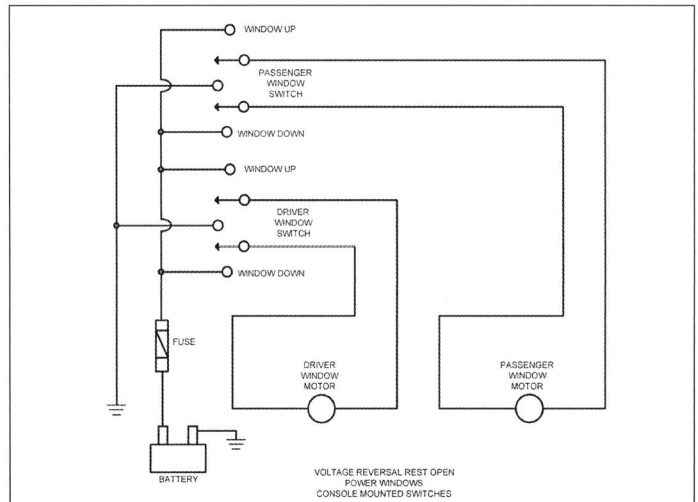

The voltage reversal rest open configuration is commonly used when power-window controls are centrally located in the vehicle. When the switch is activated, both power and ground are sent to the actuator to raise or lower the window.

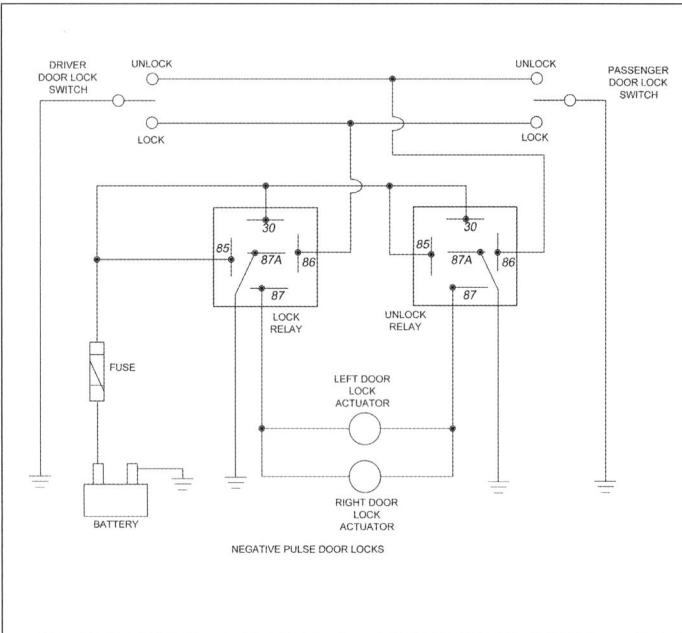

The negative pulse door-lock system is common in Japanese-manufactured vehicles. At each door-lock switch is an SPDT center off switch that is wired in parallel. When a switch is activated, a low-current ground powers the coil of the appropriate relay (lock or unlock).

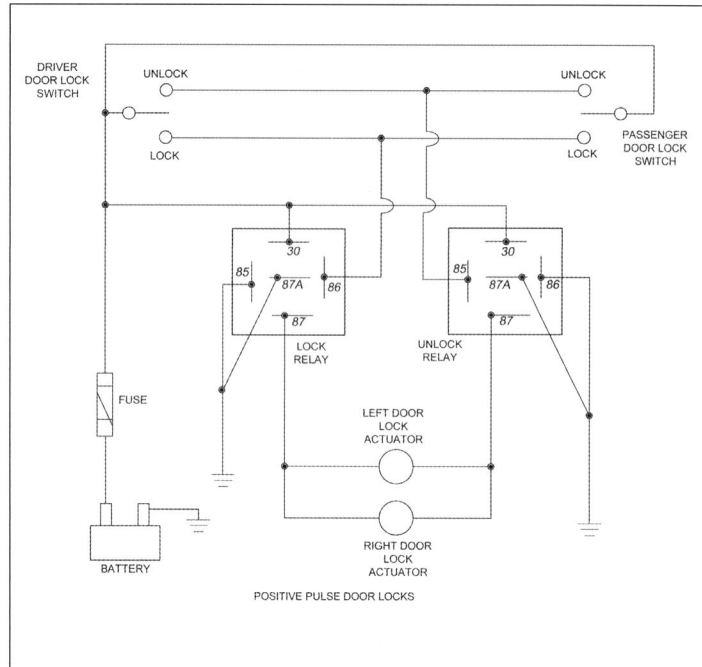

The positive pulse door-lock system is common in American-manufactured vehicles. When a switch is activated, +12-volt DC powers the coil of the appropriate relay to lock or unlock.

Negative Pulse and Positive Pulse Circuits

Negative pulse– and positive pulse–type circuits use two relays. The difference in wiring for these is between the switch and the relays. Between the relays and the actuators, wiring is the same. Since relays are used in each of these systems, the current involved is less, so smaller-gauge wiring (18 or 16 gauge) can be used.

Positive Pulse without Relays Circuit

The positive pulse without relays circuit is very similar to the positive pulse, except with no electrical relays. For this purpose, all components must be able to endure higher current, including the wires, which should be at least 14 gauge, if not 12 gauge.

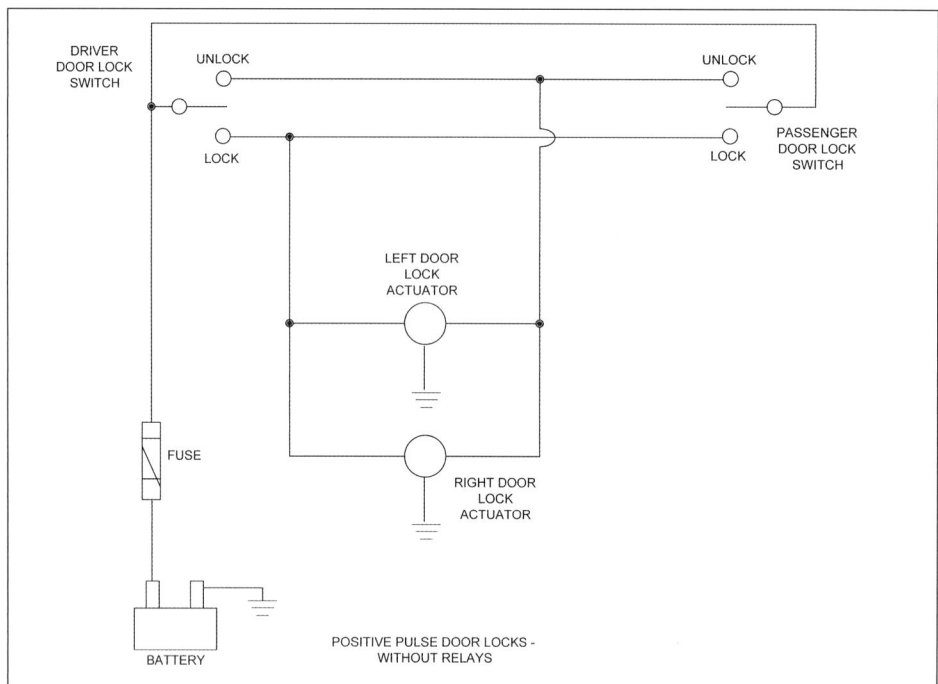

Many older GM vehicles with power door locks used three wire actuators. They included two coils (one for lock and one for unlock) but did not use relays. Operating the actuators requires between 5 and 10 amps, which requires that the wire size be at least 12 gauge. The switches must be sized accordingly as well.

Power Seats

When just one person drives a truck on a regular basis, power seats are more of a luxury than anything else. However, when a truck has multiple drivers or is driven long distances and the driver wants to adjust the seating to avoid fatigue, power seats can make adjustment significantly easier.

Power-seat configurations are two-way, four-way, six-way, and eight-way. Two-way power seats simply move the seat and seat back forward or backward. Four-way power seats can move the seat and seat back forward or backward, as well as tilt the entire seat/seat back assembly. Six-way power seats allow for separate control of the seat and seat back, providing height adjustment of the seat and tilt of the seat back. Eight-way power seats allow for the seat back to be raised or lowered independently of the seat.

Power seats can be installed in a GM truck, but wiring is greatly dependent upon the vehicle in which the seats were originally installed. The reason for this is that power seats vary between manufacturers. Some seats include one motor with a separate clutch system for each axis of movement. Other seats include one motor for each axis of movement.

When shopping for power seats from a swap meet or salvage yard, do whatever may be necessary to determine the year, make, and model of the donor vehicle. This will allow you to consult a vehicle-specific manual for instructions on how to properly wire the new seats in the truck.

Trailer Wiring

Part of the appeal of a pickup truck is the relative ease of pulling a

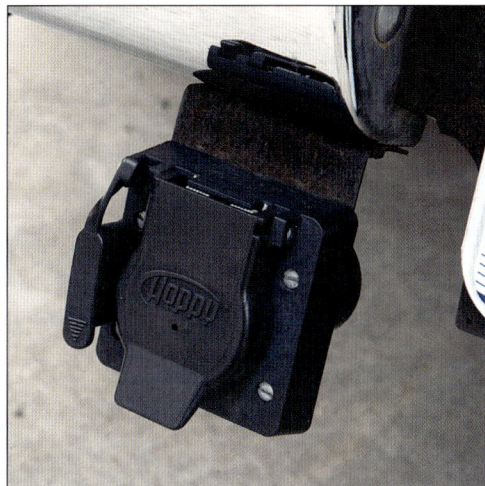

When pulling a trailer, having an electric plug on a truck makes the hook-up procedures simpler than making a temporary electrical connection. Trailer wiring plugs are available at most auto parts stores, farm stores, and home centers. Plugs are commonly available for a flat four wire, round seven wire, or a combination of the two. Use whatever works the best for the type of trailer that you will tow the most often.

This plug is a combination plug for flat-four and round-seven wire. The flat four (with the cap on in the photo) is typically be used only to provide trailer lighting (brakes, left turn signal, right turn signal, and taillights). The round seven wire provides those features along with marker and clearance lights, ground, and an auxiliary circuit (such as trailer brakes).

The center terminal on the trailer plug should always run to chassis ground. The trailer plug always has a raised notch that will slide into a keyway in the vehicle portion of the plug. This ensures that the proper trailer wires connect to the proper vehicle wires.

The large-diameter billet wheels are a giveaway to the era of this photo, but aside from the wheels, this Suburban pulling an Airstream trailer could have been taken in the mid-1960s. It's a nice setup regardless of the date.

Table 5-2: Trailer Wire Color	
Trailer Wire Color	**Purpose**
Brown	Taillights
Yellow	Left turn signal and hazard light
Green	Right turn signal and hazard light
Red	Stop lights
White	Ground
Black	Clearance and marker lights
Blue	Auxiliary circuit

trailer, whether it is a camping trailer, a fishing boat, or some type of cargo. Sure, a trailer can be hitched to a passenger car, but trailers are more commonly hooked up behind a pickup than a coupe or a sedan. However, electrically, the following information is the same for a passenger car or a pickup truck.

Unless the trailer pulling is a temporary, one-time-only situation, having an electrical plug at the back of the truck is worth the effort of the installation. This allows the user to simply plug the trailer wires into the truck's wiring system. When done properly, this connects taillights, clearance lights, brake lights, and turn signals in one simple step. When the trailer is equipped with electric brakes, they are now connected also, which makes the entire hook up very easy.

Lights

Most late-model pickup trucks come with a receiver hitch and are pre-wired for towing a trailer. That is all well and good. However, the older GM pickups to which this book applies typically did not come pre-wired for a trailer. Yes, there may

be some exceptions. Still, it is easy enough to properly wire a truck for pulling a trailer and having the electrical be a simple plug-in connection—just like with new trucks.

Most trucks use a round, seven-pin connector because this provides more circuits than a flat, four-pin connector. On the truck, this connector can be mounted on the trailer hitch, onto a tab mounted on the rear bumper, or mounted into a rear rolled pan. It just needs to be relatively close to the hitch ball for convenience and to have a minimal amount of wire that could potentially drag or get caught on something during a turn.

Trailer wiring typically follows an established color code. If the truck already has a wiring connector installed, do some testing with a voltmeter to determine what each terminal is wired to, regardless of the wire color. It would make sense that the actual location of each wire within the connector plug would be consistent; however, it is probably a safe assumption that it is not. So, if you are rewiring your truck, it may be simpler to rewire the trailer plug while you are at it.

When doing the wiring yourself, the location within the plug does not really matter, as long as the truck side matches the trailer side of the plug. If a trailer is already wired, wire the truck plug to match it. There are multiple manufacturers of these trailer plugs, and there are different designs as far as making the connections, so refer to the instructions provided with the components.

After determining the function for each terminal, connect them to the truck's wiring as follows:

Table 5-3: Trailer Plug Connections	
Terminal on the Plug	**Connection to the Truck Wiring**
Taillights	Splice into wiring that crosses from one taillight to the other
Right Turn and Hazard	Splice into wiring that powers the right rear turn signal on the truck
Left Turn and Hazard	Splice into wiring that powers the left rear turn signal on the truck
Stop Lights	Splice into wiring that crosses from one brake light to the other
Auxiliary Circuit	Connect to fuse block or fused battery lead
Clearance Marker Lights	Splice into wiring that crosses from one taillight to the other
Ground	Connect to a ground stud or other suitable ground

White/Ground

Brown/Tail Lights

Black/Clearance Marker Lights

Brown/Tail Lights

White/Ground

Black/Clearance Marker Lights

Blue/Auxiliary Circuit

Blue/Auxiliary Circuit

Yellow/Left Turn & Hazard

Yellow/Left Turn & Hazard

Red/Stop Lights

Green/Right Turn & Hazard

Green/Right Turn & Hazard

Red/Stop Lights

Connector on Truck

Plug from Trailer

Round Seven Pin Connector

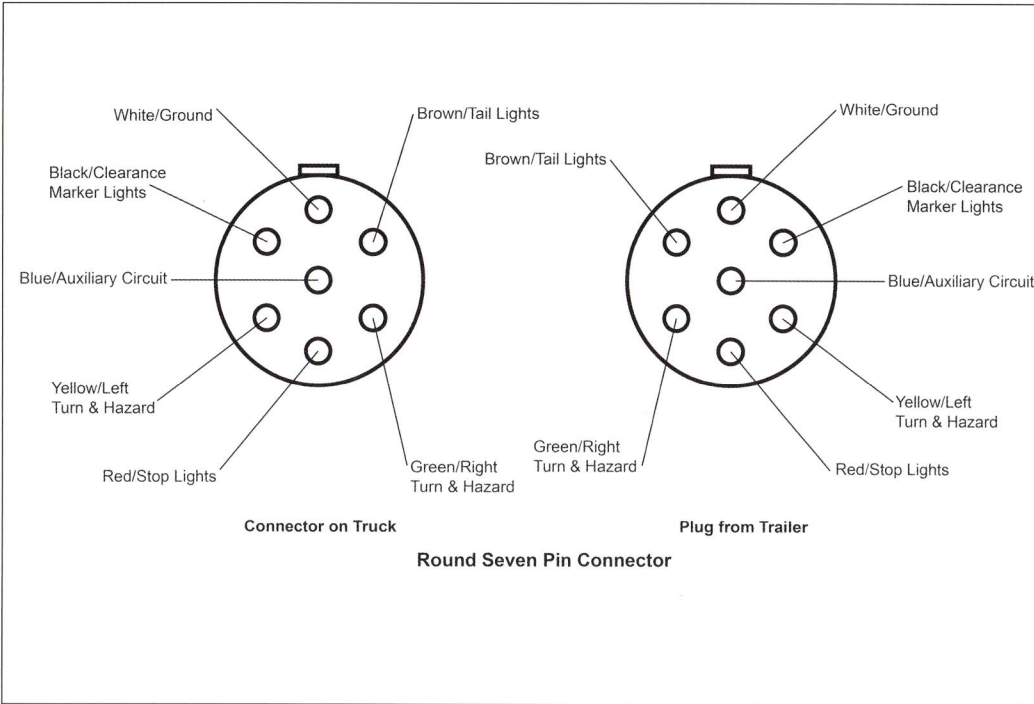

If a truck already includes a trailer-wiring plug, verify which terminals go to which circuits, and then wire the trailer to match. Conversely, if a trailer is already wired and you need to install the appropriate wiring in your truck, verify the wiring of the trailer. I believe the colors used for wiring are relatively standard, but that does not mean that they go to the same place in each plug. What matters is that each wire on the trailer plug connects with the appropriate terminal on the truck side of the plug.

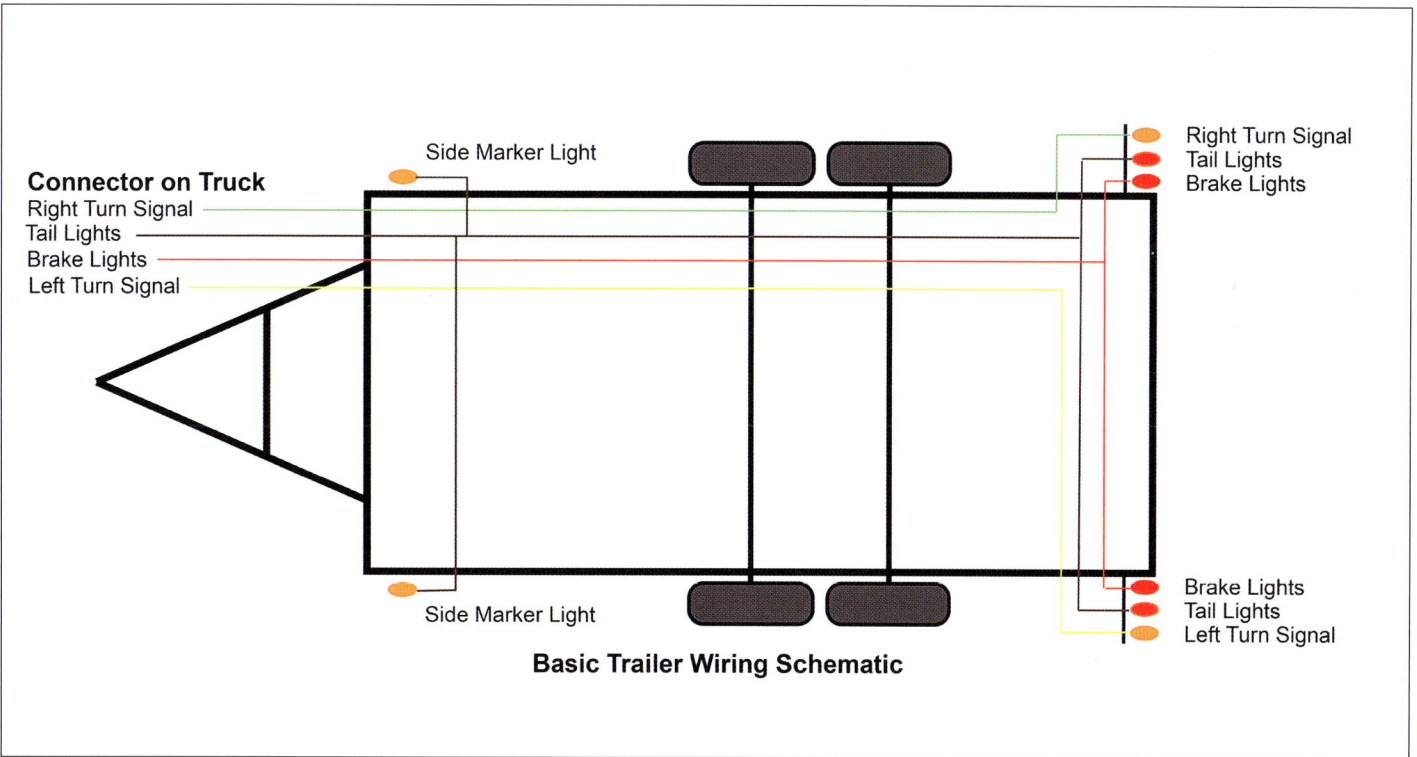

Side Marker Light

Right Turn Signal
Tail Lights
Brake Lights

Connector on Truck
Right Turn Signal
Tail Lights
Brake Lights
Left Turn Signal

Brake Lights
Tail Lights
Left Turn Signal

Side Marker Light

Basic Trailer Wiring Schematic

The actual routing of the wiring in a trailer varies, depending on the manufacturer. To keep things simple, wires are usually run down one side or the other to the destination. Then, they are run to the corresponding light on the opposite side. Ensure that all lights are grounded.

Trailer Brakes

Many drivers who are new to towing a trailer believe that their vehicle should be able to pull most trailers with no issues. While their vehicle usually can pull a trailer, stopping that trailer is where most people get into trouble. Many vehicles simply do not have the stopping power to stop a trailer that is behind them. When the trailer is heavier than the tow vehicle, that trailer can literally push the vehicle during a stopping event. This can be scary or potentially fatal.

Some trailers have brakes, while others do not. Commercially manufactured trailers that do not have brakes can usually be pulled and stopped by almost any vehicle if the trailer is not overloaded. If the trailer is overloaded, you are asking for trouble whether it has brakes or not.

Trailers with brakes have electric brakes. Unlike a truck, trailers have no practical method of applying mechanical brakes. When using a round seven-pin connector, the electric brakes connect with this plug, just like the lights.

To get the best performance out of the electric brakes, a brake-controller accessory should be installed. The brake controller is typically mounted on the lower edge of the dash but must be located within arm's reach of the driver. This controller allows the driver to conveniently fine-tune the braking based upon the loaded weight of the trailer.

When you are regularly pulling the same item, such as a boat trailer, the weight is typically going to be the same, so there is no real need for adjustment. However, when pulling a cargo trailer, the weight of the load varies based on the task at hand. One load may require hauling a few sheets of plywood and some lumber, and the next load may feature items that are significantly heavier. Installation and calibration of the brake controller is simple, but you should refer to the instructions provided with the controller to ensure the best performance.

To implement the electric brakes on a trailer, tie into the brake-feed circuit of the truck. A contemporary truck has hydraulic brakes that are applied when the brake pedal is pressed. This action causes the mechanical process of pushing a plunger into the master cylinder, which increases the pressure of the brake fluid and causes the

An electronic trailer-brake controller allows you to set the correct amount of braking force that will be applied. For example, when pulling an empty boat trailer, not as much force will be required as when the boat is on the trailer. Either one of those settings would probably be different for when pulling a travel trailer. Since the necessary pressure varies from one towing condition to another, the controller should be mounted within easy reach of the driver.

Consult the manufacturer's instructions for wiring the brake controller. The controller will have a predetermined procedure for setting the correct amount of braking force. Be sure to read through this procedure before you stop in traffic.

brake pads to grasp the brake rotor or press against the brake drums. This mechanical process also causes the brake-light switch to send an electronic signal, causing the brake lights to illuminate. That same electronic signal will be used to activate the electric brakes on the trailer.

To properly wire the trailer-brake controller, refer to the information provided by the manufacturer to connect the correct wires to the correct locations. Generically, a 12-gauge wire from the controller must connect to the brake-light switch. A 12-gauge wire from the controller must run to the electrical plug at the rear of the vehicle. A 12-gauge wire from the controller must connect to a 12-volt constant power source. In addition, a 12-gauge wire from the controller must connect to a suitable ground.

Trailer Ground

How many times have you been behind a vehicle that is pulling a trailer, and the trailer lights do not work? Chances are good that it has happened more than once. Sadly, if you run into the back of a trailer, it is still your fault—regardless of whether the trailer's brake lights work or do not.

A common cause for trailer lights not working correctly is insufficient ground or sometimes no ground at all. Rubber tires on the trailer are not going to ground the trailer. Some people mistakenly believe that the trailer will ground through the hitch. With the grease that should be on the hitch to allow for easy coupling and uncoupling, as well as turning on the hitch ball, there is no way that the hitch can provide sufficient ground.

However, there is a very easy solution. One of the terminals of a seven-pin plug is a ground that commonly goes directly to the negative side of the battery. Therefore, when wiring a trailer, use this terminal to provide a return path (ground) to a ground stud located somewhere on the trailer. This ground can be located almost anywhere on the trailer, but a convenient location is somewhere near the front of the trailer, such as the A-frame.

Drill a hole in the desired location for a 10-32 x 3/4 stainless-steel screw to pass through. Install the correct-size ring terminal onto a piece of 12-gauge wire and secure it to the ground stud with a 10-32 brass nut. Connect the opposite end of this ground wire to the ground terminal on the trailer side of the seven-pin connector.

When the trailer is hitched to the truck and the seven-pin connector is plugged in, the ground stud will now provide suitable ground. Run a ground wire from each light to the ground stud, secure a ring terminal on the end of each ground wire, and secure them all in place on the ground stud with a stainless-steel 10-32 wing nut.

Multiple ground wires can be connected to the ground stud. It is possible to connect the right-side lights at the back of the trailer (brake lights, taillights, and turn-signal lights) to one ground wire and the left-side lights to another ground wire. Then, connect all of these to one ground stud. This cleans up the wiring installation by running two ground wires the length of the trailer instead of six. In addition, when the lights are wired in this way, it is relatively easy to diagnose a bad ground issue. If, for example, all of the right-side lights quit working, chances are good that it is due to a bad ground.

To ensure that the electrical functions of the trailer always work as they should, they must be grounded. To do this, run a specific ground wire from the center terminal of the trailer plug to a stud located somewhere on the tongue of the trailer. All electric components of the trailer can then be grounded to this central ground location.

Audio and Video Applications

During the era that these trucks were made, the radio was simple. Many of these trucks came from the factory with an AM radio that had an integral speaker. A common upgrade was the installation of a new stereo. So, depending on the era, the truck may have an FM radio, 8-track tape player, cassette player, or CD player. Any of those choices simply involved swapping out the head unit, connecting the new one to power and

ground, and connecting your choice of speakers.

Audio

Car audio has changed substantially, as more options are available today than merely choosing between broadcast or prerecorded music. We now have video presentation and navigation systems to accompany music. In the context of this book,

"music" refers to all audio—whether it is news, weather, sports, or traffic information.

The options available lie entirely with the specific head unit that is being installed. In addition to the standard AM/FM/HD Radio/CD selections, options now include units that play MP3 discs and Windows Media Audio (WMA) files. Other music sources include satellite radio and streaming options via Pandora and

Vintage automotive radios were simple. As a history lesson for those who may not know, the dial on the left turned the radio on and increased the volume as it was turned clockwise. The dial on the right moved the frequency across the available channels. The five buttons allow for presetting favorite channels. There was no remote and no digital display.

This is the AM/FM/CD stereo receiver that will be installed in the 1970 C10 that will be wired with a Painless Wiring kit later in this book. This truck will simply be a work truck for the time being, so this radio will be sufficient. Most modern receivers include a plug to facilitate the wiring, allowing easy removal of the head unit from the vehicle.

Spotify via Android Auto and Apple CarPlay.

The head unit (also known as a receiver) dictates how you can listen to music. It must be compatible with the source, whether that is through a smartphone, a thumb drive, or an SD card. To listen to a CD, verify that the receiver includes a CD or DVD player. Not all new stereos include this once-common feature. For satellite radio, the receiver must be "satellite-radio ready" and have an auxiliary input for Bluetooth connectivity. For those looking for the best FM reception, a receiver with low FM sensitivity (8 to 12 decibels above a femtowatt [dBf]) is considered very good. To listen to HD Radio broadcasts, an HD Radio tuner will be required.

A Bluetooth connection allows hands-free calling when using a compatible phone, which is a feature that is very convenient when traveling. Receivers with global positioning system (GPS) navigation not only help with directions to a destination but also allow for touchscreen control of the stereo. A touchscreen also allows for the addition of a backup camera, which makes backing up a trailer much easier.

After choosing the various sources for music, the next step is to achieve the sound quality that you want. Sound quality is largely dependent upon speakers, amplifiers, and subwoofers. Not all of these components are required. It just depends on what you want and how much you want to spend.

Although aftermarket receivers are not always the best, they are typically better quality than the OEM speakers. So, if the head unit that you have does everything that you want, a new set of speakers may be all that

you need to upgrade a sound system. On the other hand, if you are doing a ground-up rebuild of a vintage truck, an entirely new system may be in order.

Amplifier

While the stock radio and speakers will suffice for many people, the sound can be greatly enhanced by including an amplifier in the audio system. The reason for this is quite simple. Most audio head units (radios) have a limited amount of power (15 to 18 watts) available to them. As they are pushed to their maximum output, the sound distorts.

As you may suspect, higher-fidelity sound requires more power. An amplifier can provide the required extra power for an audio system. If you like your music loud, consider installing an amplifier. This allows you to crank up the volume without distorting the sound. The amplifier provides a more defined and cleaner

sound at all volume levels.

Without getting too technical, the amplifier receives 12 volts of battery power. The internal components of the amplifier increase it to about 28 to 32 volts. This amount of increase depends on the equipment involved.

Within the amplifier are electric crossovers that control the frequency range that each speaker receives. In layman's terms, low-pass crossover filters block everything but the bass, while high-pass crossover filters block the bass. So, connect the subwoofers to the amplifier terminals that use the low-pass crossover filters. Connect door speakers and tweeters to the amplifier terminals that use the high-pass crossover filters.

With amplifiers typically drawing from 50 to 80 amps, larger wire is required for the power cable (directly from the battery). As with all other electrical components, the amplifier must be properly grounded.

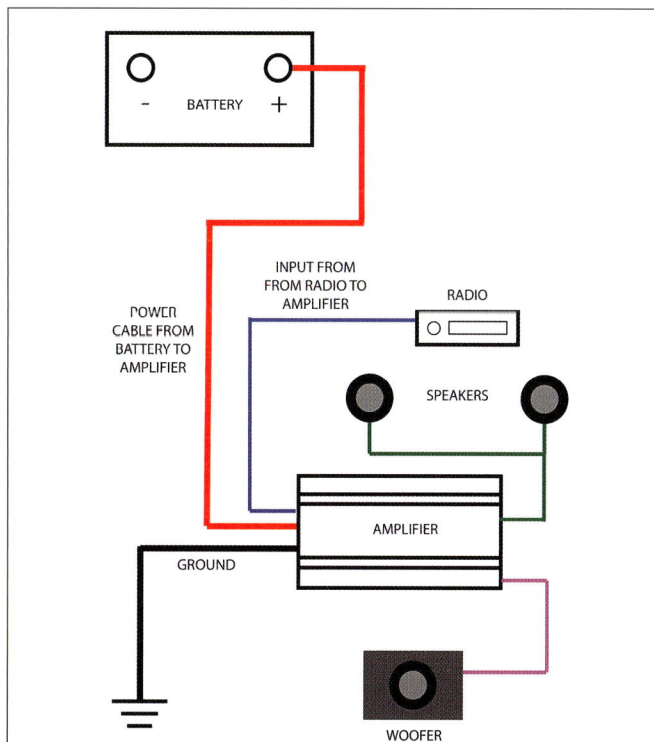

Stereo amplifiers typically have an input side and an output side. The input side includes a connection for power (the battery), input from the radio/stereo, and a ground connection. The output side includes connections for speakers and woofers.

Speakers

On these vintage trucks, the OEM speakers have probably distorted and deteriorated so much that they should be replaced. Since they are often made of paper-based materials, moisture and heat have surely taken their toll. Aftermarket speakers typically provide better sound because they are made from higher-quality materials that are less likely to distort.

While designing a truck's sound system, consider your budget and available space. When the budget and space allow, component-based speakers provide the best sound. The component-based system separates the various sound levels by incorporating individual woofers and tweeters. Full-range speakers combine the characteristics of tweeters, midrange speakers, and woofers into one speaker, which makes them more economical.

Video Monitor

A head unit with video capabilities can offer versatility to a truck's sound system. One advantage is that the in-dash video monitor can serve as a touchscreen for stereo settings and menu selections. Other advantages include having a map and voice directions with GPS navigation systems. With the availability of a map, it is easier to see which side of the street a destination is on, and it allows you to get into the correct lane sooner. Lastly, when a video monitor is used, a backup camera can also be installed.

Cameras are included with some head units but can typically be added separately, as long as you have a video port to connect to. A backup camera can be especially useful when using a hitch or backing up a trailer.

When selecting a video monitor,

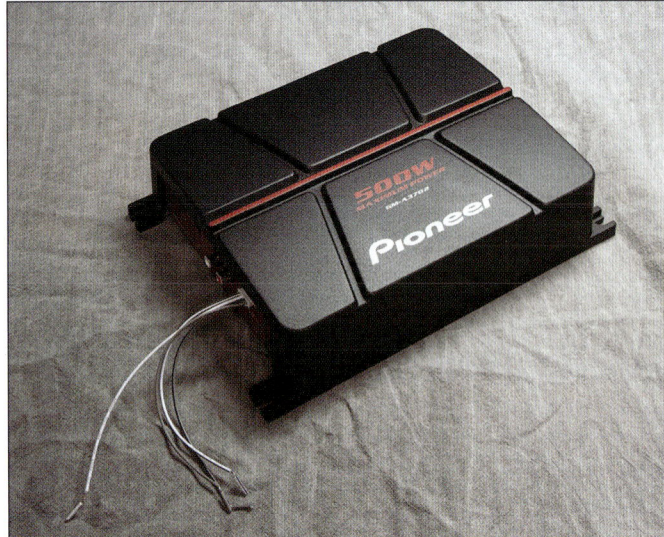

Most amplifiers are built in a relatively flat configuration, which allows them to be placed under a seat if necessary. They can be positioned in a horizontal or vertical orientation. This is a Pioneer 6M-A3702 500-watt maximum-power amplifier.

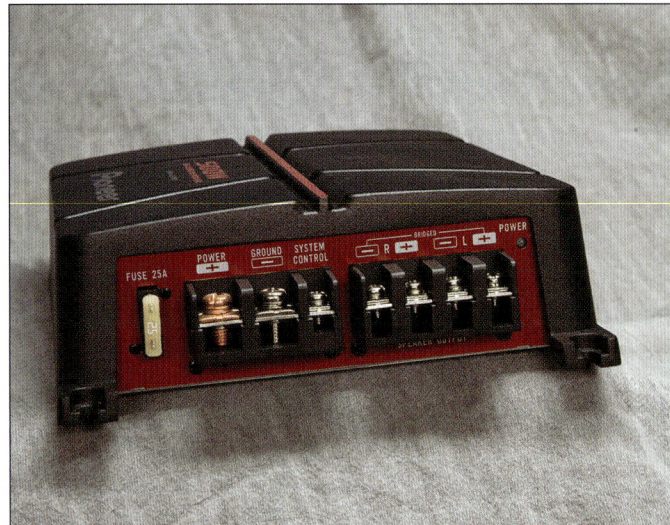

The input end of the amplifier includes the connection points for the sound from the head unit. This can be from RCA cables or from speaker-level inputs. The latter is the speaker wire that would connect from the radio head unit if an amplifier was not used.

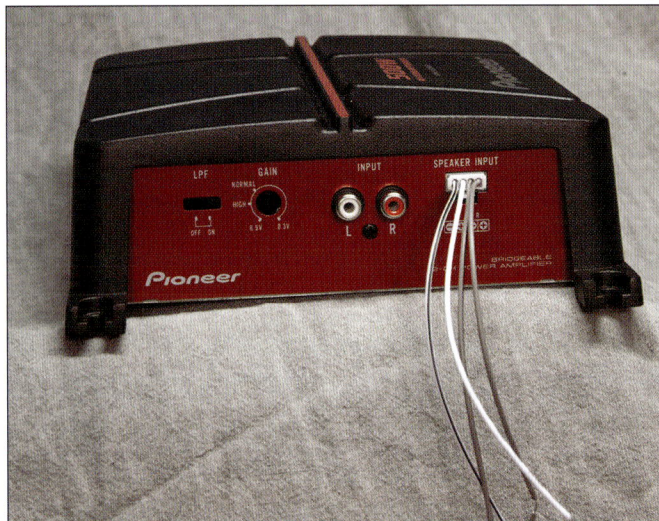

The opposite end includes the power connections (12-volt positive, ground, and remote) and the connections for the speakers. The latter will provide amplified power.

screen size and resolution are two aspects to consider. Their importance depends somewhat on how the screen is going to be used. With all things being equal, a larger screen makes the various menus and settings easier to see. Having a higher resolution makes the images sharper.

GPS

An in-dash navigation (also known as a GPS) system requires a compatible head unit that includes a built-in screen and an external GPS antenna. Most head units that provide this also provide satellite radio, so purchasing one of these units has multiple advantages. Most of these also include a remote-control device, which allows a choice of audio/video inputs and outputs.

In addition to power and ground connections, the navigation system requires connection to a vehicle speed sensor. While the vehicle is in motion, the navigation system receives between 800 and 1,000 pulses per mile. This is what informs the

navigation system in which direction and how fast the vehicle is moving.

To compensate for backward movement, older systems require an electrical connection to the backup-light signal to determine that the vehicle is moving backward. Newer systems determine this simply by the GPS satellite tracking mechanism of the navigation system. For systems that require connection to the backup-light signal, you can typically connect to this at the shifter mechanism.

The quality of the satellite signal depends largely on the placement of the antenna. The GPS antenna cannot see through metal. In addition, the GPS antenna should not be placed inside the cab when it has an electric window defroster, windshield-mounted radio antenna, metallic window tint, or solar reflective material.

For any audio/visual/navigation system to provide superior performance, the interior of the cab should be quiet. Wind noise, road noise, and any noise caused by vehicle vibra-

tions should be eliminated as much as possible. New weather-stripping material can eliminate most external noise. Installation of high-quality dampening materials can minimize noise caused by vibration. All vehicles have some natural vibration at various harmonics, so noise will not be eliminated completely. However, it can be reduced considerably.

AM/FM/CD

When installing only a receiver and one or two pairs of speakers, the wiring requirements are relatively simple. Two wires (a power wire and a ground wire) come out of the receiver. Connect the power wire from the receiver to the terminal specified for use with a stereo.

In addition, some receivers have a wire that should be connected to a keyed ignition source, which allows the radio to be on only when the vehicle is running or the ignition switch is in the accessory position. Connect the ground wire to a suitable ground source and connect the

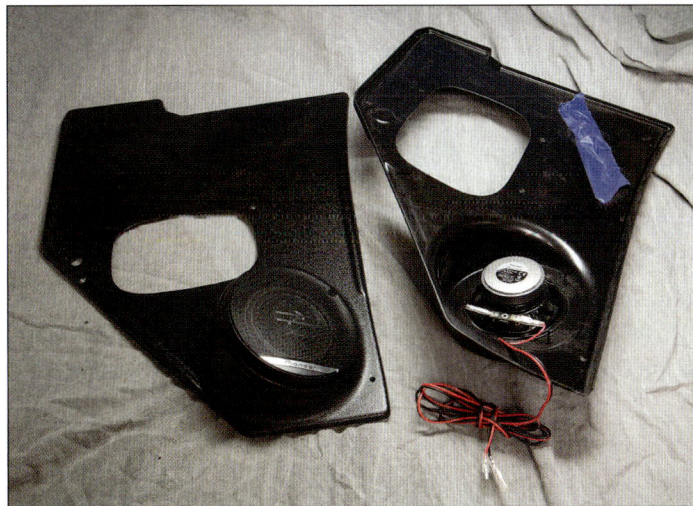
These acrylonitrile butadiene styrene (ABS) panels allow speakers to be mounted in the kick panel in front of the door on my 1955 Chevy pickup. The panels are vehicle-specific with the openings for the stock vents.

Primary stereo speakers for the 1955 truck are mounted on each side of the center console near the floor. Above and to the right of the speaker is a courtesy light that illuminates when one or both doors are opened.

radio antenna. This will be either to a designated female plug on a pigtail or directly to a port on the receiver's housing.

Wires to the speakers will run directly from the back of the receiver to each speaker. The receiver will probably have bass, treble, and fade controls at a minimum, so verify that speaker wires are connected to their corresponding speakers for these controls to work properly. In this situation, speakers can be connected by using 16- or 18-gauge multistrand copper wire.

Two wires are provided to power the radio. Always check with the stereo installation instructions to determine the best installation options for your vehicle.

An 18-gauge wire from the headlight fuse on the fuse panel provides a battery power source for the radio. This allows the time and radio presets to remain, even when the ignition is turned off.

An 18-gauge wire from the radio fuse on the fuse panel provides an ignition-switched power source. This wire has power whenever the ignition

switch is in the accessory or on/run position. For older radios that require only one power wire, it is suggested to use this wire because it will prevent the radio from draining the battery if it is left on while the truck is not running.

To provide backlighting for the radio, it is necessary to splice into the instrument-panel lighting. This provides radio lighting whenever the headlight switch is in the parking/taillights-on or headlights-on position. As with all electrical devices, the radio must be grounded.

Installing a Radio/CD Receiver in the 1970 C10

1 The 1970 C10 is my work truck, so it is not going to have a radical stereo system (at least not in this build). However, it is an AM/FM/CD receiver with Bluetooth connectivity.

2 At the lower left of the backside of the receiver is the receptacle for the power, ground, and speaker wires. At the lower right of the backside of the receiver is the receptacle for the antenna.

3 Most car-audio systems today are significantly more complicated than those that were available when these trucks were new. With the number of speakers, remote features, and other functions, more wire connections are required. Therefore, most stereo systems use a quick-disconnect plug for those connections.

Installing a Radio/CD Receiver in the 1970 C10 *continued*

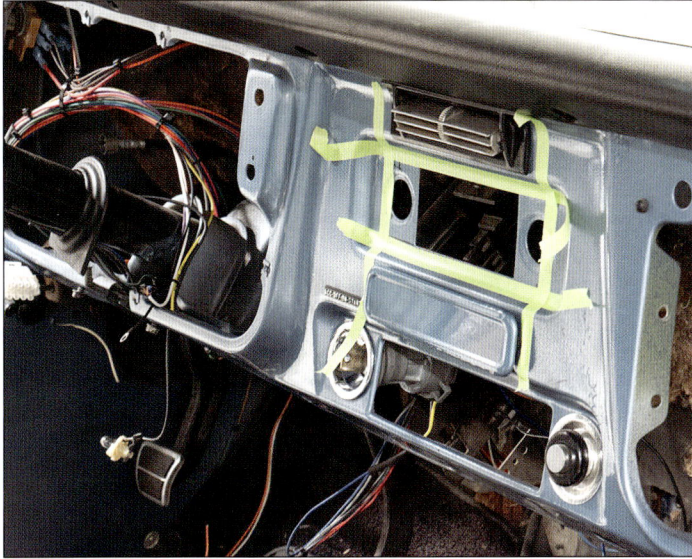

4 The new radio is significantly wider than the original, so some dash material needed to be removed. After taking some measurements, the area to be cut out was outlined with masking tape.

5 Using a pneumatic reciprocating saw with a fine blade, the necessary dash material was quickly removed.

6 The new radio was set in place from behind the dash and the faceplate was installed from the front. A length of plumber's strap suspended from a bolt on the inside of the firewall was used to secure the back side of the radio. The two power wires (constant hot and switched power) were connected to the wiring pigtail.

7 Speaker wire for the two speakers mounted behind the seat were connected to the wiring pigtail and then routed down the inside of the firewall, rearward over the transmission hump to the back of the cab, and then to the left and right speakers. Carpeting will cover the speaker wires later, but masking tape is used to secure the wires in place.

Installing a Radio/CD Receiver in the 1970 C10 *continued*

8 *These speakers will be mounted behind the seat. On the back of these speakers are the connections for the speaker wires. The red tab is for the (+) speaker wire and the black tab is for the (-) speaker wire as shown in Table 6-1.*

9 *For the time being, the speakers are merely sitting in place with some extra speaker wire stashed behind them. When the seat is installed, they may need to be moved slightly and will be secured in place at that time.*

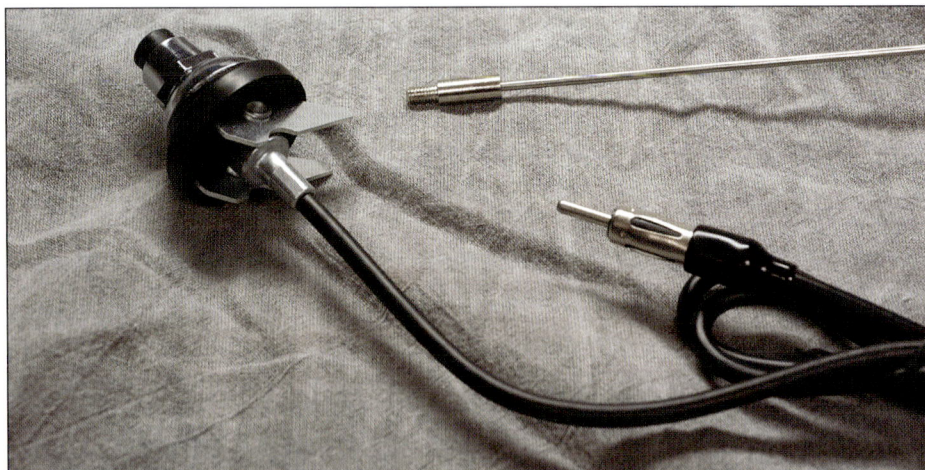

10 *The swivel base of the radio antenna mounts inside the right front fender. The antenna cable will be routed downward around the air-conditioning evaporator and into the back of the stereo receiver.*

Table 6-1: Radio Wire Color and Connection

Color	Connection
Red	12V Ignition/Accessory
Yellow	12V Battery/Memory
Black	Ground
Blue	Power Antenna/Amp Turn-On
White	Left Front (+)
White/Black	Left Front (-)
Gray	Right Front (+)
Gray/Black	Right Front (-)
Green	Left Rear (+)
Green/Black	Left Rear (-)
Violet	Right Rear (+)
Violet/Black	Right Rear (-)

TECH TIP

Ground Cable

It is certainly not a necessity to rewire your truck just to install a new stereo system, nor is it a necessity to install a new stereo when rewiring your truck. Since it is conceivable that a stereo system may be installed after a truck is up and running, be sure to disconnect the ground cable from the battery prior to installing any stereo equipment. Just remember to reconnect this cable before attempting to start the truck again. Sometimes people forget to read the instructions that come with new stereo equipment to ensure nothing is done that will void the warranty. ■

WIRING INSTALLATIONS

While rewiring a vehicle may be a daunting task, it may be easier than chasing down all of the defects and potential problems that exist in OEM wiring that is more than 10 years old.

If the truck was bought new and you know every modification that has been made to it, you may feel confident in the wiring the way it is. If you have not owned the truck for its entire life, you have no idea how many different stereos or sets of aftermarket gauges may have been installed. Even if each stereo was an improvement (from AM to FM to 8-track to cassette to CD to satellite) that does not mean that the wiring was done correctly.

How many times has a new electrical accessory been installed and then the next big thing spliced into its place a few months later? How many times have the wires been overloaded because a relay was not used or a smaller-than-necessary fuse was installed? Perhaps the original wiring is simply old, worn, and brittle.

Whether you are doing a complete frame-off rebuild (stock or custom) or merely updating an old truck, all new wiring is often worth the time and money that is spent. Whether the purpose is for confidence or reliability, it is worth it.

Multiple aftermarket companies sell wiring kits for use in these older trucks. Some kits are vehicle specific and are typically for vehicles manufactured in the 1960s and 1970s. For a wiring kit that is basically a replacement upgrade for the stock wiring harness, this can be a great way to go.

For an older truck that had few of the electrical conveniences that are enjoyed today, a universal wiring kit may be a better choice. This is a great option when a vehicle-specific kit is not available for your truck or if you are going to be installing options that were not available when your truck was assembled, such as air conditioning, an electric fuel pump,

or power doors and windows. Both vehicle-specific and universal kits often have varying numbers of circuits, allowing you to expand beyond what may have been OEM equipment in your truck.

If you are well versed in electrical theory and circuit design, you could wire your truck from scratch. If you choose to do this, draw or at least sketch out schematics for the entire system prior to running any wire.

Soldering and Crimping

There was a time when most automotive aficionados would insist that all automotive wiring applications

If you choose to solder electrical connections, use 60/40 lead-based, rosin-core solder. You will need a soldering iron or a butane torch.

should have nothing but soldered electrical connections. While a small percentage may still believe that to be true, modern wire and solderless connectors are making soldering a thing of the past. With shop classes in high school not being as common as they used to be, once-common skills such as soldering are not as prevalent. No matter which process is used, if the person does not have the ability to do it correctly, it does not matter which process is implemented. Soldered connections are no

good if they are not done correctly.

In the case of large wires (4 gauge or larger), such as battery cables, the crimping tool required may be too expensive for the hobbyist electrician. There are two workarounds for this. One is to purchase the battery-cable wire and connectors from an auto parts store and have a store employee crimp the connectors on for you. Most auto parts stores will do this for regular customers at no charge.

The second method is to use a pro-

pane or methylacetylene-propadiene propane (MAPP) gas torch and 60/40 lead-based, rosin-core solder. Simply strip enough insulation off the cable so that about 1/8 inch extends past the metal part of the terminal. Clamp the cable in a vise so that the strands are exposed and the terminal slips down over them. Heat the terminal and the cable with the blue flame of the torch until the solder begins to flow into the connection. Remove the heat and allow the connection to cool.

Soldering a Terminal on a Large Cable

1 Ensure that the terminal is the correct size for the stud that it will be mounted to and the wire that it will be soldered to. Strip and remove the appropriate amount of insulation from the wire.

2 Use a wire brush to rough up the surface inside of the terminal. Then, apply flux to the wire strands or to the inside of the terminal.

3 Place the terminal into a vise and insert the wire into the terminal. Ensure the wire is supported so that it does not fall out or pull out of the terminal.

4 Using a torch, apply heat to the terminal. When the terminal is hot enough, applying solder to the terminal will cause the solder to melt and run into the spaces between the wires and the terminal, making a solid connection.

Do-It-Yourself Wiring

Regardless of the truck vintage or the reasons for rewiring it, if you feel that it should be rewired, you can do it yourself. There is no reason to pay someone else to do it, although you can if you really prefer it. All too often on vintage trucks, a breakdown can be caused by an electrical component. When you have no knowledge of the electrical system, you may be in for a hefty tow bill. However, when it is truly an electrical issue and you are familiar with the truck's electrical system, you can often work around the problem sufficiently to get back home.

For most auto enthusiasts, a replacement wiring harness (either vehicle-specific or universal fit) is a good place to start. This will provide a fuse panel, most if not all wiring needed, some electrical connections, and instructions. Some kits provide all of this, along with all the necessary connectors, some wire ties, and better instructions. With any of these kits, some basic automotive knowledge and the ability to follow directions, rewiring a truck is a rewarding experience.

While all aftermarket wiring kits vary somewhat, the overall project for most vehicles is similar. Actual vehicle installations later in this chapter provide more details with the specific wire gauges that are used. A very generic installation to get the engine running and the lights operational would be as follows:

Install a fuse panel in a convenient location. Run wires to the engine compartment, including wires to be connected to the alternator, the starter, the coil, and the battery. Depending on the type of alternator, two or three wires will typ-

ically connect to it. Connect a wire between the fuse panel and the stud on the outside of the alternator. A second wire comes from the fuse panel, passing through a diode (to serve as a one-way flow valve) and then plugs into the alternator. A jumper wire also connects this plug to the stud on the alternator.

A power wire from the battery, a wire from the fuse panel, and a wire from the neutral safety switch connect to the starter solenoid. Another wire connects the neutral safety switch and the ignition switch, but it typically passes through the fuse panel. When the neutral safety switch is installed properly, the truck will start only when the shifter is in park or neutral.

Additional wires to the engine compartment are for a coolant-temperature sending unit, an oil-pressure sending unit, a horn, and an electric fan (when used). The coolant-temperature sending unit should be threaded into the intake manifold. A wire connects this sender

to the coolant-temperature gauge or a warning light in the dash.

The oil-pressure sending unit should be threaded into a pressurized oil gallery. A wire connects this sender to the oil-pressure gauge or a warning light in the dash. Both of these instrument senders are grounded through their mounting in the engine block or the intake manifold. Since the horn and the electric fan require considerable current, they should each use their own electrical relay and must be grounded through a wire to a suitable ground.

Choose the best route for these wires, staying away from any sources of excessive heat or any pinch points that could damage the wire. The wires are typically grouped together, using wire ties, and branching out as they approach their destination. For wires running to the engine compartment, it is common to run wires through the firewall and over the intake manifold or along the inner fender. Depending on the location of the fuse panel and the destination of the wires, running

One of the main reasons that I chose to build a center console for the 1955 Chevy truck was to provide an easily accessible fuse panel. Although the center console was under construction at the time of this photo, the fuse panel is shown bolted in place in the bottom. It will presumably be easier to replace a fuse in this center console than in the stock location under the dash.

wires along one of the front frame rails is an option.

Power for the headlights, taillights, and parking lights originates from the fuse panel after passing through the headlight switch along the way. The headlight switch also controls the interior lights but may be assisted by a jamb switch in the doors to provide light when entering or exiting the truck.

From the headlight switch, one wire runs directly to the dimmer switch. From here, power is sent to the low-beam terminal of each headlight. Power is also sent to the high-beam terminal of each headlight, as well as a smaller wire to the high-beam indicator on the dash. When parking lights are used as front turn signals, power comes directly from the fuse panel to operate the turn signals.

The headlights, taillights, and parking lights must be grounded through a wire to a suitable ground. Taillights receive power through the headlight switch and, when combined as a turn signal, also receive power from the fuse panel. One wire provides power to the right rear turn signal while a different wire provides power the left rear turn signal. Power to the brake lights comes directly from the fuse panel and is activated through a brake-light switch.

Connectors

Even when a wiring kit is purchased, you will most likely need

Sealing Heat-Shrink Tubing

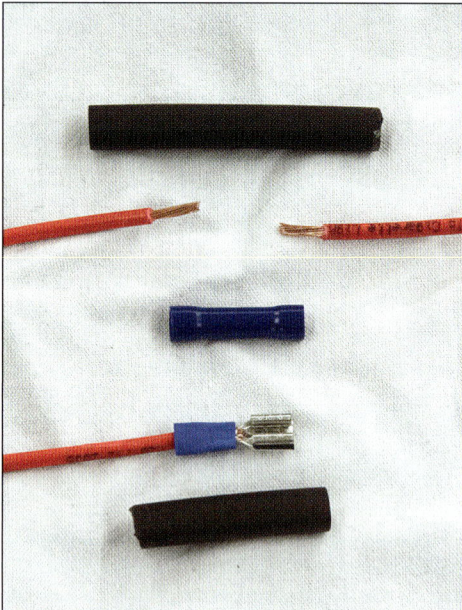

1 *Cut the heat-shrink tubing so that it is about twice as long as the butt connector. Slide the heat-shrink tubing over one wire and crimp the butt connector onto both wires. Then, slide the heat-shrink tubing so that it is centered over the connection. When crimping a terminal onto one wire, cut the heat-shrink tubing approximately one and a half times the length of the terminal.*

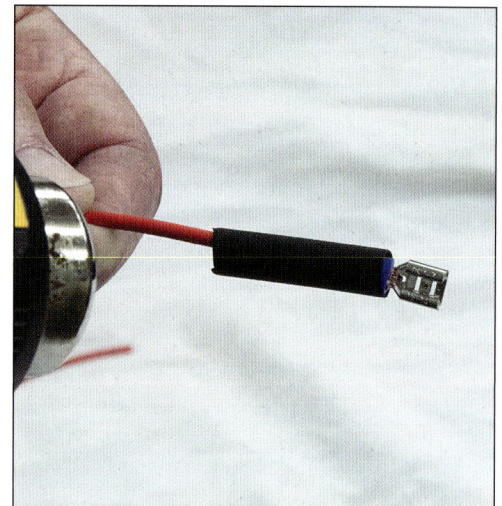

2 *With the heat-shrink tubing positioned correctly, begin to heat the tubing.*

3 *To heat the wire from all sides, move the heat source. In other situations, you can rotate the wire between your fingers.*

4 *As heat is applied, the tubing will begin to shrink around the wire. Heat the wiring from all sides for the best results.*

to purchase additional connectors. Aftermarket vendors and some auto parts stores sell electrical-connector assortments. One of these is probably a good addition to your truck's travel kit for the occasional roadside-emergency repair. However, when doing a complete rewiring job, you will be better off purchasing the connectors in bulk. Some connectors are simply used more commonly than others, making more of these connectors necessary.

Heat-Shrink Tubing

When using uninsulated wiring connectors, use heat-shrink tubing to protect the connection. To protect wiring connections from corrosion, all wiring connections that may be exposed to moisture should be protected with heat-shrink tubing.

To use heat-shrink tubing properly, cut a piece of the appropriate diameter so that it is about one and a half times as long as the connector. Slide the heat-shrink tubing over the wire before crimping on the connector, strip the wire approximately a 1/4 inch, then crimp on the connector. Finish by sliding the heat-shrink tubing over the connection and apply heat to shrink the tubing.

Avoid overheating the wire. An electric heat gun, available at auto parts stores, heats the tubing quite nicely and does not burn the wire. A heat gun works much better than a hair dryer (they do not get hot enough to work properly) and is more controllable and therefore safer than a cigarette, match, or lighter.

Not only will heat-shrink tubing protect an electrical connection by providing a bit of strain relief but it will also look more professional. While heat-shrink tubing is available in different colors, it can be purchased in bulk and in black, which probably looks more professional than a splatter of colors in your wiring.

Wire Wrap

Although it is not an absolute requirement, wrapping the wiring with a protective covering is a good idea and certainly gives the wiring project a more finished and professional look. Convoluted plastic tubing is available at most automotive parts stores in various diameters. This tubing is split so that it can be installed after the wiring has been completed. Automotive aftermarket vendors have various types of woven fabric wire loom that serves the same purpose. While it is perhaps a bit more expensive, it looks much better.

Grommets

Chafed wires lead to short circuits. To prevent chafed wires, install a rubber grommet any time that a wire or wires pass through sheet metal

Heat-shrink tubing is available in various diameters, colors, and lengths (or in a roll). My personal preference is to purchase the tubing on a roll and cut it to the length that I want.

Plastic convoluted tubing is available at most auto parts stores and farm/home centers. It is available in various lengths and diameters. It has a split, which allows you to run the wiring and then slide the protective covering over the bundle of wires. This is the cheap stuff, but it is better than nothing when it comes to protecting the wires. Other types of protective coverings are made from woven plastic or a woven cloth material. Those look significantly nicer but come with a higher price.

Painless Performance Products offers PowerBraid and ClassicBraid wire wrap. This is one of the chassis kits that includes a variety of lengths and diameters of split wrap. It is also possible to purchase rolls of specific sizes individually.

The PowerBraid wire wrap looks slightly shinier than the ClassicBraid, with the latter being more appropriate for vintage vehicles. In addition to the split wrap, the kit includes wire ties, electrical tape, and self-sealing tape.

Any time that wires pass through sheet metal or fiberglass, the wires should pass through a rubber grommet. If left unprotected, a wire passing through sheet metal will quickly vibrate enough to abrade the wire's insulation and short out. Even though the wire would not ground itself to a fiberglass component, it could still abrade the insulation, making itself vulnerable to moisture.

Evenly spaced wire ties go a long way toward making any wiring job look like it was done by a professional. These are great for keeping bunches of wires separated during the wiring process and then keeping wires together when you are finished routing them.

or fiberglass. Rubber grommets are available at auto parts stores in various diameters and for different wall thicknesses. A properly sized grommet fits the hole snugly and has sufficient room for the wires that must pass through but is not so large that lots of air is allowed to pass through.

Wire Ties

Plastic wire ties are designed to tie multiple wires together in a bundle and work much better than a length of electrical tape, as there is no residual adhesive. The plastic tie has ridges and a square head on one end with internal teeth. The tie is wrapped around the wires, and the tail is inserted into the square end and pulled tight. The internal teeth grab the ridges, securing the wire tie in place. Use a pair of diagonal side cutters to trim off the excess at the side of the square head. Wire ties are available in various lengths and colors.

When routing wires, leave the wire tie loose until all wires that are going to a particular area have been routed through it. This helps segregate various routings of wire when starting your wiring project. You might start out with wire ties every foot or so. However, by the time you are finished, having wire ties uniformly spaced every 6 to 8 inches makes for a neat and tidy installation of which you can be proud.

For wires that must run behind upholstery or beneath carpet, keep the wire bundle as small as possible. Cover any wires on the floor with duct tape to secure them in place and to help prevent any abrasion. All wires that run behind upholstery should be routed and secured behind the structural supports to which the upholstered panels mount.

Electrical Tape

While electrical tape has been used extensively in the past to bundle wires together and provide some protection for those wires, wire ties and wire wrap is a much better way to go. Electrical tape will stretch and therefore get loose, and it will also dry out and fall apart.

However, having a roll of electrical tape in the glove box or toolkit is a good practice, as it may come in handy for a temporary side-of-the-road repair. If a wire has been nicked or develops a bare spot, a couple of wraps of electrical tape will prevent the bare wire from shorting out. Also, if a wire gets cut or an issue

Electrical tape should not really be used as much as it has been used in the past because wire ties and heat-shrink tubing are significantly better choices. However, electrical tape works well to make temporary repairs to electrical work.

calls for splicing two wires together, that can be resolved with tape if the appropriate connectors are not with you.

When using electrical tape, avoid touching the sticky side of the tape and ensure that the surface to be taped is as clean as possible. Pull the tape tightly around whatever you are wrapping and ease up on the tension a bit as you get close to the end so that the tape does not stretch. This will help prevent the electrical tape from pulling loose.

A Better Ground

Ground the battery directly to the engine block or transmission (a bolt

that mounts the transmission to the engine works well). You must also run a ground strap from this point to the chassis. However, a better and more convenient method of grounding is installing multiple ground studs throughout the truck. Determine a suitable location near the front, rear, and interior of the truck to install a ground stud. Although various sizes of hardware can be used if desired, each ground stud requires a 10-32 x 3/4 stainless steel screw, a 10-32 brass nut, and a 10-32 wing nut.

Route a 12-gauge wire from the negative side of the battery (there is usually an accessory pigtail on the negative battery cable) to each ground

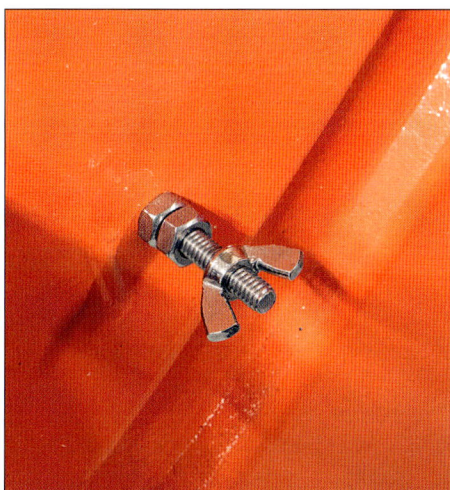

Install as many ground studs as you want (three is usually sufficient) and do so anywhere you want. Install one in the engine compartment for the front lights and any engine-related accessories. Install another in the interior (most likely under the dash) for interior accessories. Finally, install another ground stud near the rear of the truck for rear lights, the fuel sender, and any other items that are in the rear portion of the truck.

stud and install the appropriately sized ring terminal. At the desired location, drill an appropriately sized hole for the ground stud. Insert the stainless-steel screw through the ring terminal on the ground wire and into the hole. Then, secure it with the brass nut. After the process has been completed, ground wires (from all lights and accessories) that have been terminated with a ring terminal can be secured to the ground stud with the wing nut.

Vehicle-Specific Kits: Painless Wiring Kit in a 1970 Chevy Pickup

Electrically speaking, GM trucks matured a bit in the 1960 model year and even more so in the 1967 model year. Wiring first became a little more complex as factory radios and heaters were getting to be more common. By the end of the decade, air conditioning, auxiliary lighting, and towing packages were soon to become standard equipment on some of these trucks.

While a commercially available vehicle-specific wiring kit is designed to replace all the wiring in the vehicle for which it is intended, it is typically designed to replace the original fuse panel as well. The new wiring kits provide more circuits than these trucks ever had from the factory.

Remove the Old Wiring

Unlike the shop truck, which had no existing wiring in it to be removed, the work truck is a running and driving vehicle, which has some electrical issues. Prior to buying it, I was told that the gas gauge and speedometer did not work. I did not get any speeding tickets and ran out of gas only

once, so I consider that a win. Still, these issues need to be resolved, so along with installation of a new fuel tank, it will receive a new fuse panel along with completely new wiring.

As a side note, just because you are rewiring your truck does not mean you need to replace the fuel tank. The fuel-level sender may need

to be removed, as it must be compatible with the new gauges being used, whether they are new or old. I replaced the tank because the previous tank had some rust issues.

Whether using a vehicle-specific wiring kit or a universal kit, remove all the existing wiring prior to installing the new wiring. However, there

Painless Performance Products has been manufacturing vehicle-specific wiring kits for several years. Its kits include everything that is required for rewiring a vehicle, whether it is a vintage pickup truck or muscle car. Several kits are available, so determine what is needed/wanted before choosing a kit.

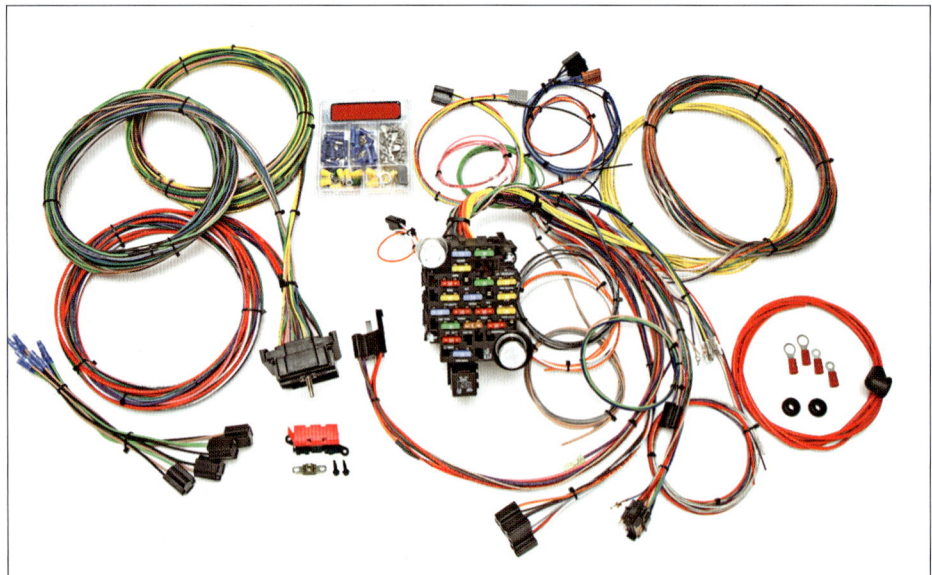

The vehicle-specific kit from Painless Performance Products includes a new fuse panel with fuses, flashers, wires, and connectors to completely rewire your truck. (Photo Courtesy Painless Wiring)

Removing the Old Wiring

1 In addition to new wiring, my work truck is receiving a Vintage Air HVAC system, a new fuel tank, electric gauges, and a stereo. These improvements are nothing elaborate and are practical for any truck.

2 Verify that the battery is disconnected before removing any existing wiring. This cannot be stressed enough! Keep the battery disconnected throughout the wiring process.

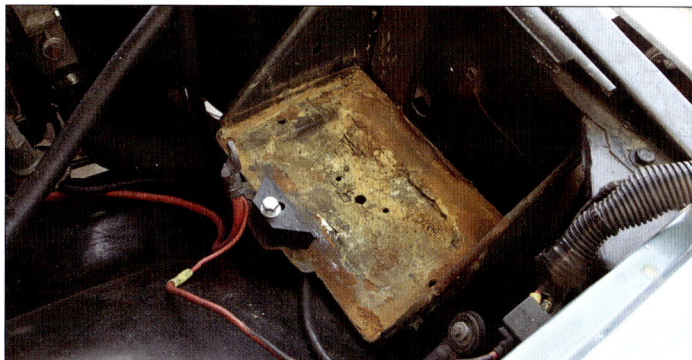

3 While the battery is disconnected, check the battery tray for damage. Most battery trays benefit from a good cleaning or even replacement if damage or rust is extensive.

4 The original fuse panel and its wiring provides evidence of why I chose to rewire this 1970 Chevy C10. The existing wiring has many splices and is a mess.

5 When it comes to wiring, neatness counts. When all of the existing wiring has been removed, the fuse panel will be replaced along with all the wiring. Even though there will be many wires in this area eventually, they will be arranged in a more orderly manner.

Removing the Old Wiring *continued*

6 With the wires removed, it is easier to see some of the stock electrical components that will be retained. The electrical connection at the base of the steering column is for the neutral safety switch and backup lights. The cylindrical switch with two prongs is the brake-light switch. On the left of the photo is the horn relay.

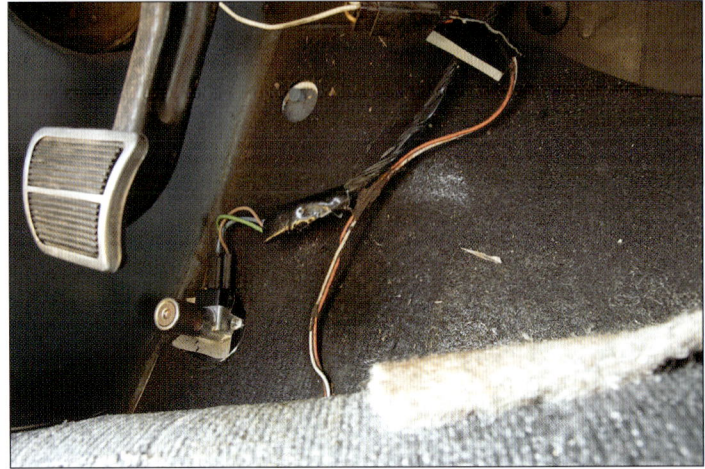

7 The dimmer switch was duct-taped to the floor, and the wires to the headlights were covered with various pieces of tape. It was certainly not a high-quality installation.

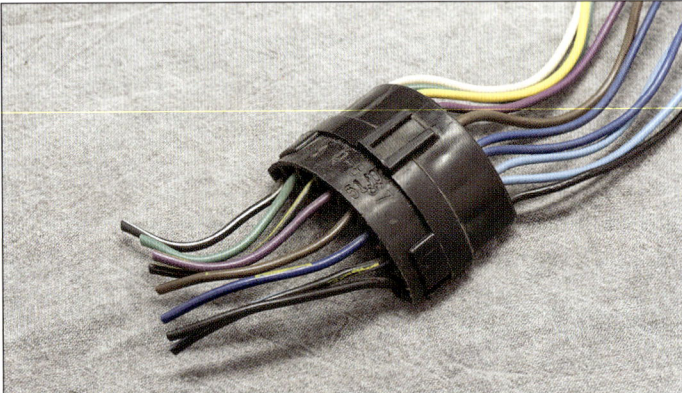

8 This is the original turn-signal switch that was removed from the truck. Some wiring kits may not include this plug, so keep this plug (and any others that may not be included) so that you are not required to find a source for a new one.

9 This truck is a factory A/C truck, but parts of the HVAC system are missing. Eventually, a new system from Vintage Air will be installed. Again, hang on to any parts that may be difficult to replace until the project has been completed.

10 While it is not mandatory to remove the steering wheel when rewiring a truck, doing so aids in accessibility. Typically, removing the horn button provides access to the nut that secures the wheel to the steering column. However, unless the steering wheel has been removed recently, a steering-wheel puller will likely be required to remove the wheel.

11 To remove the dash, the headlight-switch knob must be removed. On this 1970 C10, the knob and the shaft can be pulled out from the front of the headlight switch, after pushing in on the spring-loaded release button.

12 On the side of the headlight switch opposite the electrical connections, there is a spring-loaded release button located near the step in the metal plate. Pressing in on this button allows you to pull the headlight-switch knob and shaft out of the switch.

13 It is also necessary to remove the knob from the wiper-motor switch. This knob can be removed by loosening a small setscrew that secures it to the shaft. With the knob removed, unthread the bezel nut and pull the wiper motor switch out the back of the dash.

14 I have not owned any cassette tapes for about 30 years, so this unit will be replaced. Since the plan for this truck is to merely be a work truck, it will simply be upgraded to an AM/FM/CD player. The 1955 Chevy pickup that will also be wired as part of this book will have satellite radio.

15 This shows more stock wiring under the hood to be removed. The one solid line that comes through the large grommet goes to either the mechanical coolant-temperature sending unit or the oil-pressure sending unit. The spiral wound cable is the stock speedometer cable, which will be replaced.

Removing the Old Wiring *continued*

16 The single wire connecting to the proportioning valve of the master cylinder connects to one side of the brake-light switch.

17 The electric choke on the passenger's side of the carburetor normally requires just a power wire and a ground. However, when used with a TH400 automatic transmission, there is a little more to it. That is discussed later in this chapter.

18 This shows even more splices in the wires—in this case, the ground wire of the horn. All of the ground wires will be replaced as part of this project.

are some things to keep in mind before you begin to rip out the old wiring. There are multiple pigtails and light sockets that may not be included in the wiring kit. Verify that headlight pigtails, a quick disconnect for the steering column connections, an ignition switch, and a headlight switch are included. For items such as doorjamb switches and a dome light, remember to leave enough existing wire to connect to because you may not be able to access these components without doing considerably more work than you planned.

Before doing anything with any of the wiring, disconnect the battery. While doing so, inspect the battery tray and clean it up, or even replace it if necessary. Since the battery is going to be disconnected and is not neces-

sary for anything during the rewiring job, consider completely removing it from the truck. This will ensure that you do not inadvertently contact both terminals with anything. It would be rare for the resultant 12-volt charge to harm you, but it would definitely wake you up.

With no chance of electrical current passing through any of the existing wires, begin by removing the existing fuse panel and the wires that connect to it. With the age of these trucks, you may begin finding more splices than you can imagine, as who knows what electrical accessories have been installed and/or replaced in the life of your truck so far.

While you may choose to replace all the wiring in your truck, there are a few places where you should give

this some thought prior to simply ripping out all the wires. Regardless of whether the ignition switch is in the dash or the steering column, there are going to be some wires (the turn signals and horn at the very least) that come out of the steering column. These typically have a plug that connects them to the rest of the wire that connects to the electrical device.

A new plug may or may not be included in the wiring kit that you selected. Therefore, if you cut these wires, leave them long enough to splice to again as necessary. Any special plugs that you come across should be retained, at least until the wiring project has been completed, just to be sure that you have them if necessary.

If the truck is equipped with power door locks, power windows, or a power antenna, leave that wiring intact and simply attach the power wires for each of these to an appropriate terminal on the fuse panel. If you already have an air-conditioning system that works, leave that wiring intact as well. Trace all the wires involved back to where they connect and label them accordingly.

This specific truck has factory air, but parts of that system were removed by a previous owner, so it will be replaced entirely. Due to the location of the dome light, you should probably leave it in place, along with the power and ground wiring to it. If you do replace the wire, make the connection in a location that is convenient.

While it is not an absolute necessity, removing the steering wheel and the seat makes access to most of the interior wiring much easier. Removing the dash panel also makes the wiring project easier, especially if you plan to install new gauges. Depending on the model of the truck, the dash panel is usually secured in place by several screws that are easy to locate.

The pain about removing the dash panel is with the headlight switch that passes through it. There are two options. One is that the knob of the headlight switch can be removed from the switch shaft by loosening a small setscrew. After removing the knob and usually a threaded bezel that secures the switch to the dash panel, the headlight switch can be pulled out through the back of the dash. The second option is that the headlight-switch knob is permanently connected to the shaft that pushes into the headlight switch.

To remove the knob and the shaft, find and then push in a small, spring-loaded button located on the headlight switch. When the headlight switch is in your hand, this but-

ton is easy to find and usually pushes inward relatively easily. However, when it is behind the dash, it is difficult to see, and with any gunk on it, it may be difficult to push inward.

On GM trucks, the wiper motor switch may or may not protrude through the dash panel, depending on the vintage. Regardless of its location, the knob can usually be unthreaded or removed by removing a small setscrew. Unthread the bezel that threads onto the wiper switch shaft and then pull the switch out the back of the dash.

To remove the ignition switch from the dash, like most switches so far, there are two basic options, depending on the year of the truck. On the older trucks, remove a threaded bezel and pull the switch out from the back of the dash. On the newer vintage trucks, it is a bit more complicated but still easy to do when you have the correct ignition key.

With the key in the ignition, push a paper clip into the small hole as far as it will go and turn the ignition switch counterclockwise to the accessory position. Some people say to turn the key and then push the paper clip in the small hole. Perhaps it works either way? You should then be able to pull the key and the tumbler. Then, unthread the bezel from the ignition switch.

Install the New Wiring

With the old wires removed, the next steps are to determine where all the new wires need to go. The wiring kit from Painless Wiring has all of the wires divided into one of three sections: the engine/headlight section, the interior section, and the tail section.

Depending on where certain

items in the truck are located or whether they are even used, some wires must be moved into a different group. These variables are the dimmer switch, the turn-signal switch, the wiper-motor switch, the brake switch, the reverse switch, the external voltage regulator, the charge-indicator light, and the temperature light.

With the wires regrouped, the new fuse panel can be installed. If you later decide that additional wires should be regrouped, you can still do that. Mount the fuse panel anywhere inside the truck cab that you desire, but the original factory location is typically the best pace overall.

After selecting a location, use the metal template provided to drill two 1/4-inch holes for use in mounting the fuse panel. Hardware is provided, but assistance is required from someone else to install it when mounting the fuse panel to the firewall. Go ahead and install the two flashers in the fuse panel at this time.

Routing Wires

Before cutting or connecting any wires, each wire should be routed toward its destination. The engine/headlight-section wires typically pass through the firewall through one or two holes. Some builders route the headlight wires through the firewall so that they enter the engine compartment near the inside of the fender and go onward toward the core support. Others route them with the rest of the engine wires through the middle of the firewall so that they enter the engine compartment behind the engine. The route is purely up to the builder, but remember to use rubber grommets to protect the wires where they pass through sheet metal.

The tail-section wires can be routed through the firewall with the other wires and then routed down below the cab and along the inside of the frame rail to the rear of the truck. An option is to route the tail-section wires under a door sill and through the cab floor somewhere behind the seat. Tail-section wires are commonly routed along the inside of the driver-side frame rail, leaving the passenger-side frame rail available for fuel lines.

Any wires that remain in the cab can be routed directly toward the electrical device that they connect to without exiting the cab. The best advice to be given to anyone doing automotive electrical work is to take your time, route your wires neatly, and use plenty of wire ties. Remember to use rubber grommets when passing through sheet metal, stay away from sharp edges and hot surfaces (exhaust headers and pipes), and avoid pinch points, such as door and hood hinges.

Route the headlight wires, front turn-signal wires, and horn wire along the inside of the fender to the core support. At the core support, separate the left-side wires from the right-side wires. The right-side wires typically cross the core support, but the exact location may depend on the vintage of the truck and personal preference.

Route the taillight, turn signal, brake light, and fuel-level sender wire (if running a rear-mounted tank) to the rearmost crossmember of the truck. Again, separate the left-side wires from those that go to the right side. With all wires routed toward their general location, begin making electrical connections.

Wiring the Headlights

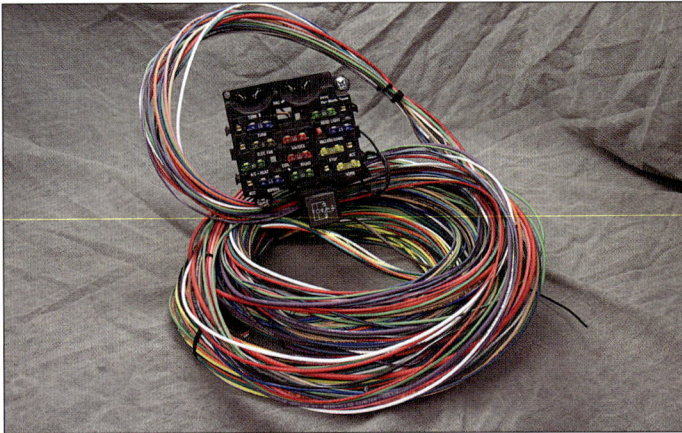

1 A new fuse panel and a bunch of new wiring will cure many past indiscretions that make me wonder how this truck ever ran at all.

2 With all of the old wiring and fuse panel out of the way, the interior side of the firewall looks much better already. The new fuse panel will be installed in the same location as the original.

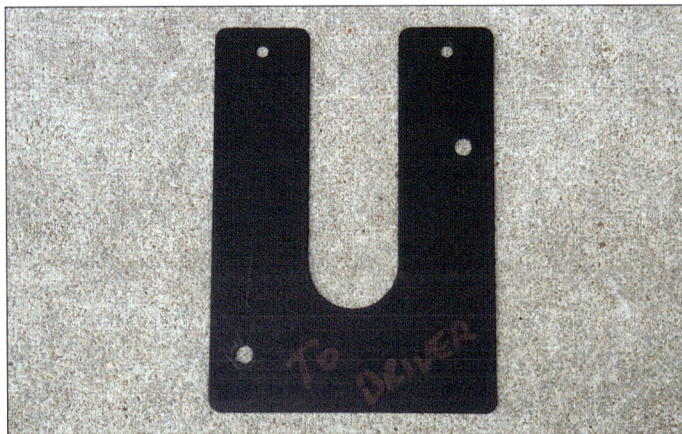

3 The Painless Performance wiring kit provides a steel template to use for drilling new mounting holes for the fuse panel.

4 After drilling the two mounting holes, secure the fuse panel in place with the two provided screws, washers, and nuts. Enlist a helper to tighten the mounting screws when the fuse panel is installed in the stock location. Do not forget to install a flasher in each of the two flasher locations at the top of the fuse panel.

Wiring the Headlights *continued*

5 A sheet-metal cover will be made to cover the stock square hole that remains from the original wiring. Use grommets any time that wires pass through sheet metal. You are asking for trouble if you do not do this.

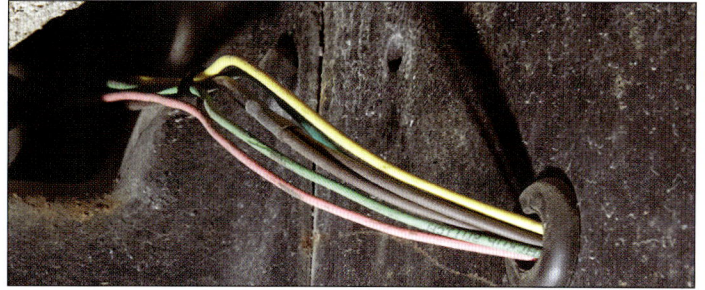

6 Route the wires that should be routed to the back of the truck down the firewall and through a rubber grommet as they go to the inside of the frame rails. The wires can then run along the inside of the frame rails to their destinations.

7 After passing the engine-section wires through the firewall, the wires that run toward the front lights can be routed along the inside of the front fender. Later, these will be protected by wire loom, but it is too soon to do that at this point in the process.

8 To route right-side headlight and turn-signal wires across the top of the radiator, loosen the two upper radiator mounting brackets. The convoluted wiring covering that is shown is the old wire, which has since been removed.

Headlight Section

There are a few things to determine before making any connections to the headlights. First, are you going to install relays into the headlight circuit? Second, are there separate wires for the right-side headlight or must you jump from the left side to the right side? This has more to do with the physical wiring connections than where the electricity goes. The Painless Wiring Kit includes low-beam and high-beam wires to go to the driver's side as well as separate wires that go directly to the passenger's side.

When installing electrical relays into the headlight wiring, a relay is needed for the high beams, and another relay is for the low beams. The 16-gauge wire (or wires) for the low-beam light connect to terminal 86 of the low-beam relay. The 16-gauge wire (or wires) for the high-beam light connect to terminal 86 of the high-beam relay.

Power for the headlights from the fuse panel connects to terminal 30 of both headlight relays. A wire from terminal 87 of the low-beam relay connects to the low-beam terminal of both headlights. A wire from terminal 87 of the high-beam relay connects to the high-beam terminal of both headlights. Each relay requires a ground.

The low-beam and high-beam wires from the dimmer switch should have power when the headlight switch is in the headlight-on position. The headlights will toggle between the low beam and high beam with each click of the dimmer switch.

Park/Side-Marker Lights

Beginning with the 1968 model year, Chevrolet and GMC pickup trucks included side-marker lights. In the front, these can be wired to serve simply as a front marker/parking light or as a parking light and turn-signal light.

When wiring as a front marker/parking light, connect the 18-gauge left parking-light wire to one side of the side-marker-light socket and to the left parking light. This wire will have power when the headlight switch is in the park/taillights-on or headlights-on position.

Connect the 18-gauge left front turn-signal wire directly to the left front turn light socket. This wire will have interrupted switched power from the turn-signal flasher when the left turn signal is activated. It will also have interrupted battery power when the hazard switch is activated. Connect the remaining wire from the side-marker light socket and the remaining wire from the turn-signal light socket to ground.

When wiring the side-marker light to operate as a turn signal, connect the left parking-light wire to one side of the side-marker light socket and to the left parking light. Connect the left front turn-signal wire to the remaining side of the side-marker light socket and then to the left turn-signal light. When connecting the side-marker light as a turn signal, it will receive its ground through the turn signal.

Wiring Side-Marker Lights

1 As you begin wiring the truck, remember to leave the wires long enough that they can be unplugged when necessary, such as during maintenance or when painting (if this is a complete frame-off restoration). Do not leave the wires dangling everywhere, either. When all is said and done, these wires will be tied up a bit nicer.

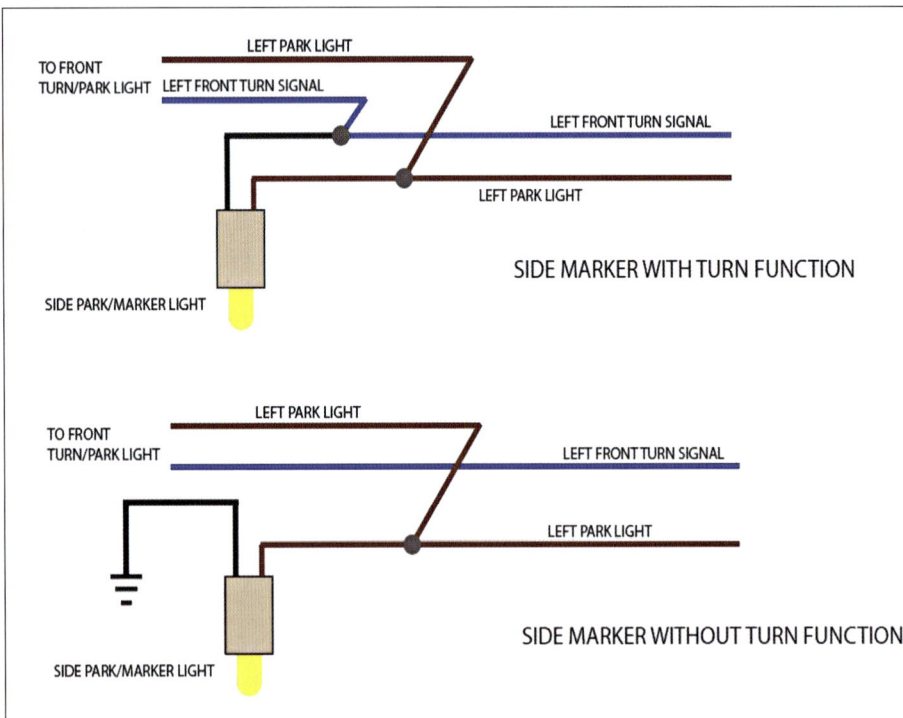

2 On trucks with side-marker lights, you have the option of using the side marker as a turn signal. With the turn function, the turn-signal wire connects to the ground wire of the side-marker light. Without the turn signal, the side-marker light must be grounded.

Wiring Side-Marker Lights *continued*

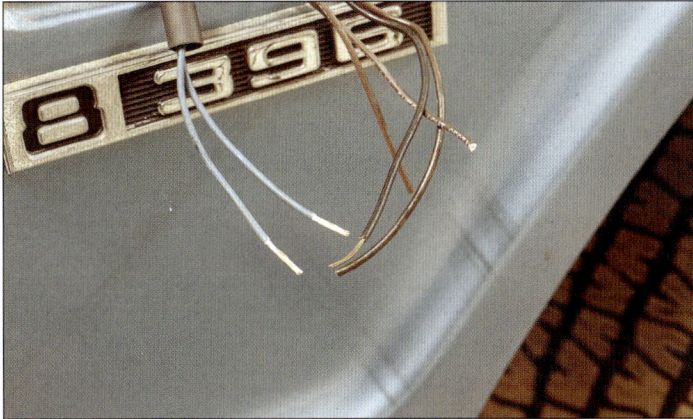

3 To use the front side-marker lights also as turn signals, the left front turn signal (the light blue wire from the fuse panel) must connect to one terminal of the side-marker light and to the left front turn signal. The front parking light (the brown wire from the fuse panel) must connect to one side of the side-marker light and to the left front parking light. When the side-marker light is powered by the turn-signal power and the parking-light power, the side-marker lights will operate as a turn signal. When the side-marker light is powered by the parking-light power and a ground wire, it will operate as a parking light.

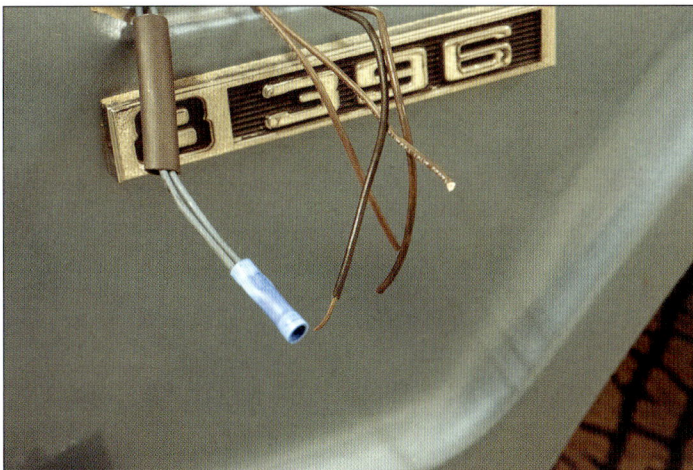

4 Cut the turn-signal wires to length, strip the insulation, slide a piece of heat-shrink tubing over the wires, and crimp on a butt connector.

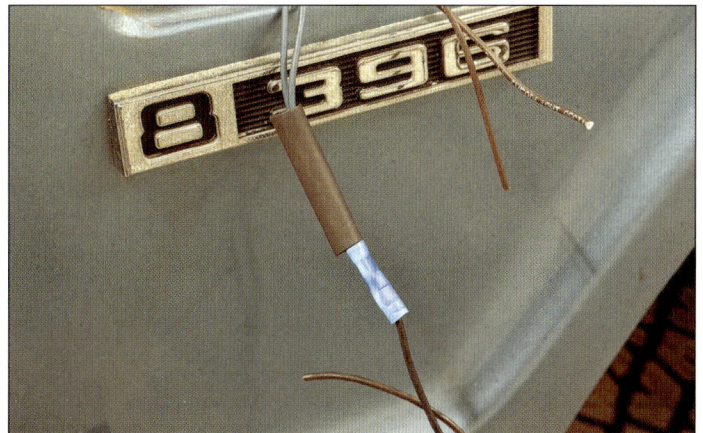

5 Strip the insulation from the side-marker-light wire, insert it into the butt connector, and crimp it in place. Repeat the previous process for the parking-light wires.

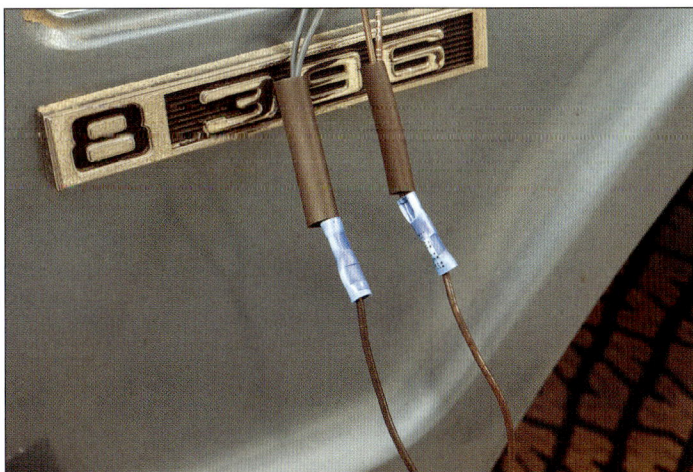

6 With heat-shrink tubing in place and butt connectors connecting the wires in the proper configuration, you are almost done.

7 Slide the heat-shrink tubing over the butt connector. Use a heat gun to apply heat to the connection until the heat-shrink tubing shrinks and seals the connection.

Wiring Side-Marker Lights *continued*

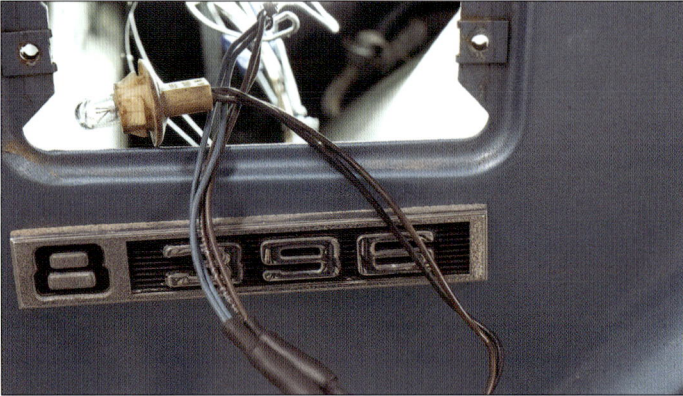

8 As wired, the front side-marker lights will now operate as turn signals.

9 Inspect the side-marker lights to ensure that they are not damaged. If they are damaged, replace them. Even if they are not damaged, it is good to clean them up.

10 The rectangular side-marker lights first appeared on GM pickup trucks in the 1968 model year and were on the front and back. In the 1973–1980 model years, a narrower side-marker light in a vertical orientation was located on the front fenders. Fleetside trucks featured a wraparound-style taillight, eliminating rear side-marker lights on all but Stepside trucks. In the 1981–1987 model years, the front side-marker light was similar in size to the previous years but in a horizontal orientation. Side-marker lights were discontinued in the 1988 model year, as the headlight and taillights were a wraparound design.

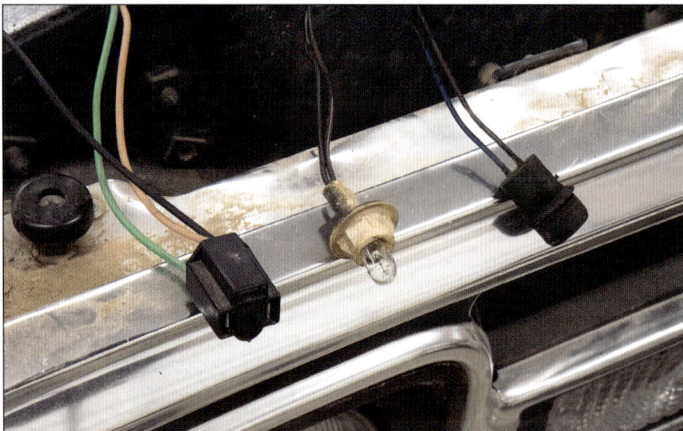

11 Wires for the three common front lights are connected and ready to be installed. On the left are the high beam, low beam, and ground with the plug for the headlights. In the middle are the side-marker power wire and turn-signal wire for the side-marker light. On the right is the parking-light power wire and ground wire for the front parking light.

12 These are the various wires that are ultimately terminated at the right, front side of the truck, including the headlight, parking light, and side-marker/turn-signal light. Note that the battery tray has been removed in this photo.

13 *While the front side-marker light can be wired to operate as a turn signal if desired, the rear side-marker light does not have that option. This is because of the rear turn signal and the brake light being integrated.*

Horn

Since the horn has a high current draw, the 14-gauge power wire comes from the horn relay that is mounted on the fuse panel and connects to the horn. When the horn button is pressed, the circuit grounds, completing the circuit and causing the horn to sound. Some horns ground through their mounting, but the aftermarket horn on this truck requires a separate ground. That ground wire will be installed later and connected to a ground stud inside the engine compartment.

Wiring the Horn

1 *This aftermarket horn requires one wire for power and one for ground. The power wire comes from the fuse panel and is connected in this photo. Since the horn is shaped somewhat like a funnel, mount the horn so that water will not collect in it.*

2 *To connect the ground wire, repeat the process that was used for the power wire, but do so with a wire that will ultimately connect to a ground stud. Cut the ground wire to length, strip the insulation 3/8 inch, slide a piece of heat-shrink tubing over the wires, and crimp on a female spade connector (in this case).*

Wiring the Horn *continued*

3 After the appropriate connector is crimped onto the wire, slide the heat-shrink tubing over the connection and apply heat with a heat gun to seal the connection. Give the heat shrink time to cool. Then, connect the ground wire to the remaining terminal on the horn.

Accessory/Fan Relay

Included in the Painless wiring kit is an 18-gauge wire that is used to provide 12-volt activation for an electric fan. This is commonly used when an air-conditioning system is installed in the truck. As such, it will be mentioned later when the HVAC system is installed. For now, it is merely tucked away near the radiator core support.

Engine Section

Within the engine section are seven wires: the wire for the oil-pressure sending unit, coolant-temperature sending unit, coil and ignition system, A/C-compressor clutch, electric choke, and two wires for a hydraulic brake-light switch.

Brake Switch

On this truck, the brake-light switch is in combination with the proportioning valve. Two wires connect to it: a 14-gauge wire that provides power from the fuse panel and a 16-gauge wire that provides power from the brake switch to the brake lights when pressure is applied to the brake pedal.

Coolant-Temperature Sending Unit

On this truck, the previous coolant-temperature and oil-pressure gauges were mechanical. When using mechanical gauges, there is nothing electrical to do, aside from the gauge lighting. However, this truck will be treated to a new set of electrical gauges, which requires a new sender for the coolant temperature and the oil pressure.

After disconnecting the coolant-temperature hose from its gauge, the sender must be removed from the engine. The coolant-temperature-gauge sender is commonly installed in the intake manifold but can be installed in either cylinder head. By using the appropriately sized open-end wrench, unthread the sender, and discard it. There may or may not be an adapter in place, and it may or may not need to be removed. Using the adapter, if necessary, insert the temperature gauge sender in place, making sure that it is tight. Teflon (tape or liquid) should not be used on the senders for electrical gauges, as the mounting is what provides the necessary ground.

Complete the installation by connecting an 18-gauge wire to the end of the sender. Depending on the sender, this may require a ring terminal or a female spade terminal. This wire sends the temperature to the gauge by way of a resistive ground signal. The gauge translates this signal to a temperature measured in Fahrenheit or Celsius, depending on the gauge.

Oil-Pressure Sending Unit

Switching out and installing the oil-pressure sending unit is very similar to the process for the coolant-temperature gauge. The difference is the sender and its location. The oil-pressure sending unit is typically larger than the coolant-temperature sending unit and is commonly located on the back of the block behind the intake

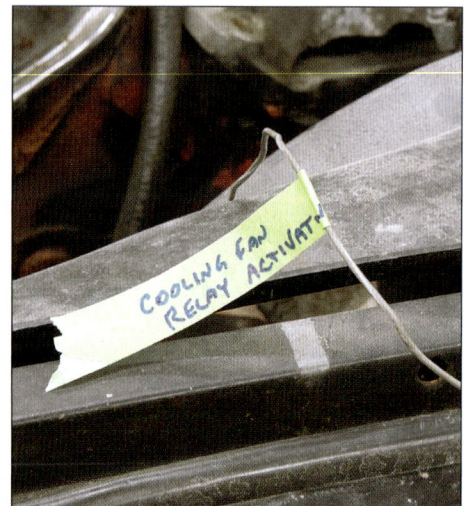

While most wiring kits have the wiring identification stamped on the wire, due to the size of the wire, the lettering can be pretty small. In addition, through the course of routing the wiring, the wires rubbing together, and merely handling the wire, some of that lettering rubs off. One solution is to label each wire with some identification tags after routing the wires, especially if the electrical connections are not being made right away.

manifold or near the oil filter. This is a situation where removal and installation are significantly easier if the engine is not in the truck.

After removing the old mechanical sender, install the new oil-pressure sending unit, and install the correct connector onto the 18-gauge wire. This wire will send a ground signal to the oil-pressure gauge.

Electric Choke

When using an electric choke, an 18-gauge wire provides power when the ignition switch is in the on/run position. The power wire connects to the positive terminal on the choke, while the negative terminal of the choke must be connected to ground. This electric current heats the choke thermostat, causing the choke to slowly open, helping the engine to start.

Coil and Tachometer

In this application, a 14-gauge wire from the 30-amp coil fuse on the fuse panel provides a switched ignition power source. This wire should have power anytime that the ignition switch is in the on or start position. When a tachometer is used, an 18-gauge wire sends a signal from the coil to the tachometer. There are four possible configurations to correctly connect this switched ignition power to the coil.

In this sample wiring application, which uses a high-energy ignition (HEI) coil, the power wire connects directly to the positive side of the coil. No ballast resistor is required. The tachometer signal wire connects to the negative side of the coil.

If you do not have them, purchase the special plugs that fit correctly into the coil at the auto parts store. Since this is for the ignition, spend the extra

money to ensure that the connection has the retainer mechanism and stays in place. These came with a short pigtail, so only a standard butt connection is necessary to install them.

When using a traditional coil that is remote from the distributor and no ballast resistor, the wiring is completed much like with an HEI ignition. The power wire connects directly to the positive side of the coil and the tachometer signal wire connects to the negative side of the coil.

When using a ballast resistor, the power wire connects directly to the input terminal of the ballast resistor. The second section of the power wire connects to the output terminal of the ballast resistor and to the positive side of the coil. A separate wire connects to the "R" or "I" stud on the starter and to the output terminal of the ballast resistor or to the positive side of the coil. As with other applications, the tachometer signal wire connects to the negative side of the coil.

The fourth method of connecting the coil and tachometer involves an ignition-system box. Wiring may vary by the manufacturer. Follow the specific instructions provided with the ignition system.

Alternator

Before discussing the wiring of the alternator, it should be mentioned as a reminder that when using any other belt-driven accessories (namely the A/C compressor), the belt-driven accessories and their pulleys and belts must be properly aligned. To do this, with a GM engine, determine if you are using a long water pump or a short water pump.

When simply rewiring a stock motor, this is not an issue. However, when rebuilding where the water pump may have been changed, use

the correct brackets to achieve the correct alignment. You simply cannot use an alternator bracket for a long water pump or an A/C-compressor bracket for a short water pump or vice versa. There are several aftermarket companies that manufacture bracketry, so choose something that fits your budget and taste for your truck.

Regardless of the type of alternator that you use, the output connection is the same. A 6-gauge wire connects to the alternator's output stud and to the MIDI fuse and then goes on to the battery. It is necessary to first slide the rubber alternator boot over the end of the 6-gauge wire, strip approximately 3/8 inch of the wire's insulation, and then crimp on the appropriately sized ring terminal to fit your alternator. With this size of wire, it may be necessary to use a hammer crimper.

If you do not have a hammer crimper, a local auto parts store may provide this service. Place the ring terminal on the output stud and secure it with a nut. Then slide the rubber boot over the nut and ring terminal.

There are two additional wires necessary to connect the alternator: the 14-gauge regulator power sense wire and the 16-gauge regulator exciter wire. The regulator power sense wire has power all the time and is connected slightly differently, depending on which alternator is being used. The flow of electricity is typically the same, but the actual connection plugs are different. The 16-gauge regulator exciter wire has switched ignition power from the fuse panel when the ignition key is in the start or run position.

MIDI Fuse

An inline MIDI fuse provides a fused link between the alternator and the battery. It can be located wherever it physically fits and can be wired inline between the alternator and the battery. A 10-gauge wire connects to one terminal of the MIDI fuse and the fuse panel.

Having constant battery power, this wire provides battery power to the fuse panel and is converted to switched power at the ignition switch. A 6-gauge wire connects to the same terminal of the MIDI fuse and the output terminal of the alter-

nator. This provides power from the alternator to the battery.

Connect another 6-gauge wire to the opposite terminal of the MIDI fuse and to the positive terminal of the battery or to the battery post on the starter solenoid. Note that this 6-gauge wire from the MIDI terminal to the starter solenoid does not replace the battery cable directly from the positive side of the battery to the battery post on the starter solenoid.

Starter Solenoid

A 12-gauge wire between the starter terminal "S" and the neutral safety switch provides switched power to the starter solenoid when the ignition switch is in the start position. This electric current activates the starter solenoid, causing the starter to turn over the engine. If using the ballast resistor bypass wire, it should be connected to the "I" or "R" post of the starter solenoid.

Wiring Miscellaneous Engine Components

1 On this truck, the brake-light switch is contained within the proportioning valve. The switch is the male portion of a bullet connector. Cut to length the power wire from the fuse panel and the wire that provides power to the brake lights and strip off 3/8 inch of the insulation.

2 Slide heat-shrink tubing over both wires, slide on the female portion of a bullet connector, and crimp the bullet connector on to both wires. Use a heat gun to shrink the tubing.

3 Insert the bullet connector over the electrical connection.

4 This is the mechanical coolant-temperature sending unit and its hose that provides information to the temperature gauge. The gauges in the truck when I purchased it were not stock, but they were mechanical. If you were replacing the gauges with mechanical gauges, this sender can be reused.

Wiring Miscellaneous Engine Components *continued*

5 This is what the mechanical coolant-temperature sending unit looks like as it is being removed from the intake manifold. Since it has a mechanical gauge, there is no electrical wire between the sender and the gauge. However, mechanical gauges still require electricity for the dash lights.

7 Insert the adapter (if required) and tighten it completely into the intake manifold. Then, insert the new sender and tighten it completely. The senders for electric gauges ground through the intake manifold, so do not use any Teflon on the threads.

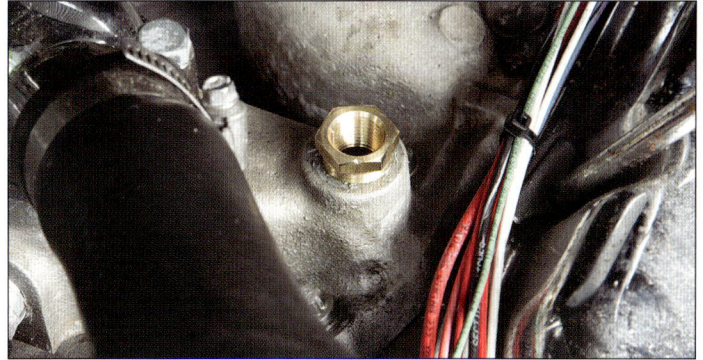

6 You may or may not require an adapter for the new coolant-temperature sending unit. If you are replacing an existing sending unit (mechanical or electrical) and it requires an adapter, find something that threads into the intake manifold correctly and take the new sender to the auto parts store to ensure that you get the correct adapter.

8 Install the ring terminal onto the coolant-temperature sending unit and secure it with a lock washer and nut. Now you can move on to the oil-pressure sending unit.

9 Wiring the oil-pressure sending unit requires a ring terminal. Whether the oil-pressure sending unit is mounted at the top of the engine block or near the oil filter, it is susceptible to moisture, so the electrical connections should be protected with heat shrink.

Wiring Miscellaneous Engine Components *continued*

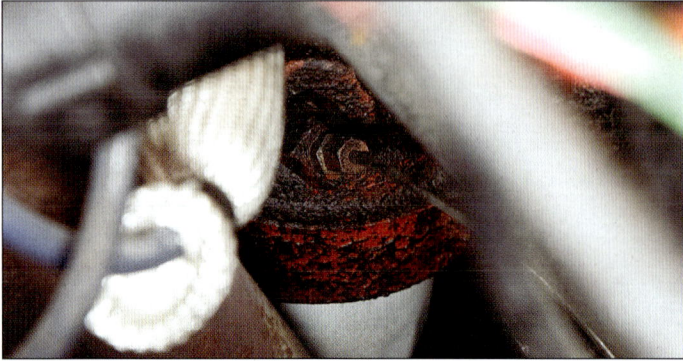

10 On the vintage big-block in the 1970 C10, the oil-pressure sending unit is located near the oil filter. This is the original sending unit for the mechanical gauges. It must be removed and a new sending unit for electric gauges must be installed. The sending unit grounds through the engine block, so do not use any sort of Teflon to seal the sender. Make sure that you get the sending unit and any adapter secured tightly.

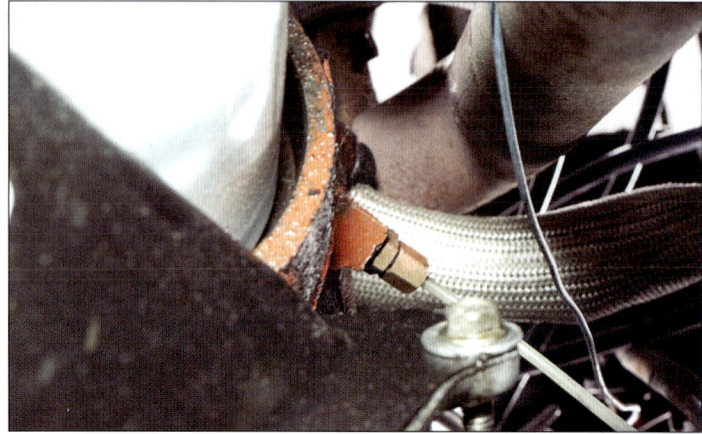

11 This fitting is the original from the mechanical oil-pressure gauge. In my attempt to remove it, the brass fitting began to round off the corners. Located near the oil filter, this fitting is not easy to access. I was able to remove the ferrule and the hose that led to the mechanical gauge.

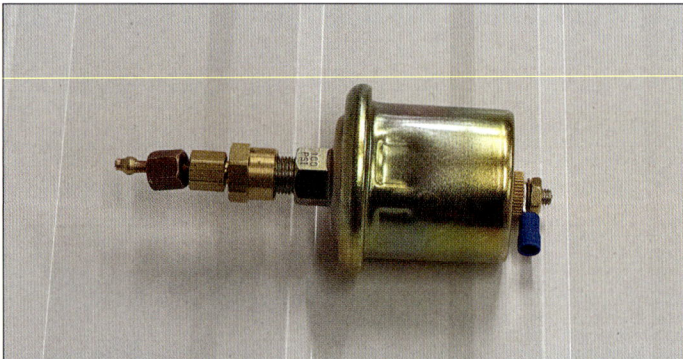

12 Todd at High Ridge NAPA properly assembled the necessary adapter (a length of copper pipe) between the pipe thread and the inverted flare fitting. The ferrule at the left end of the photo is the same one that is in the previous photo. A lesson learned is that with a length of the small hose, the oil-pressure sending unit could be mounted in a more convenient location, as long as the hose is secured to the fitting on the block with an inverted flare.

13 The electric choke on most carburetors has two spade connections that are clearly marked plus and minus. On this choke, the positive (power) terminal is a male spade terminal, while the ground terminal is a female connection. Verify that you used the correct connectors.

14 Connect the choke power wire from the fuse panel to the plus side of the electric choke. Connect a ground wire from the minus side of the electric choke to a suitable ground.

15 On the stock GM HEI-distributor coil cap, the tachometer and battery connections are embossed (albeit difficult to see when in position). The spade connection closest to the firewall when in place is the battery (+) connection. The spade connection in front is the negative (-) for the tachometer (if used).

16 When installing new wiring in the coil, it is significantly easier to install the wires by removing the distributor cap and flipping it over so that you can see what you are doing.

17 On this HEI coil, the red wire is the ignition hot wire that runs directly to the fuse block. From the negative side of the coil is a signal wire that runs directly to the tachometer.

18 Slide the rubber alternator boot over the end of the 6-gauge wire, strip approximately 3/8 inch of the wire's insulation, and crimp on the appropriately sized ring terminal to fit the alternator.

19 GM alternators are simple in construction. The housing is secured to the alternator bracket by one bolt and tightened to an adjustable arm with a second bolt. The pulley can be for a V-belt (shown) or for a serpentine belt. The pulley can easily be swapped out by using an impact wrench to remove the nut. Be sure to use an impact wrench to secure the replacement pulley.

Wiring Miscellaneous Engine Components *continued*

20 Two wires (the regulator power sense and regulator exciter) typically connect to the two spade connectors on the alternator with a plug. The alternator output wire connects to the output stud on the back of the alternator with a ring terminal.

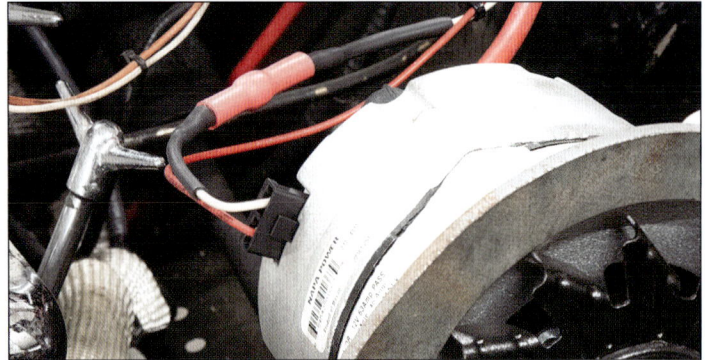

21 Strip the ends off each alternator wire, crimp on the appropriate connectors, and push the terminated wires into the alternator plug. Then, push the alternator plug into the receptacle until it clicks. Note that with a new plug, it may take multiple tries to fully insert the plug.

22 Two wires connect to the same terminal of the MIDI fuse. These are a 10-gauge wire that connects to the fuse panel and a 6-gauge wire that connects to the output terminal of the alternator. On the remaining terminal of the MIDI fuse, connect a 6-gauge wire to the positive terminal of the battery or to the battery post on the starter solenoid.

23 The MIDI fuse can be mounted almost anywhere, so you can hide it or make it convenient. For the work truck, I chose to simply make it convenient and mounted it on the driver-side inner fender. Note, not all connections are made at this time. This wire shown is the 12-volt power from the fuse panel.

24 Connect the 6-gauge wire to the same terminal on the MIDI fuse that the 12-volt power from the fuse panel comes from. This wire will connect to the output terminal of the alternator. Run a 6-gauge wire from the remaining terminal on the MIDI fuse to the starter solenoid and connect it to the S terminal.

25 *Remove the nut from the screw on the back of the alternator, place the ring terminal of the 6-gauge wire from the MIDI over the stud, and secure it with the nut that was previously removed. Then, slide the rubber boot over the connection.*

26 *When all of the wires are routed and electrical connections made, secure the wires with wire ties and snap the cover onto the MIDI fuse.*

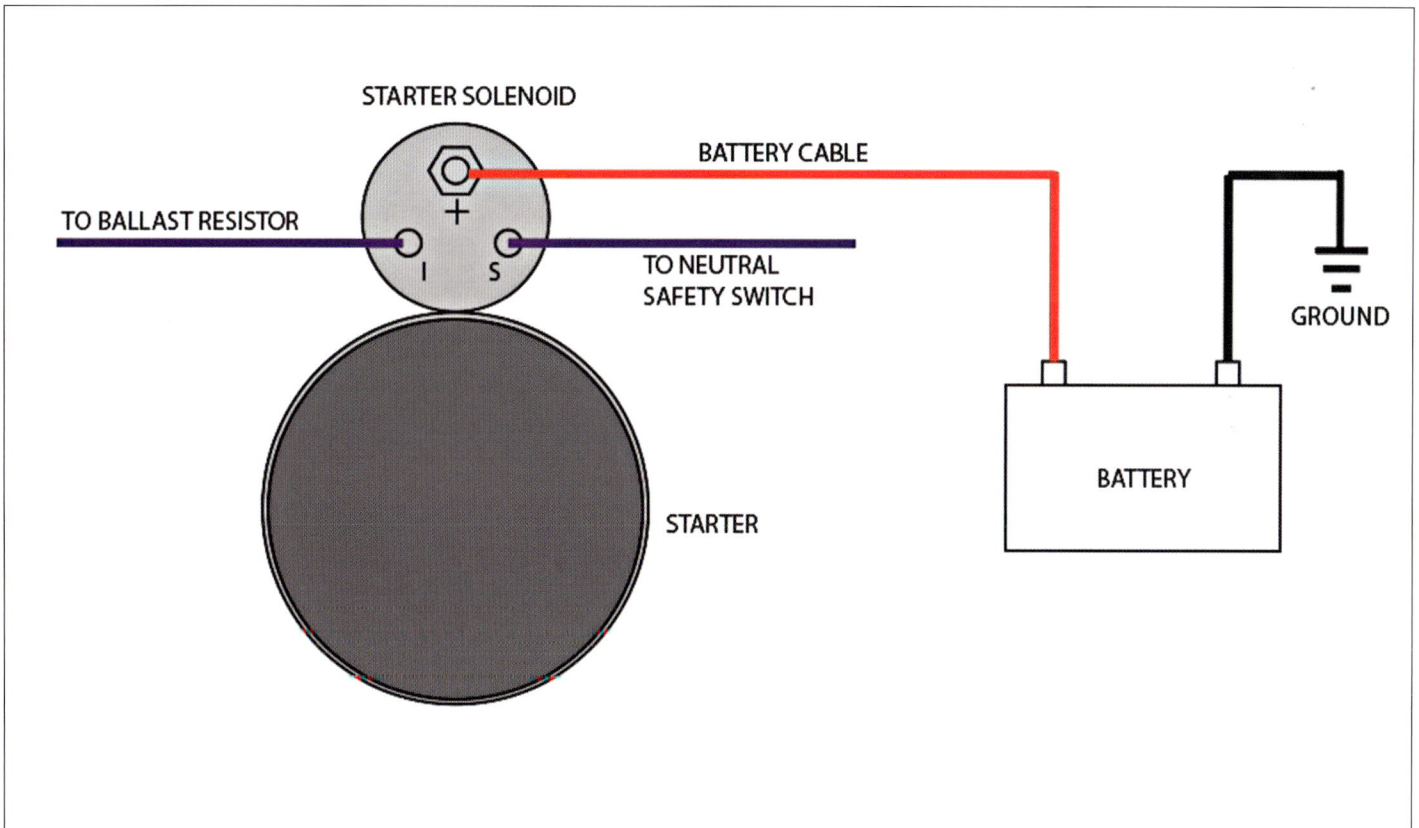

STARTER SOLENOID

BATTERY CABLE

TO BALLAST RESISTOR

TO NEUTRAL
SAFETY SWITCH

STARTER

BATTERY

GROUND

27 *A 6-gauge battery cable connects the positive terminal of the battery to the large terminal on the starter sole-noid. One leg of the neutral safety switch connects to the "S" terminal on the starter solenoid. If used, the ballast resistor bypass wire connects to the "I" terminal of the starter solenoid.*

Wiring Miscellaneous Engine Components *continued*

28 The starter solenoid sits atop the GM starter. The positive cable from the battery connects to the largest terminal on the starter solenoid. The 6-gauge wire from the MIDI fuse also connects to this terminal. The "S" terminal on the starter solenoid (on the right side of the photo) is where the neutral safety switch wire connects. The remaining terminal is where the ballast resistor wire should be connected (if used).

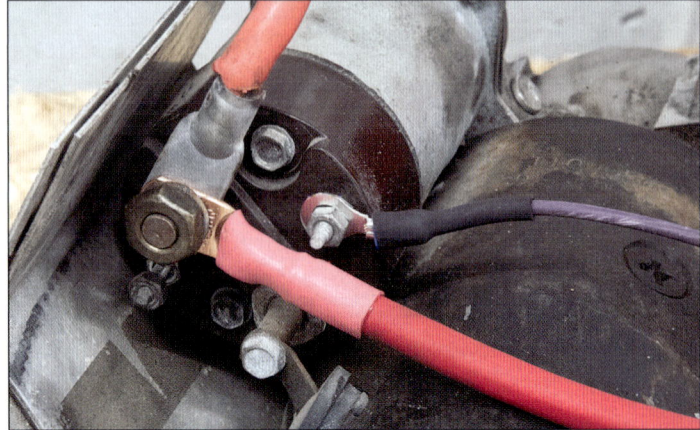

29 While it would be close to impossible to show these wires on the truck with the starter in position, this shows where the wires would be connected. The positive cable from the battery and the 6-gauge wire from the MIDI fuse both connect to the largest terminal on the starter solenoid. The wire from the neutral safety switch connects to the "S" terminal.

Interior Section

The interior section contains nine common components: a dimmer switch, a headlight switch, a brake switch, turn signals, a hazard switch, a horn button, an ignition switch, a reverse switch, and a neutral safety switch.

Dimmer Switch

A 14-gauge wire between the headlight switch and the dimmer switch provides power to the dimmer switch when the headlight switch is in the headlight-on position. Connect this wire to the center terminal on the dimmer switch. Either of the two remaining terminals on the dimmer switch can be used for the low-beam headlights and the remaining one for the high-beam headlights.

A 14-gauge wire from the dimmer switch provides power to each low-beam headlight when the headlight switch is in the headlight-on position and the dimmer switch is in the low-beam position.

A 14-gauge wire from the dimmer switch provides power to each high-beam headlight when the headlight switch is in the headlight-on position and the dimmer switch is in the high-beam position. The wiring system also provides power to the high-beam-indicator light on the dash when the high-beam lights are receiving power.

Headlight Switch

The headlight switch directs electric current to multiple locations: the front parking/marker lights, taillights, backlighting for the gauges and radio, and, of course, the headlights. Vintage GM trucks typically use either an early or a late GM headlight switch, although no one has conclusive evidence of when the change in switch styles actually occurred. There

is nothing to worry about with this because the only difference is where the parking-light wire connects.

A 14-gauge wire between the headlight-switch Power B+ terminal and the stop/tail fuse on the fuse panel provides constant battery power to the parking lights, taillights, and gauge backlighting.

An 18-gauge wire between the headlight switch and the front parking lights provides constant battery power to the parking lights whenever the headlight switch is pulled to the parking light–on position or the headlight-on position. This allows the front parking lights to be on by themselves or in combination with the headlights being on.

A 14-gauge wire between the headlight switch and the taillights provides constant battery power to the taillights whenever the headlight switch is pulled to the parking light–on and headlight-on position. This allows the taillights to be on only when the headlights are on.

An 18-gauge wire between the headlight switch and the gauge backlighting provides constant battery power to the gauge backlighting whenever the headlight switch is pulled to the parking light–on position and the headlight-on position. This allows the gauge backlighting to be on only when the headlights are on.

A 14-gauge wire between the headlight-switch Power B+ terminal and the center terminal of the dimmer switch provides constant battery power to the headlights whenever the headlight switch is pulled to the headlight-on position.

A 12-gauge wire between the headlight-switch Power B+ terminal and the headlight fuse on the fuse panel provides constant battery power to the headlight switch.

When using a factory-style switch, each wire will have a separate terminal to connect to. When no separate terminal is provided for gauge backlighting, connect that wire to the taillight wire at the headlight switch. When separate terminals are not provided, gauge backlighting, parking lights, and taillights can all be connected to the same terminal on the headlight switch.

Turn-Signal Switch

The vintage GM trucks that this book covers may have integrated turn-signal/brake lights or separate turn-signal/brake lights. The difference is that the integrated lights will typically have one light socket per side with a dual-filament bulb, while separate lights may have two or three light sockets.

In an integrated turn-signal/brake light vehicle with a dual-filament bulb, the brighter filament is for the turn signals and brake light, while the dimmer filament is for the taillights. In a separate turn-signal/brake-light vehicle, one socket will typically have a dual-filament bulb and one socket will have a single filament. In the latter case, the brighter filament bulb is for the brake light, while the dimmer filament is for the taillights. The single-filament bulb is for the turn signal.

An 18-gauge wire between the turn-signal switch and the left front turn-signal light provides power to the signal light. The signal light receives power whenever the turn-signal lever is in the left turn position and the ignition switch is in the on/run position. Power is also provided at any time that the hazard switch is activated.

An 18-gauge wire between the turn-signal switch and the right front turn-signal light provides power to the signal light. The signal light receives power whenever the turn-signal lever is in the right turn position and the ignition switch is in the on/run position. Power is also provided any time that the hazard switch is activated.

A 16-gauge wire from the brake switch provides power to the turn-signal switch for vehicles equipped with integrated turn-signal/brake lights. Power is provided any time that the brake pedal is activated.

A 16-gauge wire between the turn-signal switch and the left rear turn-signal light provides power to the signal light. The signal light receives power whenever the turn-signal lever is in the left turn position and the ignition switch is in the on/run position. Power is also provided at any time that the hazard switch is activated. For vehicles equipped with integrated turn-signal/brake lights,

power is provided any time that the brake pedal is activated.

A 16-gauge wire between the turn-signal switch and the right rear turn-signal light provides power to the signal light. The signal light receives power whenever the turn-signal lever is in the right turn position and the ignition switch is in the on/run position. Power is also provided any time that the hazard switch is activated. For vehicles equipped with integrated turn-signal/brake lights, power is provided any time that the brake pedal is activated.

A 16-gauge wire from the turn-signal flasher on the fuse panel provides power to the turn-signal switch. This wire is an ignition power wire but has power only when the turn-signal switch is activated.

A 16-gauge wire from the hazard flasher on the fuse panel provides power to the hazard switch. This wire is a battery power wire but has power only when the hazard switch is activated.

An 18-gauge wire provides a ground-activation signal to the horn relay whenever the horn button makes contact with a ground source.

Hazard Switch

When using a stock GM hazard switch, connect a wire from the hazard flasher to the three poles of the hazard switch. Then, connect wires from the left front turn signal, right front turn signal, and the brake feed to the remaining three terminals of the hazard switch. If a stock GM hazard switch is not available, use a three-pole, single-throw switch and wire it in the same manner.

Horn Button

The 18-gauge wire that provides a ground-activation signal to the horn simply connects to the horn button on the steering wheel when the horn button has only one wire. When the horn button has two wires, a ground wire must be connected to the second wire and a ground source.

Ignition Switch

The ignition switch serves two distinct purposes: it sends power to the starter solenoid to start the engine, and it controls power to the switched ignition fuses in the fuse block.

A 12-gauge wire from a buss bar on the fuse panel feeds battery power to the ignition switch when connected at the BAT terminal. This wire has power at all times.

A 12-gauge wire from the IGN terminal of the ignition switch provides switched power to the fuse block. This wire provides power to the various switched power circuits (except the radio fuse) whenever the ignition switch is in the on/run position.

A 14-gauge wire from the COIL IGN terminal on the ignition switch provides power to the coil fuse on the fuse panel. This wire provides power whenever the ignition switch is in the on/run or the start position.

A 12-gauge wire sends power to the neutral safety switch when the ignition switch is in the start position. Note that if the truck has an ignition switch in the steering column, two wires must be used for the neutral safety switch to work correctly. One of these wires connects the ignition switch and the neutral safety switch, while the second wire connects the neutral safety switch to the starter solenoid.

A 12-gauge wire sends power to the radio fuse on the fuse panel. It has power whenever the ignition switch is in the accessory position or the on/run position.

Reverse Switch

On a column-shifter truck with an automatic transmission, the reverse switch and neutral safety switch are commonly contained in one assembly that mounts near the base of the steering column. The operation of the two switches is based upon the position of the shifter linkage. Each switch (reverse and neutral safety) has two electrical connections.

The reverse switch is normally open and provides electric current to the backup (reverse) lights. An 18-gauge wire comes to the one terminal of the reverse switch from the gauges fuse on the fuse panel. This wire provides switched ignition power only when the ignition switch is in the accessory or on/run position.

A second 18-gauge wire runs from the remaining terminal of the reverse switch to the backup lights at the rear of the truck. When the shifter is moved into reverse, the switch closes, providing electrical power to the backup lights. On most floor shifters, the reverse switch is commonly located on the shifter, but it still works using the same principle as the column-mounted switch.

With the reverse switch and the neutral safety switch being part of the same assembly, a common mistake is to have the reverse lights connected to the neutral safety switch. When the backup lights are illuminated and the transmission is in neutral or park, the lights are connected to the neutral safety switch.

When a truck does not have backup lights, there is a choice to make regarding the wire from the reverse switch. Simply coil it up and stow it away or use it for a switched 12-volt power source. Since the reverse switch turns the power on, any accessory would work only while the truck is in reverse. This could be used to operate a backup camera, a warning light, or a beeper.

Note that when using a 4L60E/4L80E transmission, a starter relay must be installed, unless the factory switch from a GM-keyed steering column is also used. The reverse switch is unable to withstand the amperage required by the solenoid.

Neutral Safety Switch

The neutral safety switch operates in the same manner as the reverse switch. The electrical circuit closes and is energized depending on the position of the shifter. In this case, the circuit is closed when the shifter is in the park or neutral position.

A 12-gauge wire from the ignition switch connects to one terminal of the neutral safety switch. This wire has power only when the ignition switch is in the start position. A second 12-gauge wire connected to the second terminal of the neutral safety switch connects to the "S" terminal on the starter solenoid.

Instrument Panel

The instrument panel includes wiring for the gauges, turn signals, high-beam indicator, gauge lighting, and accessory power. Gauge wiring varies, depending on the gauges being used.

An 18-gauge wire from the headlight switch provides power to the dash lights. This wire has power whenever the headlight switch is in the parking/taillights-on position or the headlights-on position. This wire can also be spliced into to provide a lighting source for a radio and/or a gear-indicator light on a floor shifter.

An 18-gauge wire from the fuel-level sender serves as a ground signal for the fuel gauge. The amount of

Wiring the Interior

1 A floor-mounted dimmer switch is common on the trucks that this book is directed toward. In addition, if the steering column has been updated to a later model with a column-mounted dimmer switch, the wiring is essentially the same. The power wire from the headlight switch connects to the center terminal. One remaining terminal provides power to the low-beam headlights, while the remaining terminal provides power to the high-beam headlights.

2 Vehicle-specific carpet kits have a hole in the carpet for the dimmer switch to protrude through. Although it is not mandatory to use the three-terminal plug, its use results in a clean installation.

3 In their stock configuration, the headlight switch in vintage GM trucks mounts in the dash, being secured in place by tightening two bezel rings against the dash sheet metal. The switch is typically mounted in the dash so that the connections can be seen from beneath the dash. Some replacement switches include a quick-disconnect plug for service.

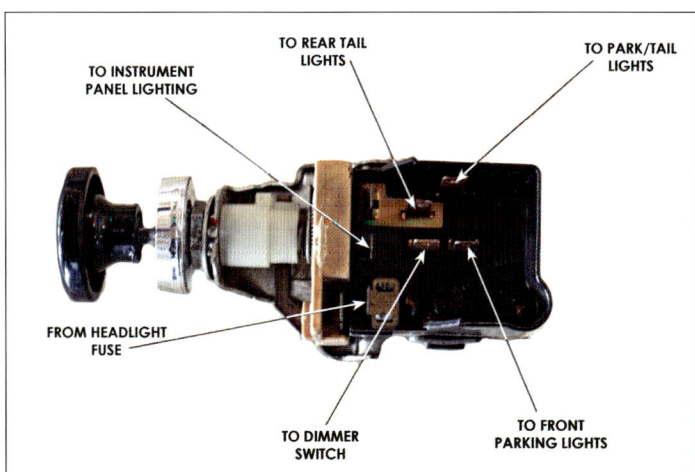

TO INSTRUMENT PANEL LIGHTING
TO REAR TAIL LIGHTS
TO PARK/TAIL LIGHTS
FROM HEADLIGHT FUSE
TO DIMMER SWITCH
TO FRONT PARKING LIGHTS

4 On the early GM headlight switch, the spade connector for the front parking lights is located near the middle of the switch at the opposite end of the switch knob.

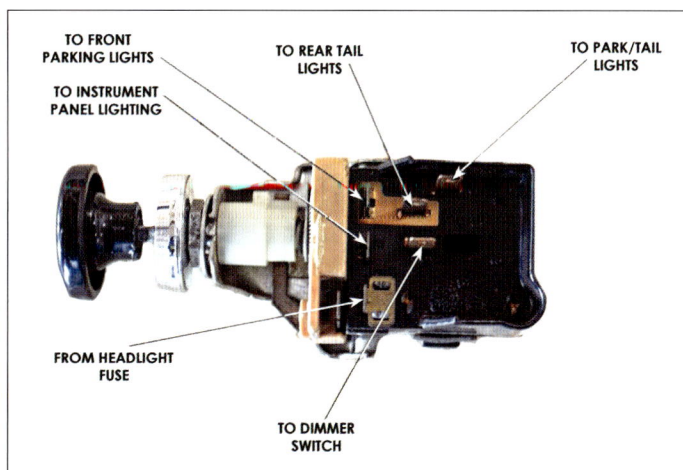

TO FRONT PARKING LIGHTS
TO INSTRUMENT PANEL LIGHTING
TO REAR TAIL LIGHTS
TO PARK/TAIL LIGHTS
FROM HEADLIGHT FUSE
TO DIMMER SWITCH

5 On the late GM headlight switch, the spade connector for the front parking lights is located near the side of the switch, much closer to the switch knob.

Wiring the Interior *continued*

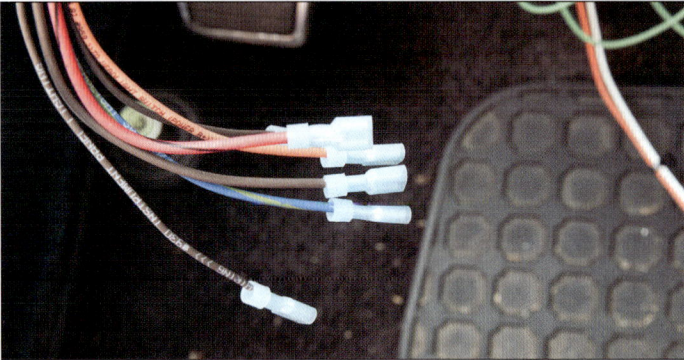

6 These five wires are now ready to connect to their respective spade connectors on the headlight switch.

7 Some replacement headlight switches include a quick-disconnect plug that allows termination of the wires at that plug. Then, simply plug it in or disconnect it without concern about where each wire belongs. However, this replacement headlight switch does not have a quick-disconnect plug.

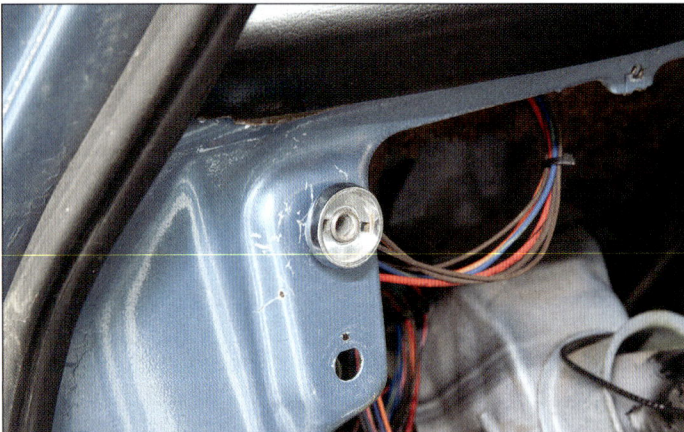

8 After wiring the headlight switch, position the wires safely behind the dash and out of the way. This one is not quite ready to install in the gauge panel, so the bezel is installed temporarily to hold everything in place. The knob will be installed after the gauge panel has been installed.

9 The first six wires listed previously connect to the turn-signal switch via this curved connector that is often mounted to the steering column, with the additional wire stashed behind the dash.

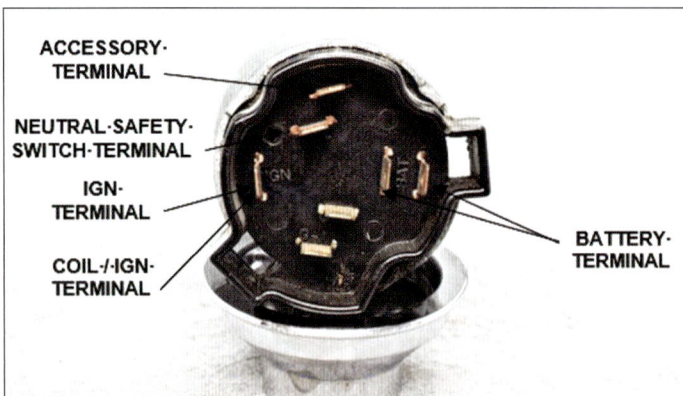

ACCESSORY-
TERMINAL

NEUTRAL-SAFETY-
SWITCH-TERMINAL

IGN-
TERMINAL

COIL-/-IGN-
TERMINAL

BATTERY-
TERMINAL

10 The stock dash-mounted ignition switch in the 1970 C10 has multiple electrical contacts. These spade connections are where the electrical power connects to the ignition switch. Various accessories will be powered depending upon the position of the key in the ignition switch.

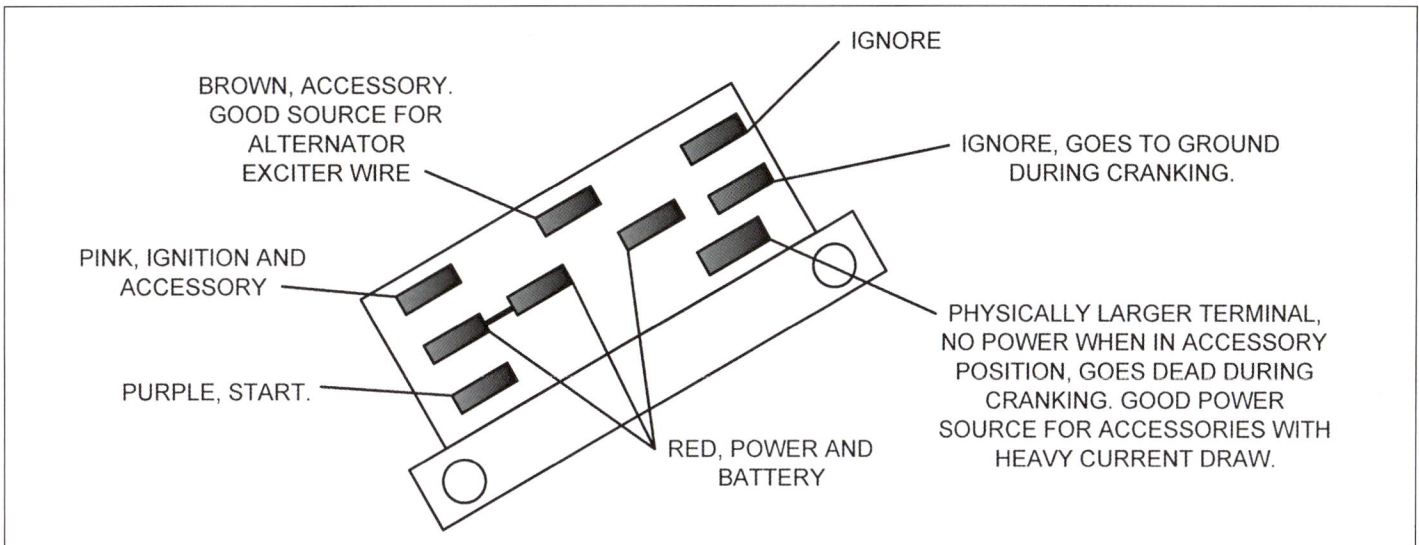

IGNORE

BROWN, ACCESSORY.
GOOD SOURCE FOR
ALTERNATOR
EXCITER WIRE

IGNORE, GOES TO GROUND
DURING CRANKING.

PINK, IGNITION AND
ACCESSORY

PURPLE, START.

PHYSICALLY LARGER TERMINAL,
NO POWER WHEN IN ACCESSORY
POSITION, GOES DEAD DURING
CRANKING. GOOD POWER
SOURCE FOR ACCESSORIES WITH
HEAVY CURRENT DRAW.

RED, POWER AND
BATTERY

11 When using a later steering column that includes a column-mounted ignition switch, the ignition-switch connections must be made on the column.

12 The ignition switch is wired and ready to install. Stow the extra wire and use wire ties as necessary to tidy up all of the wires behind the dash.

13 To install the ignition switch, slide the collar over the front of the ignition switch and hold the two behind the dash panel. Insert the threaded bezel into the front of the dash and thread it onto the collar, sandwiching the dash sheet metal between. Then, slide the tumbler into place and twist it until it locks into place.

14 On the reverse switch, use the two terminals that are perpendicular with each other. A wire from the gauges fuse on the fuse panel connects to one of the terminals. Connect the 18-gauge wire that runs to the backup lights at the rear of the truck to the remaining terminal of the reverse switch.

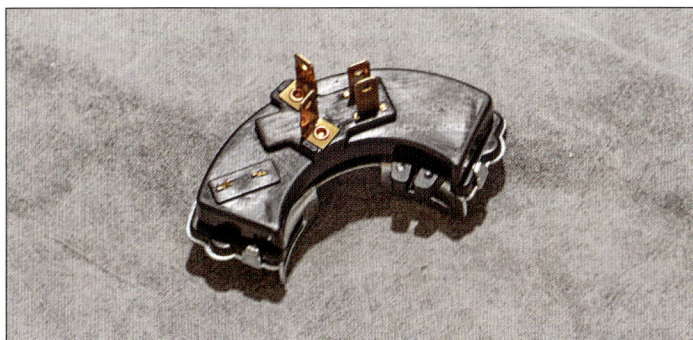

HOW TO WIRE CHEVY & GMC TRUCKS: 1947–1987

Wiring the Interior *continued*

15 In the 1966 model year, backup lights were standard on light-duty trucks for the first time, as part of a federal mandate. On Stepside trucks, the backup lights were located in the back of the fender that first year but moved to the taillight bracket the following year.

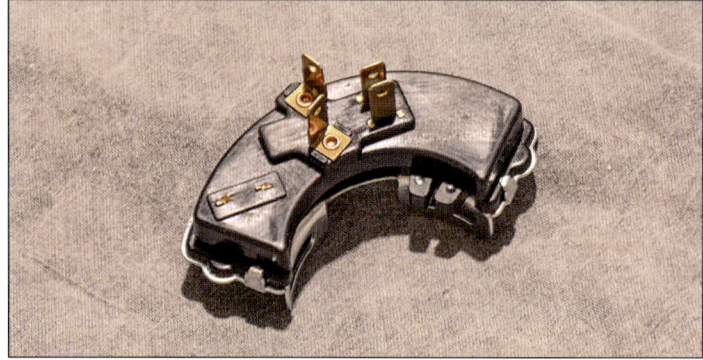

16 On the neutral safety switch, use the two terminals that are parallel to each other. Connect the 12-gauge wire from the ignition switch to one terminal of the neutral safety switch. Connect the wire from the "S" terminal on the starter solenoid to the second terminal of the neutral safety switch.

17 Make the connections to the neutral safety switch early in the wiring process. With the neutral safety switch located at the base of the steering column, it can get congested with all the other wires passing through that area.

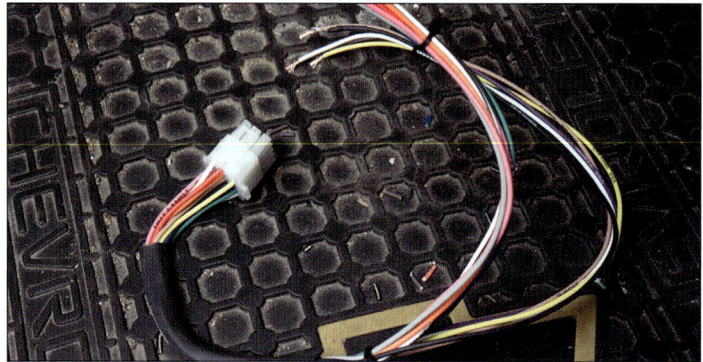

18 This group of wires connects to the various gauges and dash lights located in the dash panel. The extra length of wire allows for the dash panel to be removed for quick access to those components. The quick-disconnect plug allows the dash panel to be completely removed for service.

19 With the dash wiring terminated with a quick-disconnect plug, the panel itself can be quickly and easily removed. On the left side of the panel are the speedometer, oil-pressure, coolant-temperature, and left turn-signal indicator. On the right side of the panel are the tachometer, fuel lever, voltmeter, and right turn-signal indicator. Across the top is the hold for the headlight-switch knob, high-beam headlight indicator, and windshield-wiper control knob.

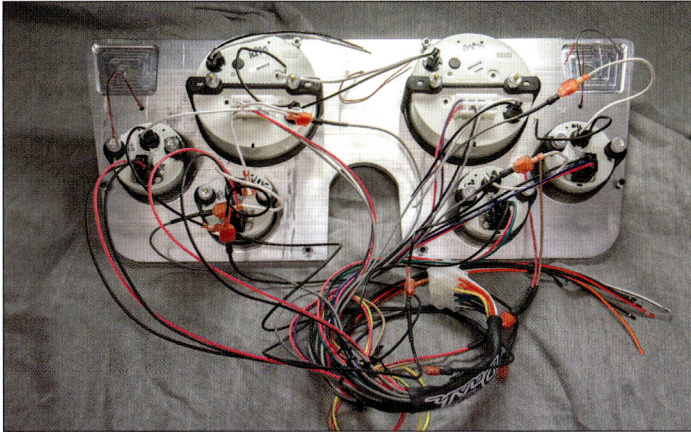

20 It is certainly acceptable to label the backs of the gauges to make it convenient to service them if the need arises.

21 Rather than connecting individual wires, this series of AutoMeter gauges uses a plug for the tachometer connections. The layout of the spade terminals varies for different components, so verify that you connect the correct terminals when wiring the plug.

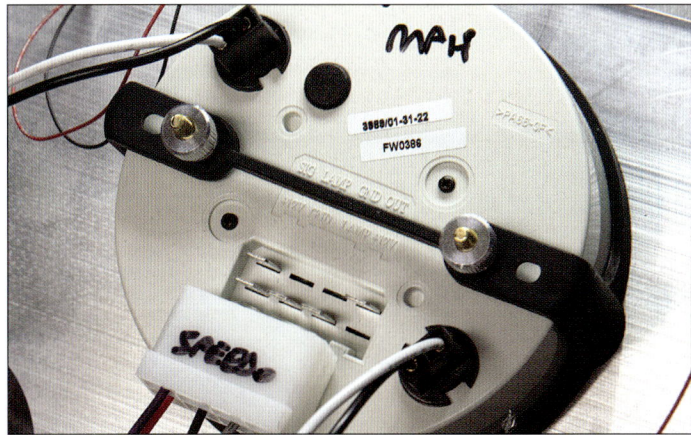

22 The speedometer also uses a plug for convenient wiring. Note that it uses a different layout to avoid plugging the tachometer wires into the speedometer and vice versa.

23 At the top of this voltmeter is the light socket for the gauge illumination. At the bottom is the connection for the gauge. In the case of the voltmeter, the pink sender wire is coming from a key-on power source. The black wire is a ground.

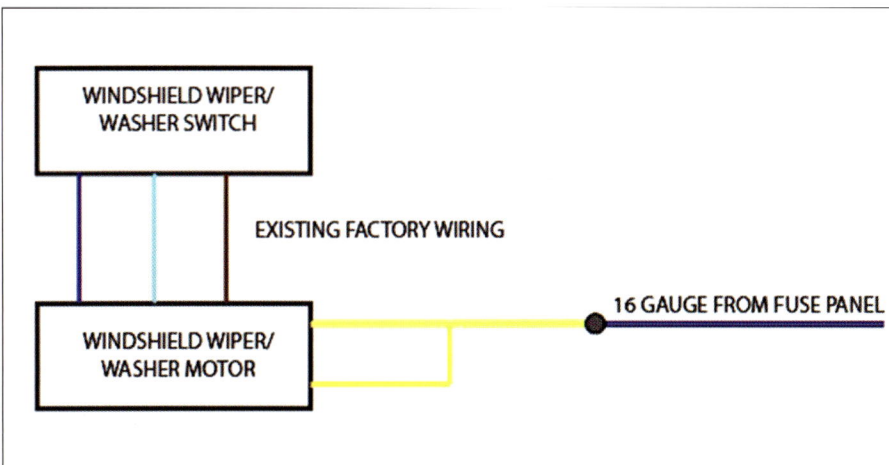

24 Multiple factory wires are between the windshield-wiper/washer switch and the windshield-wiper/washer motor. As long as those are connected properly, there should be just one connection to make, and that is the power wire from the fuse panel.

fuel in the tank causes the resistance to ground to vary, thereby operating the fuel-level gauge.

An 18-gauge wire from the gauges fuse on the fuse panel provides switched ignition power to the instrument cluster. This wire is commonly connected directly to the voltage gauge and then daisy-chained to the other gauges to provide power. Remember that all other gauges will require their owner gauge-sender wire. Think of this wire as a sender to the voltage gauge.

An 18-gauge wire from the engine coolant-temperature sending unit serves as a ground signal for the engine temperature gauge. Temperature of the engine coolant determines the resistance to ground, which operates the temperature gauge.

An 18-gauge wire from the negative side of the ignition coil serves as a ground signal for the tachometer.

An 18-gauge wire from the engine oil-pressure sending unit serves as a ground signal for the engine oil-pressure gauge. The pressure of the engine oil determines the resistance to ground, which operates the oil-pressure gauge.

An 18-gauge wire provides power to the high-beam-indicator light. This wire has power whenever the turn-signal switch is in the headlights on position and the dimmer switch is in the high position.

An 18-gauge wire provides power to the left turn-indicator light. This wire has power whenever the turn-signal switch is in the left turn position.

An 18-gauge wire provides power to the right turn-indicator light. This wire has power whenever the turn-signal switch is in the right turn position.

A 16-gauge wire from the turn fuse on the fuse panel provides a switched ignition power source for accessories. This wire will be energized anytime the ignition switch is in the on/run position.

When the instrument panel is wired with some extra length of wire and quick disconnects, both installation and future service can be made much simpler. The extra length of wire allows easy removal of the screws that secure the instrument panel in place and allow it to be pulled out far enough to service any of the dash components when necessary.

Using quick disconnects allows complete removal of the instrument panel from the dash, which is convenient when painting the truck or refinishing the dash.

The speedometer is usually driven by a cable that runs from the transmission and can be mechanical or electrical. For a mechanical speedometer, the cable contains a flexible shaft that is limited to broad, sweeping curves in its placement. Depending on the available room behind the speedometer, it may be necessary to obtain a 90-degree adapter to keep from kinking the cable where it connects to the back of the speedometer. The cable for an electric speedometer contains a group of wires, rather than a flexible shaft, which can make the cable easier to route.

Sender wires for the remaining gauges are typically 16 gauge and run directly from the sender to the back of the gauge. The oil-pressure sending unit threads into an oil gallery that is located in the engine block. On GM engines, it is typically located on the engine block near the oil filter. The coolant-temperature sending unit is commonly located on one of the cylinder heads. The fuel-level sender is part of the float assembly. Note that the fuel-level sender typically has its own ground stud and therefore requires that a ground wire be connected to it. All these senders connect to a sender terminal on the back of the gauge.

The voltmeter is slightly different, as it receives a signal from a specified terminal on the fuse panel and is connected to the gauge or instrument power terminal on the gauge, rather than on a signal terminal. Turn-signal indicator lights receive their signal from the fuse panel, while the high-beam indicator receives its signal from the dimmer switch.

Electrical power is indeed the signal for the voltmeter, but all of the gauges require electric power in addition to the signal feed to operate. This electric source can be wired in series from the voltmeter to the oil-pressure gauge, the speedometer, the coolant-temperature gauge, and the fuel level, as well as any other gauges. It can also be continued to serve as power for the dash lights.

As with all of the other electrically operated items, the gauges and their lights require a ground to operate correctly. Just like the power wire (but connected to the ground terminal instead), the ground wire can be run in series from one gauge to the next.

After the truck has been wired and is operational, let the truck run for a while and make a mental (or written) note regarding the normal readings for the truck. Knowing these baseline levels goes a long way toward helping diagnose problems later. Different readings might mean something is wrong with the truck or may simply mean that a gauge has lost its ground.

Aftermarket Gauges

While additional gauges are available, a typical gauge package includes a speedometer, an oil-pressure gauge, a water-temperature gauge, a fuel-level gauge, and a voltmeter. Electrical gauges typically have four or five wires to each gauge.

These wires and their source are as follows:

Table 7-1: Gauge Wires and Source	
Gauge Power	Switched 12-volt power source
Gauge Ground	This will vary by gauge manufacturer
Signal	From the specific gauge's sensor/sending unit
Gauge Light Power	12-volt power source from the instrument lighting circuit
Gauge Light Ground	From a common ground source or the negative side of the battery

Accessories

Five other accessory wires may be necessary to complete the wiring, depending on the vehicle. These are for the wiper switch, cooling-fan-relay activation, and the HVAC system.

A 16-gauge wire from the wiper fuse on the fuse panel provides ignition-switched power to the wiper motor or wiper switch.

Tail Section

Tail-section wires run to the back of the truck to power the turn signals, taillights, backup lights, license-plate light (tag light), and the fuel-level

Interior lights are wired so that they always have power, meaning that they are ground activated. When a doorjamb switch is used, the plunger of the doorjamb switch expands when the door is opened, closing the circuit and causing the lights to illuminate. When the door is closed, the plunger compresses, opening the circuit and causing the lights to go off. When a doorjamb switch is not used, the dome light and interior lights can be controlled by the headlight switch.

Since the fuse panel is on the left side of the toe board and the wires from the dome light are accessible on the left rear side of the cab, it makes sense to run the wire inside of the weatherstripping that goes around the driver's door opening. This will eventually be protected by carpeting and a doorsill.

sending unit. Although it is not at the back of the truck, this section of wires also includes dome-light wiring.

For the taillight, brake light, and backup lights, the respective power wires must each be routed toward the back of the truck. At some point, each wire must then be spliced to run power to the driver's side and to the passenger's side.

Dome Light

An 18-gauge wire from the hazard/dome fuse on the fuse panel provides constant battery power to the dome light. This wire should also be used to provide constant battery power to any interior courtesy lights. An 18-gauge wire from the doorjamb switch or the headlight switch serves as a ground to complete the circuit, causing the dome light and/or courtesy lights to illuminate.

Since it is not easy to access the dome-light connection to completely rewire it, it is good practice to leave some amount of the existing wires to connect to, rather than attempt to fish the new wire between the inner and outer roof panels.

Of course, this brings about another question. Which wire is power, and which is ground? If you have access to a battery charger, you can easily determine the answer. Connect the alligator clip for the positive side of the battery charger to one dome-light wire and the alligator clip for the negative side of the battery charger to the remaining dome-light wire. Apply power to the battery charger, and the dome light should illuminate. When it does, you simply know that the light bulb works.

To determine which wire is positive, disconnect the alligator clip for the negative side of the battery charger, and ground the dome-light wire. With the battery charger on, the dome light should illuminate. When it does, you now know which wire is power and which one is ground. If the dome light does not illuminate, switch the wires and try again.

Another thing to consider when routing wires for a pickup truck is that at some time the bed may need to be removed. That is never a big deal and can typically be done by four average people. However, depending on how the wires are routed, removing the bed may require cutting some wires. A better option is to use a quick-disconnect plug for the wires that go to the rear of the bed.

This quick-disconnect can be placed in a location that has convenient access. Then if/when the bed is ever removed, simply disconnect the wires and lift off the bed. This is better than cutting the new wiring in the future and adding more splices to it.

Wiring the Rear of the Truck

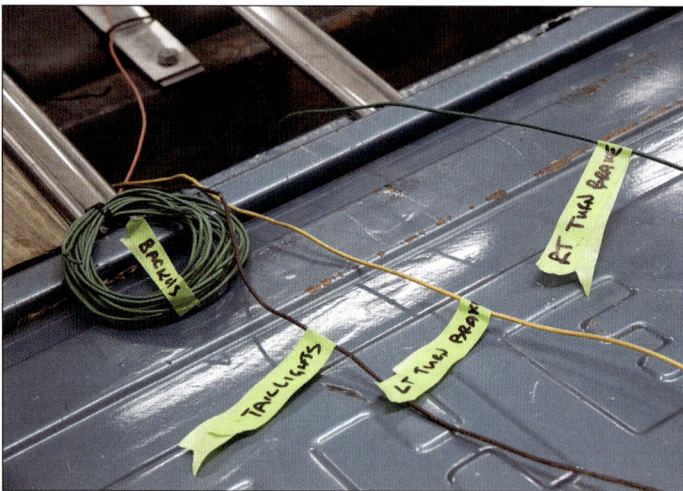

1 Begin by determining which wires should be included with the disconnect. In this case, the wires are for the taillights, left turn signal, and right turn signal. The fuel-sender wire to the underbed fuel tank is not included in the wiring disconnect, as it will always run directly to the fuel tank, whether the bed is on or not.

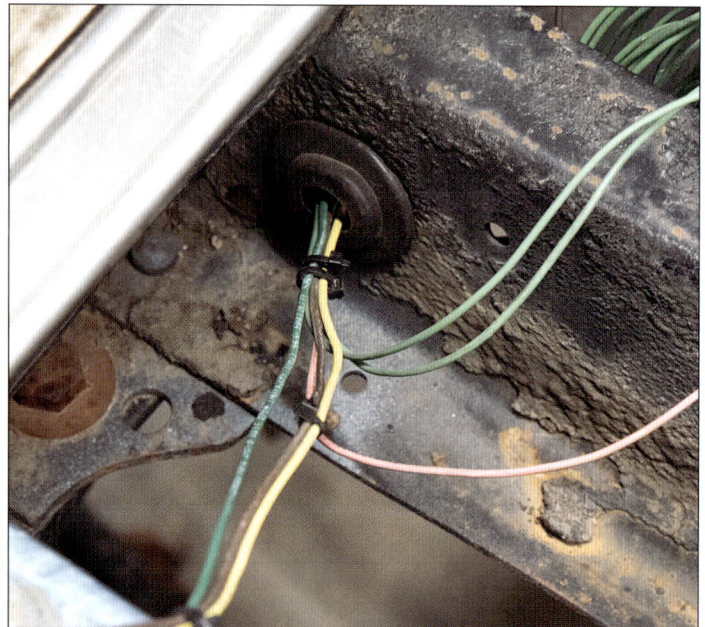

2 Route all wires that run to the back of the truck inside the driver-side frame rail and through this rubber grommet in the rearmost frame crossmember.

Wiring the Rear of the Truck *continued*

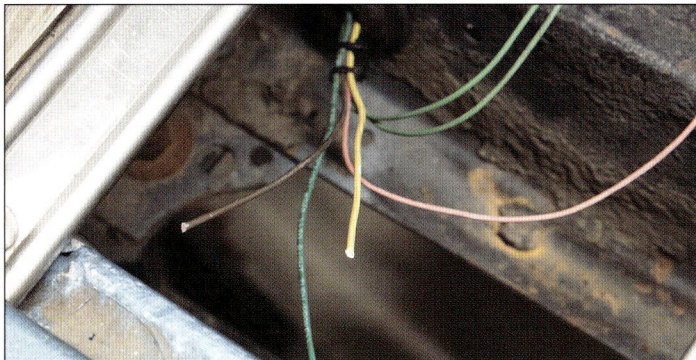

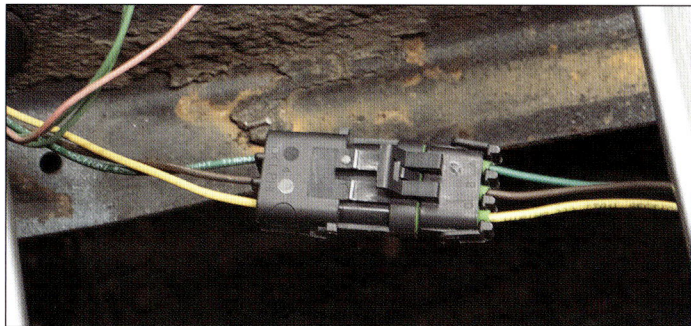

3 After selecting a location for the weathertight connection, cut the three aforementioned wires that will go through the quick disconnect to the desired length. Any remaining wires should be left intact and routed to the frame-mounted locations.

4 Install the weathertight connection as explained in chapter 1. With the rear lights connected in this manner, the bed can be removed if desired without damaging the electrical wiring. Simply disconnect the wires, unbolt the bed, and lift the bed to remove it. There is no need to cut any wires.

5 The power-in wire to the rear left side-marker light and the power-out wire that continues onward to the left taillight are connected to the side-marker-light pigtail inside of the fender. The stock configuration for the ground wire is to connect to the inside of the side-marker-light recess.

6 With the new wiring, a power wire to the rear left side-marker light and back out toward the left taillight will run through the stock hole that has been enlarged slightly with a rubber grommet added.

7 Insert the new power wires (in and out) through the hole and slide a piece of heat-shrink tubing over them.

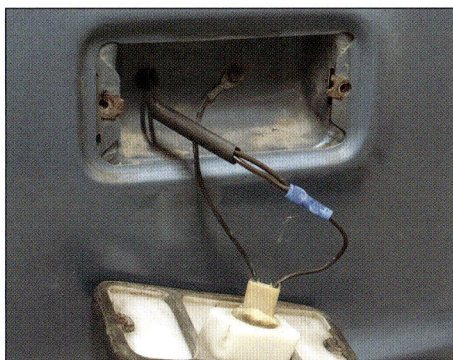

8 Crimp on a butt connector to the single wire from the light socket and to the two power wires. Give each wire a slight tug to ensure that the crimp will hold.

9 Slide the heat-shrink tubing in place over the connection and use a heat gun to apply heat to seal the connection.

Wiring the Rear of the Truck *continued*

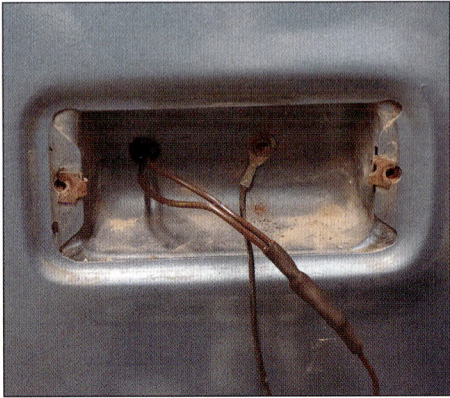

10 Although the factory ground wire is simply secured to the body sheet metal with a sheet-metal screw, this will fail eventually if/when any rust develops. A better method is to run a ground wire to a chassis ground stud.

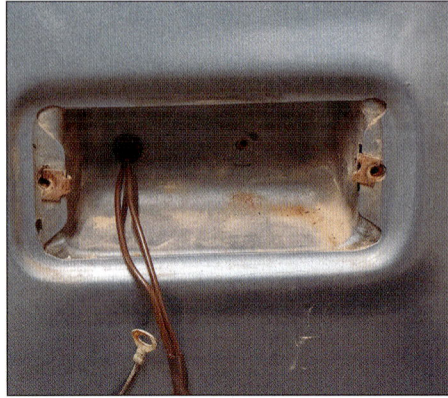

11 Disconnect the sheet-metal screw that secures the ground wire to the sheet metal inside the recess for the side-marker light.

12 Drill a hole large enough for the ground wire to pass through. Since the wire will be passing through sheet metal, the new hole must be large enough to install a rubber grommet as well.

13 Push an appropriately sized rubber grommet into place in the enlarged hole.

14 Pass the new ground wire through the rubber grommet and the hole in the sheet metal.

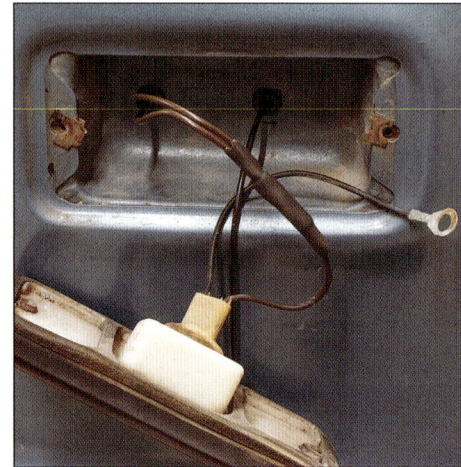

15 Remove the original ring connector from the ground wire.

16 Strip 3/8 inch of the insulation from the end of the original ground and the new wire. Slide a piece of heat-shrink tubing onto one wire or the other, use a butt connector to connect the two wires, slide the heat-shrink tubing into place, and seal the connection.

17 A ground stud has been installed near the center of the rear frame crossmember. The stainless-steel screw passes upward through an existing hole in the crossmember. A wire with a ring terminal has been routed back to the negative terminal of the battery. The ring terminal of the ground wire is secured with a washer and a stainless-steel nut.

18 Terminate the new ground wire with a ring connector and route the new ground wire to the nearest ground stud. Secure this ground wire and any others to the ground stud with a second stainless-steel nut or a wing nut.

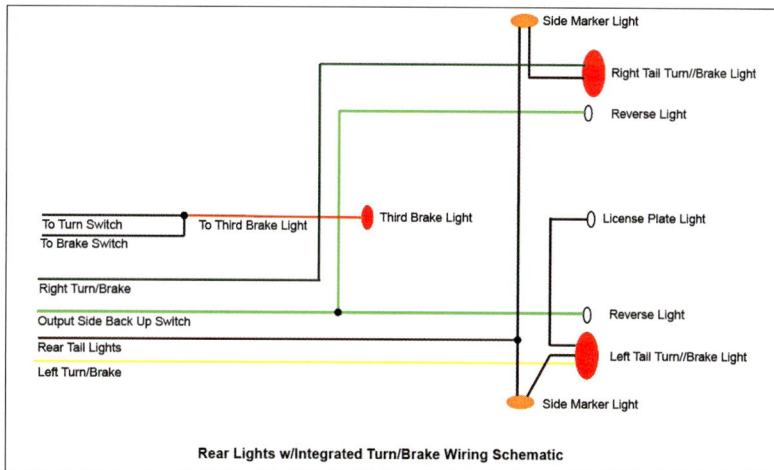

Rear Lights w/Integrated Turn/Brake Wiring Schematic

19 The 1970 C10 has integrated turn signals/brake lights, so this schematic will be used for this project. Note that the third brake light is not connected directly to the other brake lights.

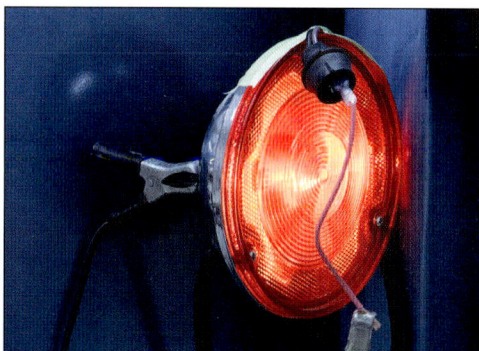

20 With the negative wire of the battery charger connected to one of the taillight mounting bolts and the positive wire of the battery charger connected to one of the taillight terminals, turn the battery charger on. Presuming that the bulb in the taillight is good, the taillight should illuminate. When it does illuminate, repeat the test with the battery charger's positive wire connected to the opposite taillight wire. Whichever terminal provides the brightest light is the turn signal/brake light.

21 After performing the test, it was obvious which terminal provided the brightest light. With the taillight terminal plug situated to resemble a "T," the horizontal terminal provided the brightest light, confirming that it is the turn-signal/brake-light wire. The vertical terminal, therefore, is for the taillight wire.

Wiring the Rear of the Truck *continued*

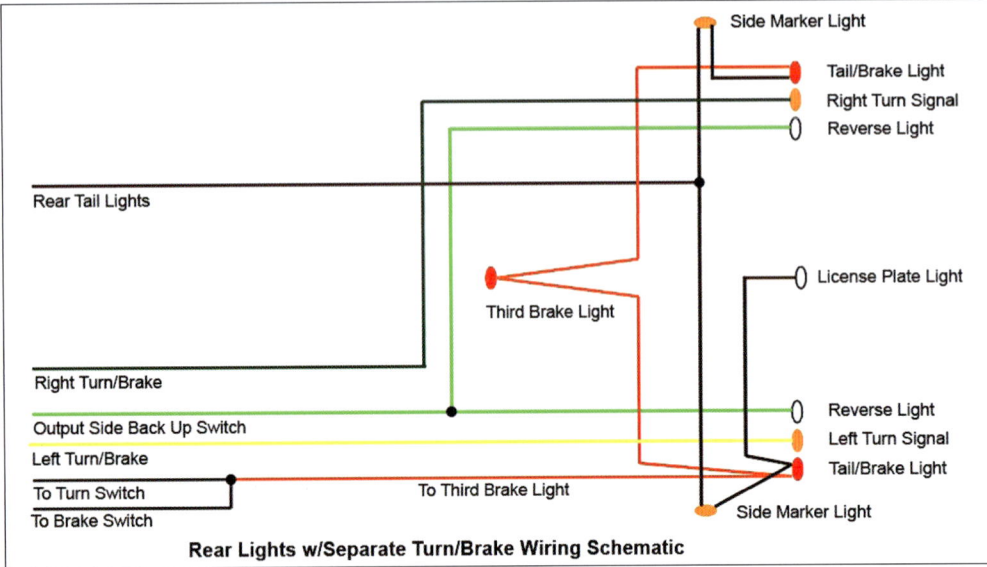

Side Marker Light
Tail/Brake Light
Right Turn Signal
Reverse Light

Rear Tail Lights

License Plate Light

Third Brake Light

Right Turn/Brake

Reverse Light
Left Turn Signal
Tail/Brake Light

Output Side Back Up Switch
Left Turn/Brake
To Turn Switch
To Brake Switch

To Third Brake Light

Side Marker Light

Rear Lights w/Separate Turn/Brake Wiring Schematic

22 I cannot think of any vintage GM pickup trucks that use separate turn and brake lights in their stock configuration. However, this would apply to a medium- or heavy-duty truck or a vintage Chevrolet Impala, while a Chevrolet Bel-Air would use the integrated turn/brake configuration.

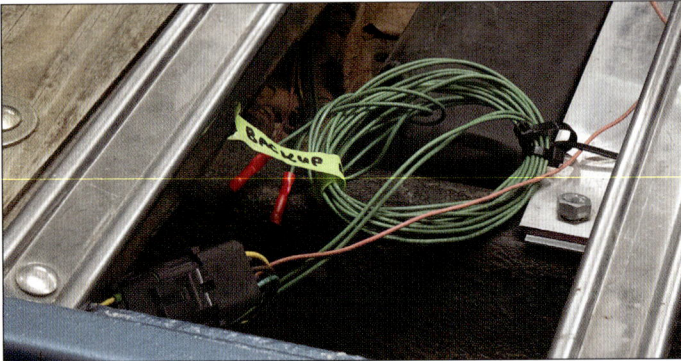

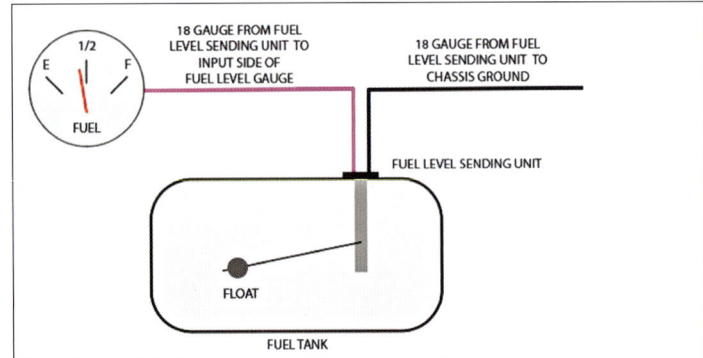

18 GAUGE FROM FUEL LEVEL SENDING UNIT TO INPUT SIDE OF FUEL LEVEL GAUGE

18 GAUGE FROM FUEL LEVEL SENDING UNIT TO CHASSIS GROUND

FUEL

FUEL LEVEL SENDING UNIT

FLOAT

FUEL TANK

23 Since this truck does not currently have backup lights, those wires were terminated with butt connectors to ensure that the wires do not short out to anything. They were then coiled up and secured below the bed in case they are needed later, such as for a backup camera.

24 The fuel-level sender wiring may sound complicated if you are not familiar with electrical terminology, but the wiring itself is quite simple. Connect an 18-gauge wire to the electrical connection of the fuel-level sending unit. Route this wire to the back of the fuel gauge and connect it to the input signal terminal. You must also connect a ground wire to one of the mounting screws of the fuel-level sending unit.

25 Route the fuel-level sender wire to the center terminal of the fuel-level sender. Cut the wire to the correct length and strip 3/8 inch of the insulation from the wire. Slide a piece of heat-shrink tubing over the wire and crimp on the appropriately sized ring terminal. Slide the heat-shrink tubing over the connection and apply heat to the tubing to seal the connection.

26 Repeat the process to connect a ground wire to the secondary connection point on the fuel-level sender.

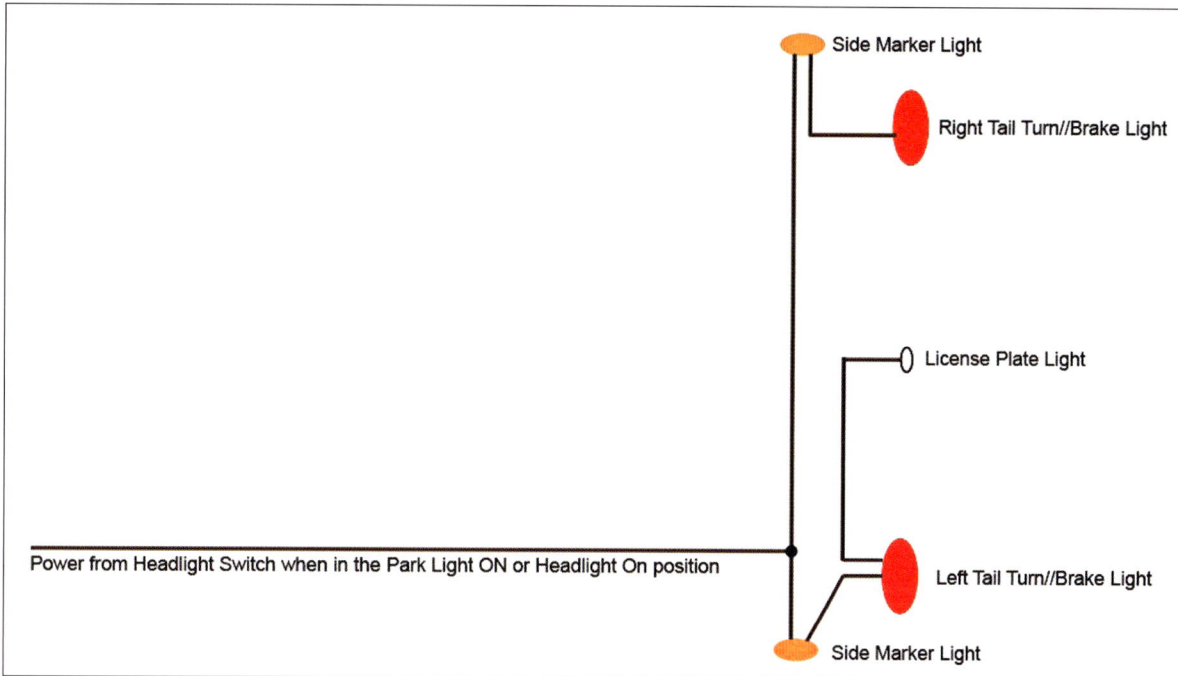

Side Marker Light

Right Tail Turn//Brake Light

License Plate Light

Power from Headlight Switch when in the Park Light ON or Headlight On position

Left Tail Turn//Brake Light

Side Marker Light

27 *Power for the license-plate light comes directly from the headlight switch and can be accessed by splicing into the wire that provides power to the rear side-marker lights and taillights.*

28 *The power wire was missing from the original license-plate light, so a new light assembly was purchased. The replacement light came with a male terminal. To take advantage of that if the bumper ever needs to be removed, incoming wire was terminated with a female bullet connector.*

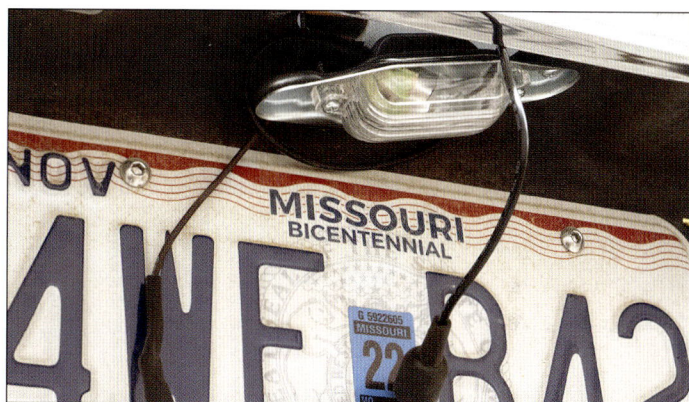

29 *Pass the power wire down through the license-plate panel in the bumper, connect the two wires, and push them to the backside of the license-plate panel. Then, secure the license-plate light in place with two sheet-metal screws.*

30 *From the test performed on the left side taillight to determine which wire is for the turn signal/brake light and which one is for the taillights, we can verify that is the situation on the right side taillight. The horizontal portion of the plug is for the turn-signal/brake-light wire, while the vertical portion is for the taillight wire.*

When pre-wiring a truck with a trailer wiring plug, run that wiring at this time. You will need to tap into wires for the taillights, right turn signal, left turn signal, brakes (when using a brake controller) and brake lights, a fused battery lead, and a suitable ground.

Left Side-Marker Light (When Applicable)

The left side-marker light receives its power from the headlight switch and should illuminate whenever the headlight switch is in the parking/taillights-on or headlight-on position. A 16-gauge wire from the headlight switch connects to one wire of the left side-marker light. From there, this power wire connects to the left taillight and also to the license-plate light. The remaining wire of the left marker light must be connected to adequate ground.

Left-Turn/Brake Lights

A 16-gauge wire from the turn-signal switch provides power to the left turn signal whenever the ignition switch is in the on/run position and the turn-signal switch is in the down or left position. If the truck has integrated turn/brake signals, this wire also has power whenever the brake pedal is pressed, or the hazard switch is activated. Connect this wire to the left-turn/brake light.

When wiring the rear lights, it is necessary to determine which terminal to connect the turn-signal/brake wire to and which terminal to connect the taillight wire to. The turn-signal/brake light will typically be brighter than the taillight, so with a battery charger, determine which wire is which.

Connect the alligator clip from the positive side of the battery char-ger to one of the wires of the taillight assembly and turn on the battery charger. One of the filaments in the taillight should illuminate. If it does not, ensure the taillight assembly is grounded and try again. When one of the filaments illuminates, notice how bright it is. Repeat the test with the positive side of the battery charger connected to the opposite wire. Whichever wire is connected to the battery charger when the light is brightest is the terminal for the turn-signal/brake light.

A 16-gauge wire from the brake-light switch provides power whenever the brake pedal is pressed or the hazard switch is activated. It is used to provide power to both brake lights on trucks with separate turn-signal/brake lights and/or to a third brake light when used. When the truck has separate turn-signal/brake lights, additional wire is required to splice to both brake lights and the third brake light when used.

Taillights

A 16-gauge wire from the headlight switch connects to each taillight and to the license-plate light. It has power whenever the headlight switch is in the parking/taillights-on or headlight-on position. When side-marker lights are used, the same wire is used.

Backup Lights

An 18-gauge wire from the reverse switch provides power to the backup lights. This wire has power whenever the ignition switch is in the on/run position and the shifter is in the reverse position.

This truck does not currently have backup lights, nor do I plan to install them. However, there are other accessories that would use the same wires if added later, such as a backup camera. You can make the decision that you are never going to use these wires and remove them from the wire bundle or you can coil up the wires and secure them out of the way. I chose the latter.

Fuel-Level Sender

An 18-gauge wire from the fuel-level sending unit connects to the fuel-level gauge to provide a ground signal. The fuel-level float moving across a resistor sends a resisted signal to the fuel-level gauge. It is critical that the fuel-level gauge and the fuel-level sender are compatible for the fuel-level gauge to provide correct readings. The fuel-level sending unit must also be connected to an adequate ground.

License-Plate Light

Power for the license-plate light is the same wire that provides power to the taillights. It has power whenever the headlight switch is in the parking/taillights-on or the headlight-on position. If your truck has two license-plate lights, simply splice in a second wire to provide power to the second light.

Right Side-Marker Light (When Applicable)

The right side-marker light receives its power from the headlight switch and should illuminate whenever the headlight switch is in the parking/taillights-on or the headlight-on position. A 16-gauge wire from the headlight switch connects to one wire of the right side-marker light. From there, this power wire connects to the right taillight and also to a second license-plate light (if used). The remaining wire of the right marker light must be connected to adequate ground.

Right-Turn/Brake Lights

A 16-gauge wire from the turn-signal switch provides power to the right turn signal whenever the ignition switch is in the on/run position and the turn-signal switch is in the up or right position. If the truck has integrated turn/brake signals, this wire also has power whenever the brake pedal is pressed or the hazard switch is activated. Connect this wire to the right turn-signal/brake light.

A 16-gauge wire from the brake-light switch provides power whenever the brake pedal is pressed or the hazard switch is activated. It is used to provide power to both brake lights on trucks with separate turn-signal/brake lights and/or to a third brake light when used. When the truck has separate turn-signal/brake lights, additional wire will be required to splice to both brake lights and the third brake light when used.

Universal Wiring Kits: Affordable Street Rods Kit in a 1955 Chevy Pickup

In 2005, I purchased a 1955 Chevy pickup as a project. It had the original frame, suspension, and body but no drivetrain. Progress was slow for various reasons. The original suspension was replaced with independent front suspension (IFS) and a rear 4-link with coilovers in 2014. In 2016, all of the sheet metal that required replacement was welded in place. A major push to get the truck finished was made in 2020 and 2021, fueled by my book *Chevy Trucks 1955–1959 Build & Modify* with CarTech. Again, for various reasons it still is not finished, but you will see the wiring aspect of it in this book.

With the shop truck being full of electrical components, I chose to go with the Wiremaster Power Panel from Affordable Street Rods. I have used this kit in multiple builds, and it has served me quite well. Installation is very straightforward, and since the wires are not pre-terminated at the fuse panel, you can run the essential circuits right now and then add the wires for the other circuits whenever you choose. Besides the circuits for making the truck's engine run and the lights illuminate, the shop truck will have heat and A/C, satel-lite radio, power windows, and some convenience plugs for charging a cell phone.

Take note before ordering a Wiremaster Power Panel that there are two from which to choose. The Wiremaster Power Panel includes 32 terminal connections, while the Wiremaster Power Panel II includes only 24 terminal connections. When planning to include any combination of air conditioning, power seats, power windows, or an electric fuel pump, go with the

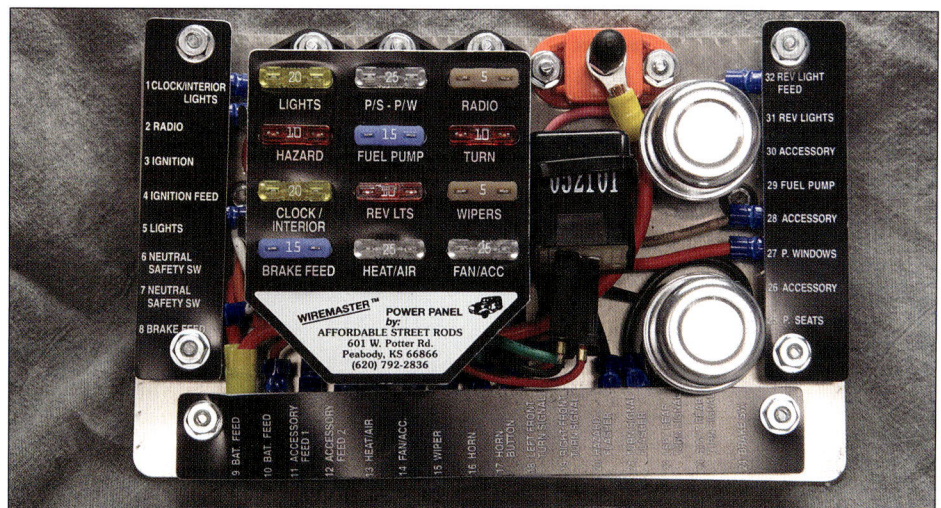

The Wiremaster Power Panel provides 32 terminal connections, including circuits for an electric fuel pump, power windows, and power seats.

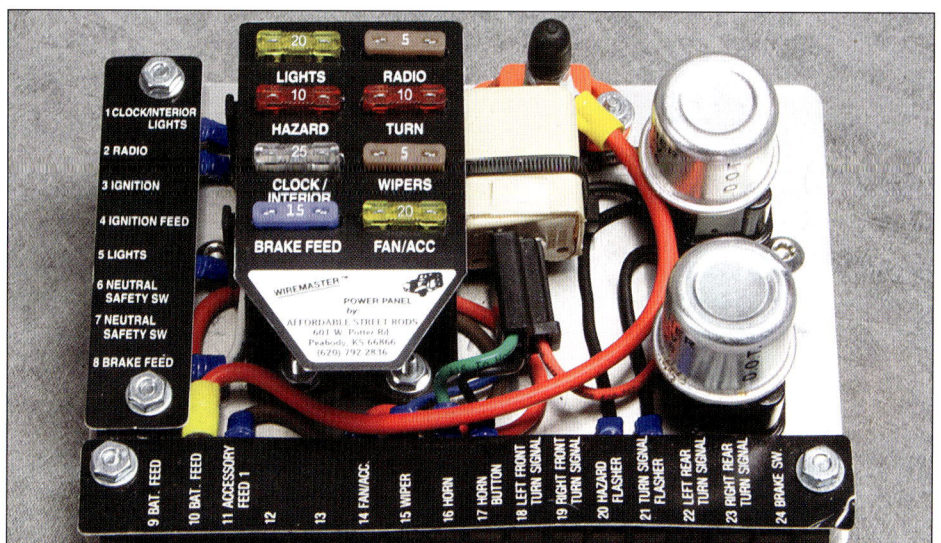

The Wiremaster Power Panel II works well for vehicles that do not include air conditioning, an electric fuel pump, power windows, and power seats.

Wiremaster Power Panel. The overall size of the panels is basically the same, but there are more available terminals on the slightly longer panel.

Whichever wiring panel is chosen, it is better to determine as accurately as possible which electrical circuits are needed and then to purchase accordingly. Wiring is not difficult, but it is not something to do halfway and then realize that you do not have an appropriate circuit and are required to retrofit a different panel (although, it is possible). If air conditioning, power seats, an electric fuel pump, or other similar electrical components will be run, start with a bigger electrical panel.

A big difference between the vehicle-specific kit and a universal kit is that the instructions for the former kit instructs you to wire items in a specific order while the latter kit instructs you to wire one wire at a time. To clarify, the vehicle-specific kit instructions started wiring components at the front of the vehicle and ended with components at the back, using the specific wires. The universal kit instructions start with the wire from terminal #1, then #2, etc.

With either kit, there is the option to connect the wires in the order that you see fit. As with most things that you may be unfamiliar with, follow the instructions that come with the product you are installing.

Wiring a truck using either of the Wiremaster kits allows you to complete as much wiring as necessary to get the vehicle operating and then wire in other accessories later as they are installed. After mounting the panel, color-coded and numbered wires are connected to the like-numbered terminals. Then, they are routed to and connected to the appropriate accessory, making for

easy installation. Simply loosen the screw at the terminal, slide the appropriate wire connector beneath it, tighten the screw, and route the wire to the component. After routing the wire, it can be cut to the appropriate length and then an appropriate connector can be crimped on.

Placement of the fuse panel quite often becomes not a question of where the best location for the panel is, but rather where there is space left over that has not been allotted

to something else. These trucks typically located the fuse panel under the dash on the driver's side. This may be practical during assembly, as many of the wires run to the steering column or the dash, so the under-dash location's close proximity saves a few feet of wire per vehicle.

However, anyone who has ever had to attempt to wrap themselves around the steering column in addition to contorting sufficiently to access one of these fuse panels does

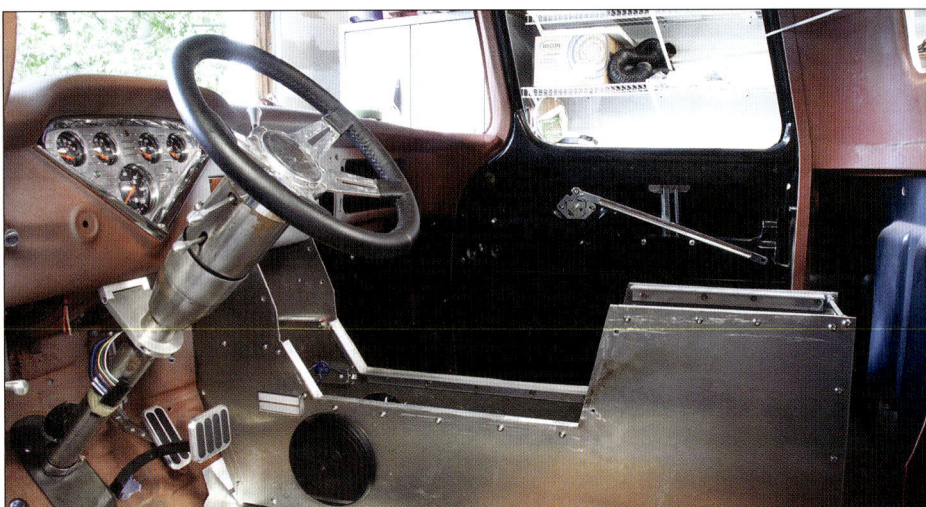

The center console (which will house the fuse panel) was mocked up early in the build process to verify that it will suffice.

On the 1955 Chevy truck, the universal Wiremaster fuse panel is positioned in the bottom of the console between the bucket seats. This location will make it easy to replace fuses if necessary.

not appreciate having the steering column in the way. Occasionally, a fuse or a flasher may need to be replaced, so keep the fuse panel accessible. Typical locations for the fuse panel are under the dash, under the seat (as long as the seat can be removed for access to the panel), in a console between bucket seats, or behind the seat.

Install the New Wiring

A universal kit is perhaps more adaptable to connecting the wires in the order that you desire. For example, you can first get the engine running and then address the other components later. Since this truck is a completely new build, I started with terminal one and worked my way around the fuse panel. Since you are making the initial connections at the fuse panel, instead of connecting to preconnected wires, this will physically be easier to do, especially if your hands are large or the fuse panel is mounted in a confined area.

Other kits may be different, but the Wiremaster Power Panel includes

tagboard labels that cover the terminals on the fuse panel. This serves as a convenient identification system for each terminal and then covers the terminals. Simply use the appropriate-size nut driver to remove the nuts and washers that secure the labels, but be sure to retain these labels for reference.

To connect each wire, loosen the terminal screw enough to slide the fork connector of the wire beneath

it. Then, tighten the screw. Some terminals may have multiple wires connected to them. The end of each fork connector has a 90-degree bend at the very end. When multiple wires are connecting to one terminal, position the fork connectors back-to-back so that the connectors are flush.

Connect and Route Wires

The wires with most universal wiring kits are labeled on the wire in

I have owned the shop truck for more than 15 years. Hopefully, it will finally be running and completed by the time you are reading this.

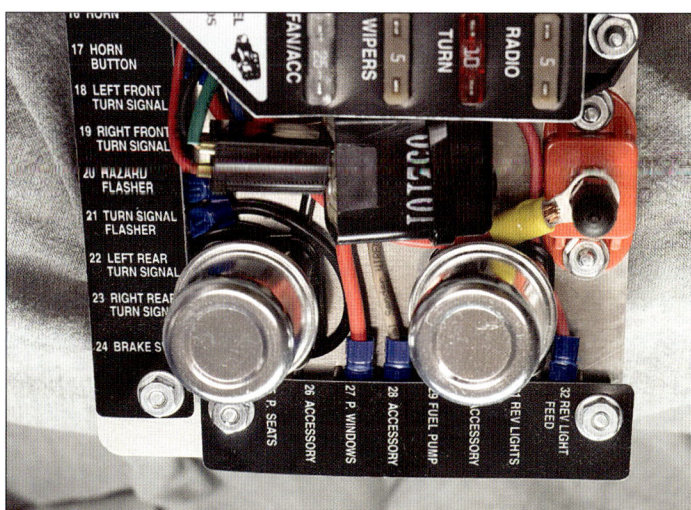

All terminals of the Wiremaster Power Panel are covered with a tagboard cover that identifies the purpose of the terminals.

To connect a wire to the terminal, loosen the screw for the specific terminal slightly, slide the forked terminal connection of the correct wire below the screw, and retighten the screw. The wires are numbered to match the terminal numbers.

addition to a tag attached to each length of wiring. The instructions with the kit also typically include the wire size as well as the color of the wire. Therefore, when the identification tag is separated from the wire, it is possible to still identify the wire and its purpose.

While the gauge size of the wire is important, the electricity passing through it does not care what color the wire is. For that purpose, the color of the wires will not be mentioned, but the gauge size will be. This was done to avoid confusion for anyone who may be using a different kit or is perhaps even doing their own custom wiring job.

During the process of wiring the truck, you will learn that you must match actual wire colors with the colors mentioned in the instructions. A specific instance of this is for the wires that connect to the headlight switch, dimmer switch, headlights, and turn signals.

Terminal 1: Clock/Interior Lights

Three wires connect to this terminal. A 16-gauge wire provides power to the clock and courtesy lights and is considered battery hot. In other words, when the battery is connected and charged, anything connected to this wire has power.

The dome and courtesy lights receive electrical current at all times. They illuminate whenever a ground is introduced to the circuit, such as by way of a door light switch or by rotating the knob on the headlight switch fully counterclockwise. To wire these lights, use a 16-gauge wire to connect each light to terminal 1 on the fuse panel. To provide a ground source, connect a 16-gauge wire from the headlight switch to

each door light switch and then to each dome and/or courtesy light.

A second wire that connects to this terminal is a 16-gauge wire that provides 12 volts of constant power to the radio. A third wire that connects to this terminal is a 14-gauge wire that provides power to a cigarette lighter. Note that this could also be used for a power terminal for charging a cell phone or computer, depending on the outlet that it is connected to.

In the shop truck, this terminal will be used to power both a cigarette lighter plug and a USB charging port. Various accessories and gadgets can be powered by this type of plug.

This terminal is protected by the 25-amp fuse labeled clock/interior. If not using a clock or interior lights, this terminal would provide sufficient

amperage to provide power for auxiliary lighting or other accessories that would require power, whether the engine is running or not.

Terminal 2: Radio

A 16-gauge wire connected to this terminal provides 12 volts of switched power to the radio. In most applications, this provides power when the ignition key is in the start, run, or accessory position. This terminal is protected by the 5-amp fuse labeled "radio."

Note that these recommendations are for simply having decent sound in the pickup truck while driving. If planning to add a bed full of speakers, heavier-gauge wiring and connections directly to the battery may be required.

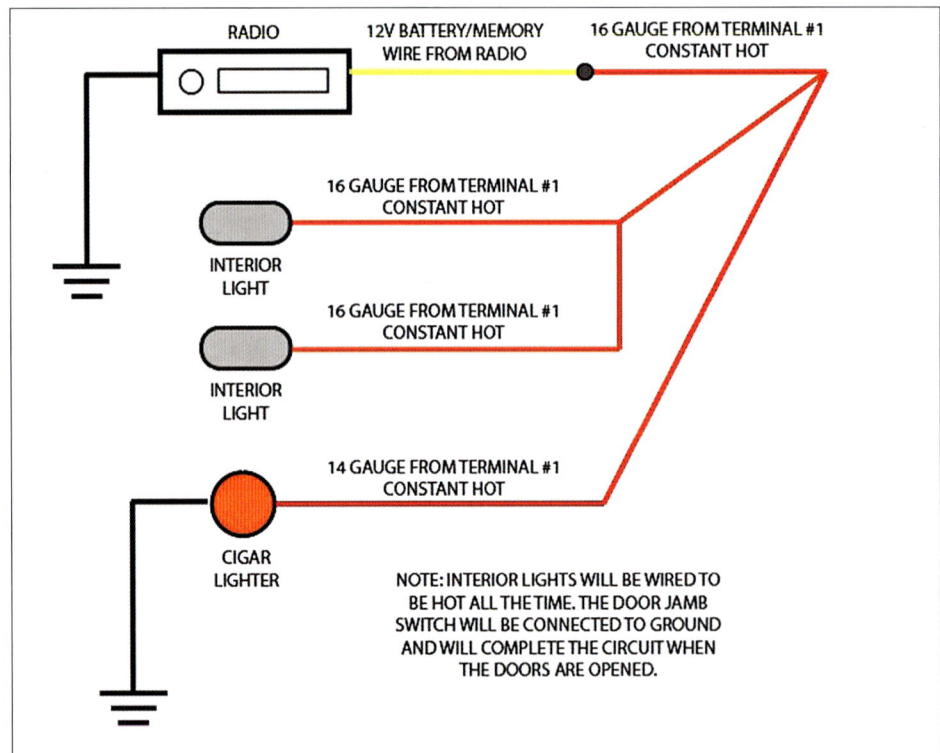

Terminal 1 provides constant hot power to the 12-volt battery/memory wire of the radio to run the clock and retain radio presets. This terminal also powers the cigar lighter or, in this case, an accessory terminal and a USB charging port. Note that terminal 26 could be used to power these last two items.

A USB charging port (left) and a port for powering a device (right) are both designed to fit into a cigarette lighter. Either one simply requires drilling a mounting hole and then connecting a power and a ground wire to the terminals. Either one or both of these accessories can be connected to terminal 1 or terminal 26.

The accessory USB charging port and cigarette-lighter accessory will be convenient while on the road.

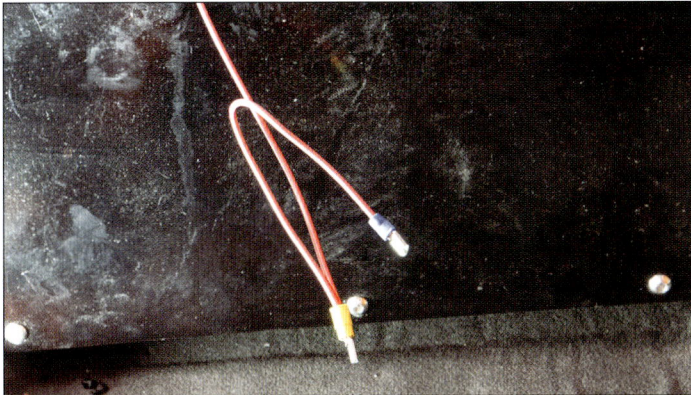

At the other end of the jumper wire, another female spade terminal is crimped on.

The female spade terminals are slid into place over the spade terminals of each charging port. Ground wires will be connected in a similar fashion to the accessory terminals and to a ground stud located somewhere in the center console.

The accessory USB charging port and cigarette-lighter accessory port are located beside each other, so one power wire is run from the fuse panel to one of the ports. A jumper wire is then added with a female spade terminal crimped on.

RADIO   12V IGNITION/ACCESSORY   16 GAUGE FROM TERMINAL #2
WIRE FROM RADIO   12V SWITCHED POWER

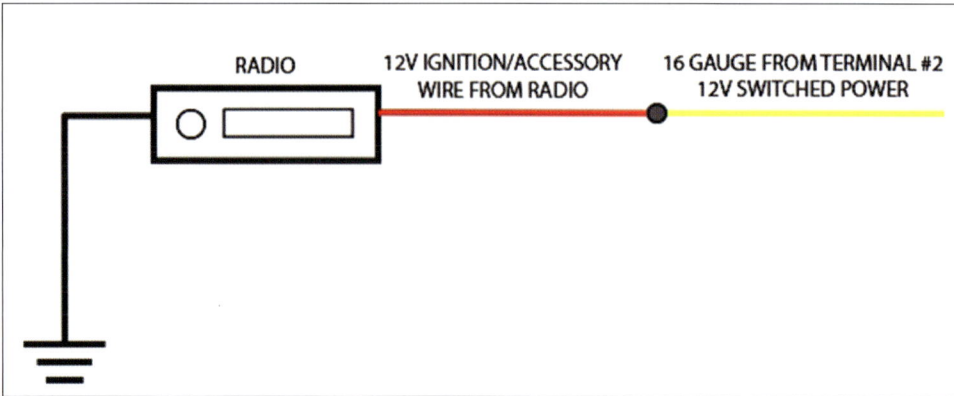

A 16-gauge wire from terminal 2 should be routed to the 12-volt ignition/accessory wire for the radio or stereo head unit. This will provide power to the unit when the ignition switch is in the start, run, or accessory position.

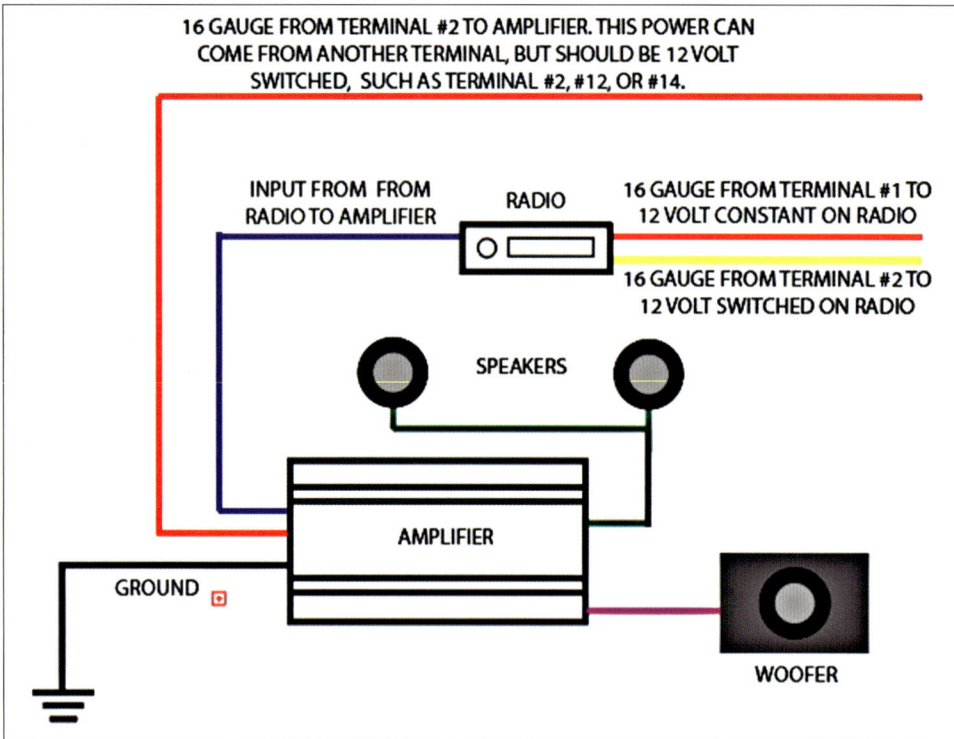

16 GAUGE FROM TERMINAL #2 TO AMPLIFIER. THIS POWER CAN
COME FROM ANOTHER TERMINAL, BUT SHOULD BE 12 VOLT
SWITCHED, SUCH AS TERMINAL #2, #12, OR #14.

INPUT FROM FROM   RADIO   16 GAUGE FROM TERMINAL #1 TO
RADIO TO AMPLIFIER   12 VOLT CONSTANT ON RADIO

16 GAUGE FROM TERMINAL #2 TO
12 VOLT SWITCHED ON RADIO

SPEAKERS

AMPLIFIER

GROUND

WOOFER

A 16-gauge wire from terminal 1 provides 12-volt constant power to the radio for the clock and presets. Another 16-gauge wire from terminal 2 provides 12-volt switched power for the radio. To power the woofer, a 16-gauge wire from a 12-volt switched terminal such as terminal 2, 12, or 14 should be used.

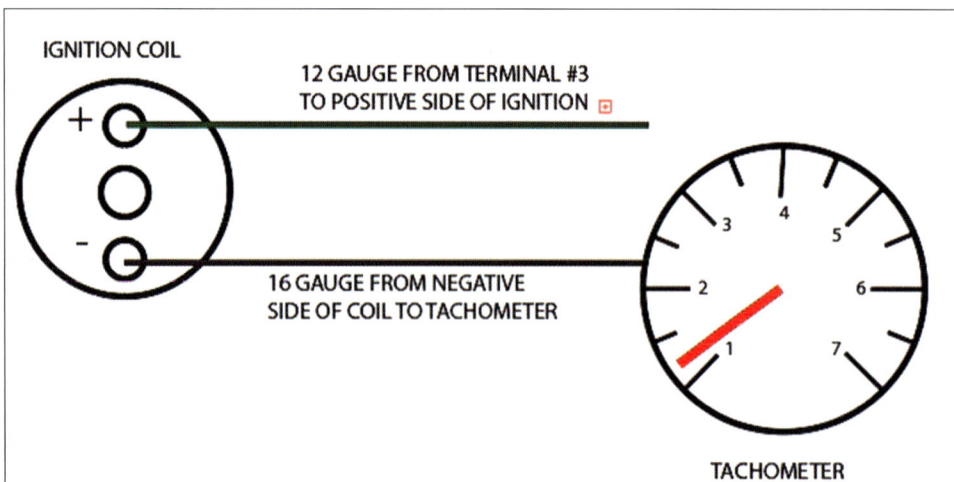

IGNITION COIL

12 GAUGE FROM TERMINAL #3
TO POSITIVE SIDE OF IGNITION

+

-

16 GAUGE FROM NEGATIVE
SIDE OF COIL TO TACHOMETER

3   4   5

2   6

1   7

TACHOMETER

Wiring a tachometer is relatively easy. Run a 12-gauge wire to the positive side of the ignition coil. Then, connect a 16-gauge wire between the negative side of the coil and the input terminal of the tachometer.

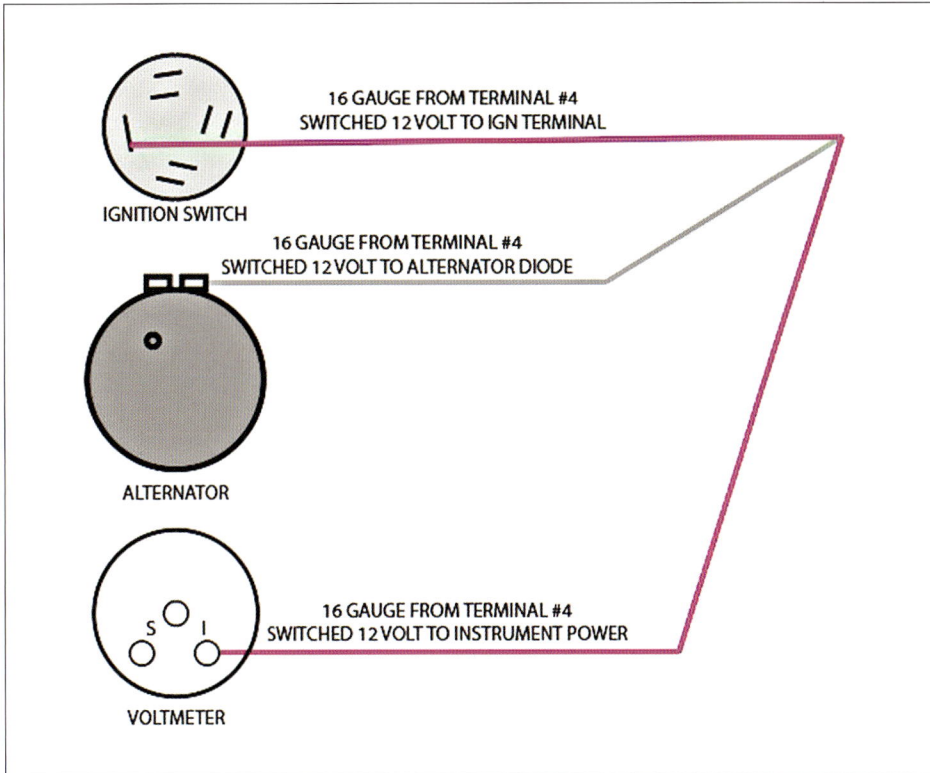

The 16-gauge wires from terminal 4 connect to the ignition switch, to the alternator, and to the voltmeter gauge. On the ignition switch, the wire connects to the ignition terminal. At the alternator, the wire connects to the regulator exciter. On the voltmeter, the wire connects to the input terminal.

The wire from terminal 4 connects to the IGN terminal on the ignition switch. In this photo, the IGN terminal is at the top.

Run a 16-gauge wire between the negative post of the coil and the input terminal of the tachometer to power the tachometer.

A pigtail such as this is used to connect the switched 12-volt power from the fuse panel when using a one-wire alternator. The red wire connects to the charging stud of the alternator.

Terminal 3: Ignition

A 12-gauge wire connected to this terminal connects to the positive side of the coil. When using an HEI ignition system, connect this wire to the battery terminal on the distributor cap. When using the older points-style ignition system, connect this wire to the ballast resistor used to reduce the voltage going to the positive side of the ignition coil.

When using an engine computer, such as an MSD ignition box, use this wire as the hot wire. This provides power when the ignition key is in the run or start position.

Terminal 4: Ignition Feed

This terminal has power when the ignition switch is in the start or run position. A 12-gauge wire connects this terminal to the IGN terminal of the ignition switch.

A 16-gauge wire connected to this terminal provides power to the gauges. Remember that gauges require power as well as a signal. For electrical gauges, this requires two wires. For mechanically driven gauges, an electrical power wire is required along with the mechanical sender connection.

A third 16-gauge wire connects to the alternator diode, when used. This wire is not required when using a one-wire alternator. However, if the engine does not shut off when the ignition key is turned to the off position, installing this diode will commonly cure the issue.

Terminal 5: Lights

Lights can be wired in multiple configurations to produce various results. For instance, headlights can be wired with or without relays. Some people believe that wiring them with relays will yield brighter light. Use

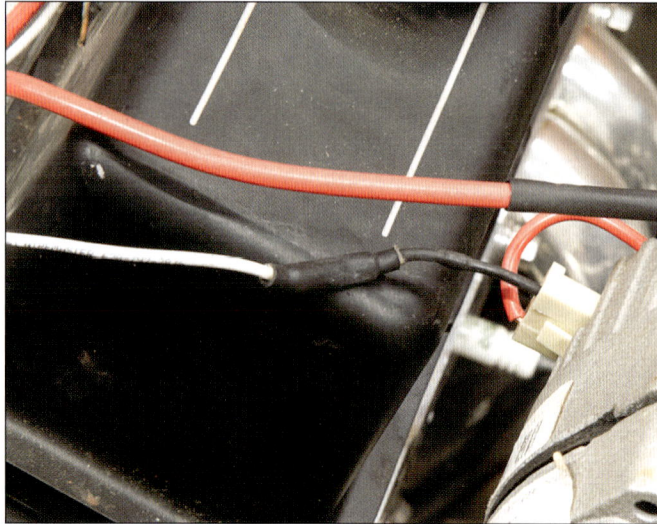

When a diode is required, install it in the wire (white in this photo) that comes from the fuse panel. Be sure to install the diode in the correct orientation.

This is a diode that has not yet been installed. The end of the diode with a flag or a stripe on it is the cathode end, which should be located closest to the wire that is receiving power.

Terminal 4 (the ignition feed) serves as a signal wire to the voltage meter in the dash. It is then connected to each of the other gauges to serve as 12-volt power to each of those gauges. They receive their signal via individual wires from their specific sensor.

of some of today's brighter bulbs requires relays to prevent overloading the headlight switch.

Use a 12-gauge wire connected to this terminal and to the headlight switch to provide constant power to the switch.

Headlight Switch

A separate 12-gauge wire connects the headlight switch to the dimmer switch. An additional 12-gauge wire provides power from the dimmer switch to the high-beam headlights, while another 12-gauge wire provides power from the dimmer switch to the low-beam headlights. This terminal is protected by the 20-amp fuse labeled "lights."

Dimmer Switch

Use a 12-gauge wire to connect the low-beam terminal of the dimmer switch to the low-beam terminal on each headlight. This can be done by running the wire from the dimmer switch to the driver-side headlight and including another wire to run

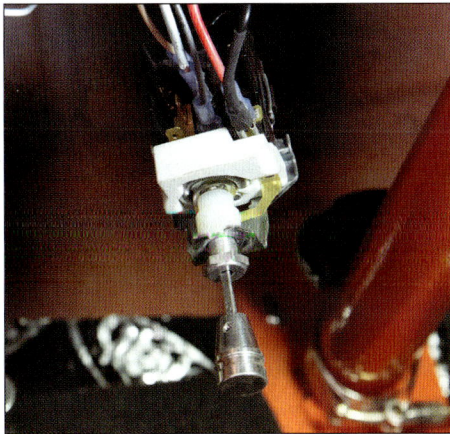

The headlight switch receives power from terminal 5 on the fuse panel. The headlight switch then divides the power to the headlights, taillights, and parking lights, depending on the knob position.

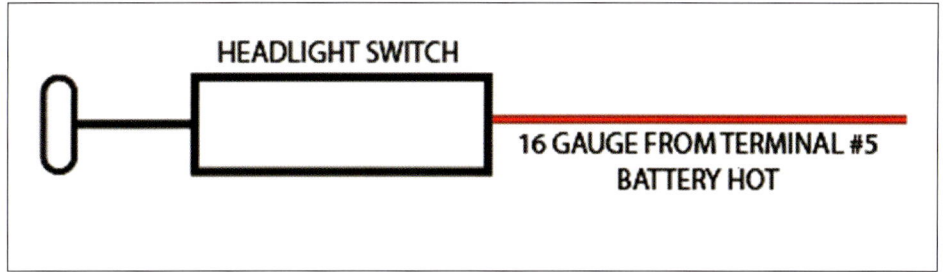

A 16-gauge wire from terminal 5 provides constant power to the headlight switch. Verify which terminal on the headlight switch is to receive the incoming power.

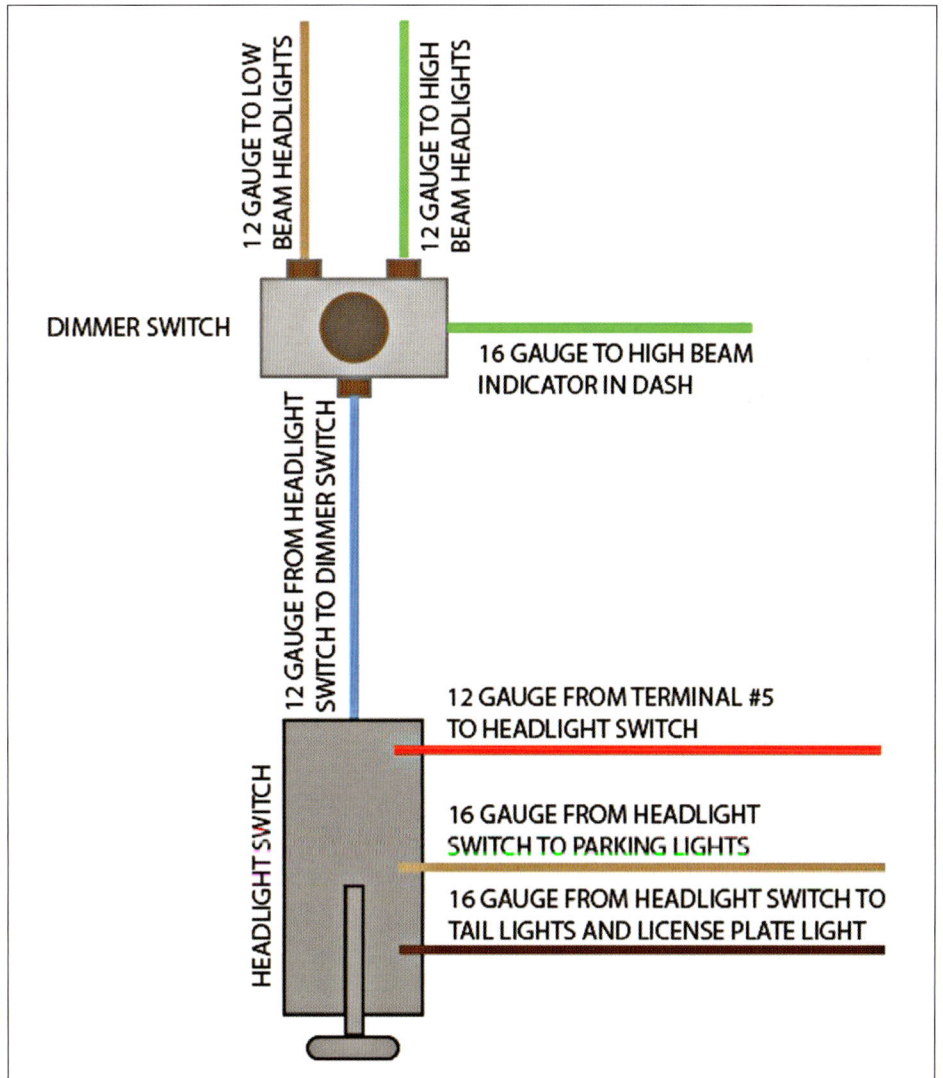

Headlight switches vary in their terminal configuration, so rely on information provided with the headlight switch to determine which terminals the various light wires should be connected to. The headlight switch receives its power from terminal 5. One 16-gauge wire runs to the front parking lights, while a second 16-gauge wire runs to the taillights and license-plate light.

to the passenger-side headlight in the female connector for the driver's side. Next, cut the second wire to the correct length and crimp on a female connector for the passenger-side light. Use this same process to provide power to the high-beam circuit.

When connecting the dimmer switch to the headlights, two wires are needed (one for high beam and one for low beam). These wires can be routed in one of two ways. One method is to run two wires from the dimmer switch for high beam and another two wires for low beam. This method provides power to each light (driver's side and passenger's side) individually. While this method may require a bit more wire, it is potentially safer, as damage to one headlight will not prevent the other headlight from working.

A second method is to run both wires to a point and then add a connector that has two wires exiting from the opposite end. One of these wires would then be routed and connected to the driver-side headlight, while the other wire would be routed and connected to the passenger-side headlight. A version of this method routes high- and low-beam wires to the driver-side light and then connects to the passenger-side light.

To provide power to the high-beam-indicator light on the dash, connect a 16-gauge wire to the terminal of the dimmer switch that is used to connect the high-beam lights.

License-Plate Light

The license-plate light or lights should be tied into the 16-gauge wire from the headlight switch that provides power to the taillights. License-plate lights are typically located above the middle of the license plate recess when using one light or one to each side when using

The two lower connections on the dimmer switch provide power to the high- and low-beam headlights. The third terminal provides a connection point for power coming in from the headlight switch.

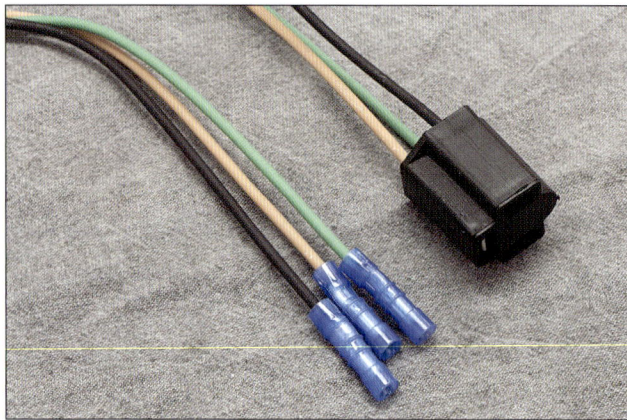

Most wiring kits include two pigtails for the headlights. For dual headlights, purchase the extra headlight pigtails at a local auto parts store. Simply crimp the appropriate headlight wires to the corresponding wires on the pigtail.

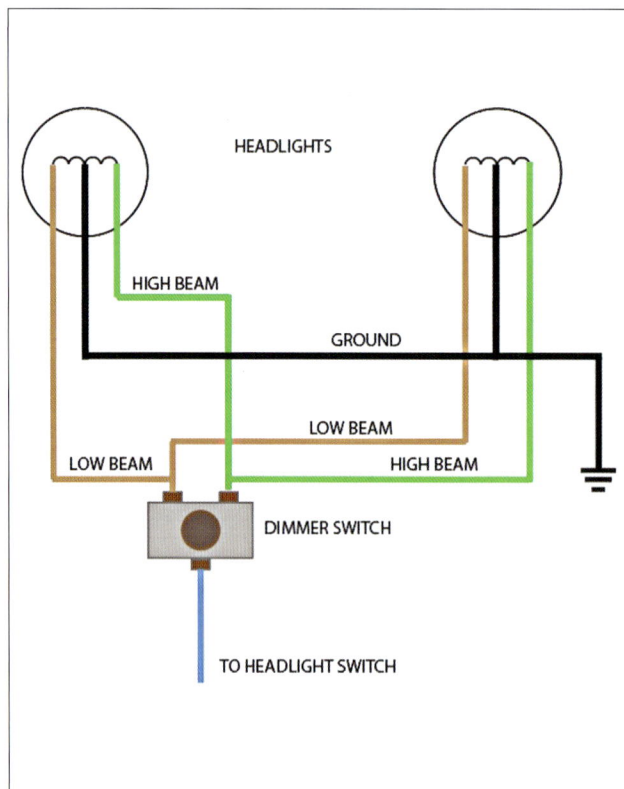

The basics of wiring the headlights are to connect one terminal of the dimmer switch to each low-beam headlight bulb and the remaining terminal to each high-beam headlight bulb. Connect a suitable ground to the third terminal on each headlight.

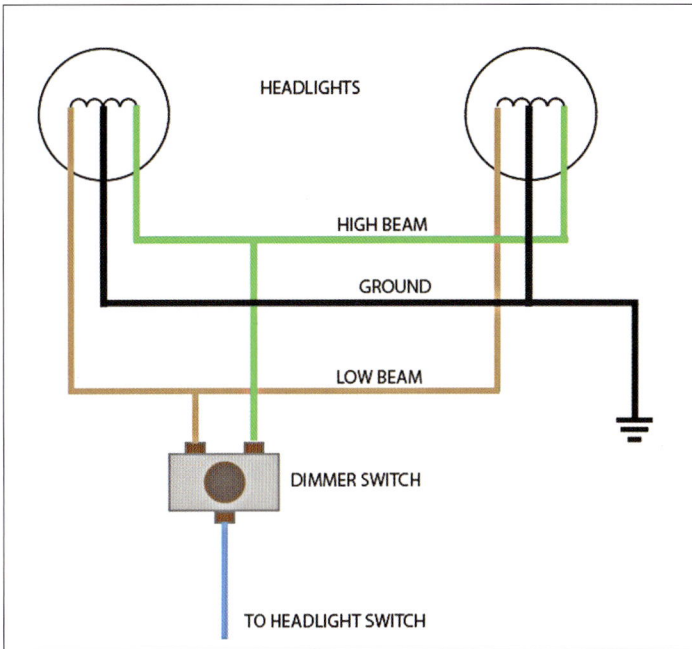

HEADLIGHTS

HIGH BEAM

GROUND

LOW BEAM

DIMMER SWITCH

TO HEADLIGHT SWITCH

Typically, the common high-beam wire and the common low-beam wire both run to a point and then split to run to the appropriate terminals on each headlight. Where they are split is a matter of preference and convenience.

When connecting the headlight wires, leave enough extra wire so that it is possible to remove the headlight's retaining ring and pull the headlight out with one hand and have enough room to unplug the light from the pigtail with the other hand. The extra wire can always be stashed inside the headlight bucket.

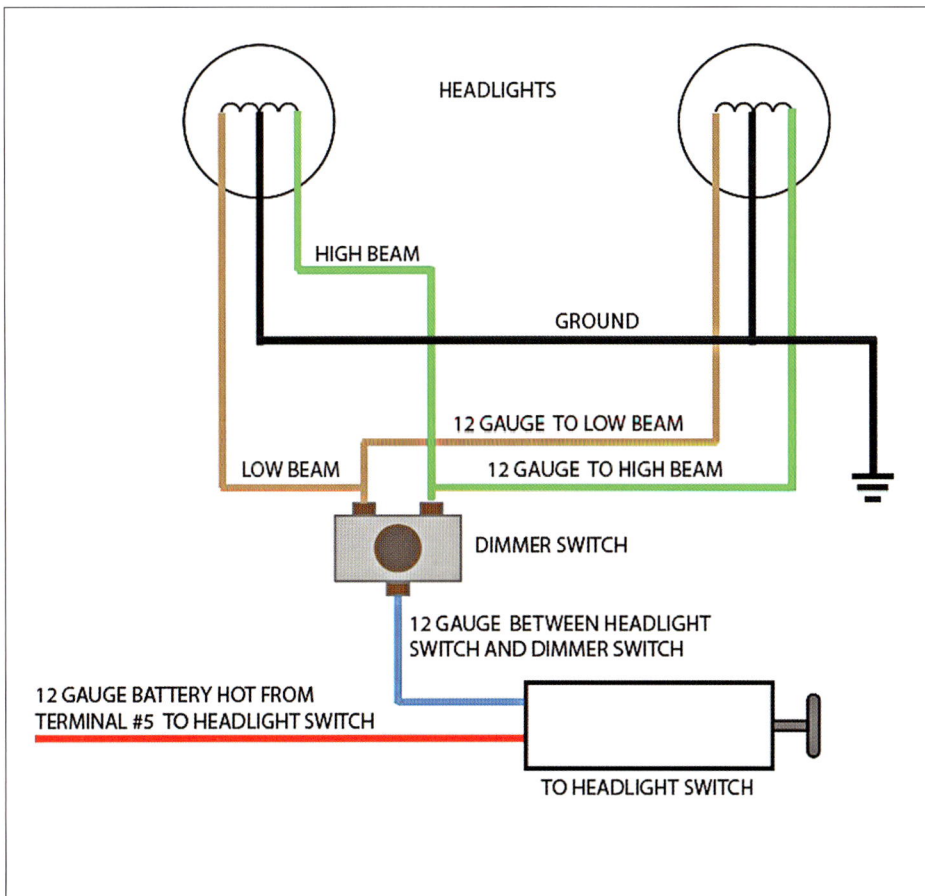

HEADLIGHTS

HIGH BEAM

GROUND

12 GAUGE TO LOW BEAM

LOW BEAM

12 GAUGE TO HIGH BEAM

DIMMER SWITCH

12 GAUGE BETWEEN HEADLIGHT
SWITCH AND DIMMER SWITCH

12 GAUGE BATTERY HOT FROM
TERMINAL #5 TO HEADLIGHT SWITCH

TO HEADLIGHT SWITCH

A 12-gauge wire from the headlight switch provides switched power to the input side of the dimmer switch. A 12-gauge wire runs from one output terminal of the dimmer switch to each of the high-beam headlights. At this same terminal on the dimmer switch, connect a 16-gauge wire to the high-beam-indicator light. A 12-gauge runs from one output terminal of the dimmer switch to each of the low-beam headlights.

The 1955 Chevy truck will feature a rolled pan that will have a recessed panel for the license plate, so it will require lights to be installed to illuminate the license plate. The location for the two lights have been determined, a hole for the wires has been drilled for each one, and a rubber grommet has been installed in each hole.

The aftermarket lights have been set in place. After the rolled pan has been painted, each light will be secured in place with two screws, lock washers, and nuts.

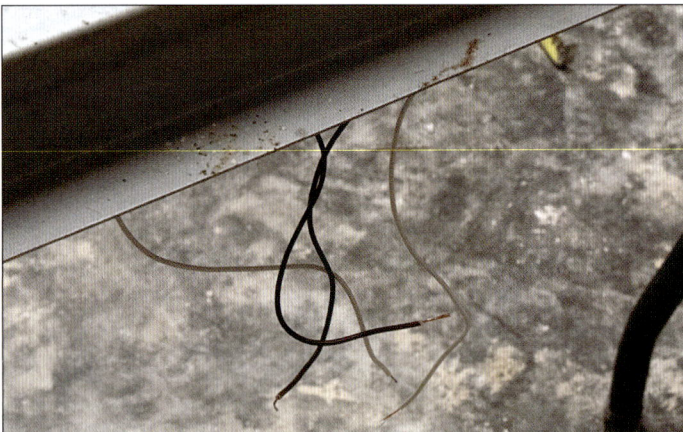

It should not matter in this case, but the white wires will eventually be connected to the taillight circuit to provide power whenever the headlight switch is in position to have the headlights on. The black wires will be used to connect to a ground.

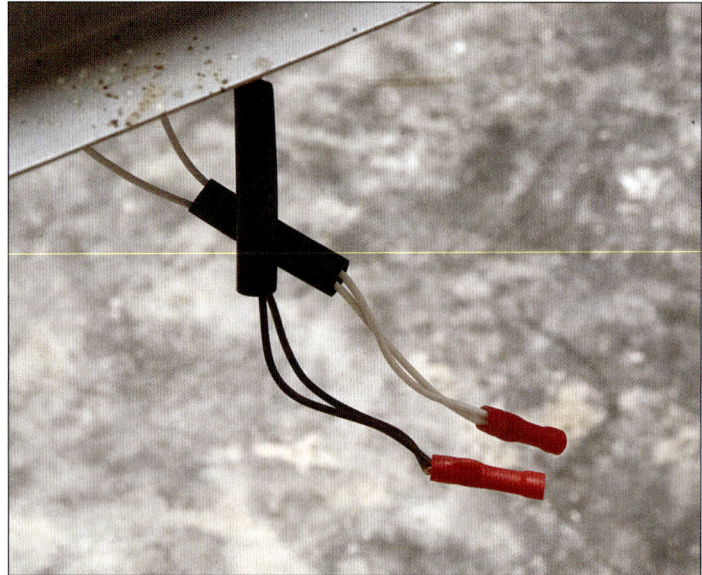

Two white power wires are ready to be connected to power, while two black wires are ready to be connected to ground. The heat-shrink tubing will be heated in place after the connections have been made.

two lights. Some folks use an illuminated license plate frame that has its own light. However, this must still be connected to the truck's taillight wiring.

Terminal 6: Neutral Safety Switch

A 12-gauge wire connected to this terminal connects to the starter solenoid. A second 12-gauge wire connects to the neutral safety switch. This terminal is merely a connection point for these two wires.

Terminal 7: Neutral Safety Switch

A 12-gauge wire connected to this terminal connects to the neutral safety switch. This terminal is merely a connection point for these two wires.

During the process of starting the engine when the ignition switch is in the start position, electrical current flows to this terminal and onward to the neutral safety switch. When the automatic transmission is in neutral or park (or a standard transmission is in neutral or the clutch is depressed), the neutral safety switch allows the electrical current to pass to terminal 6. From there, the electrical current passes to the starter solenoid, allowing the starter to spin the engine.

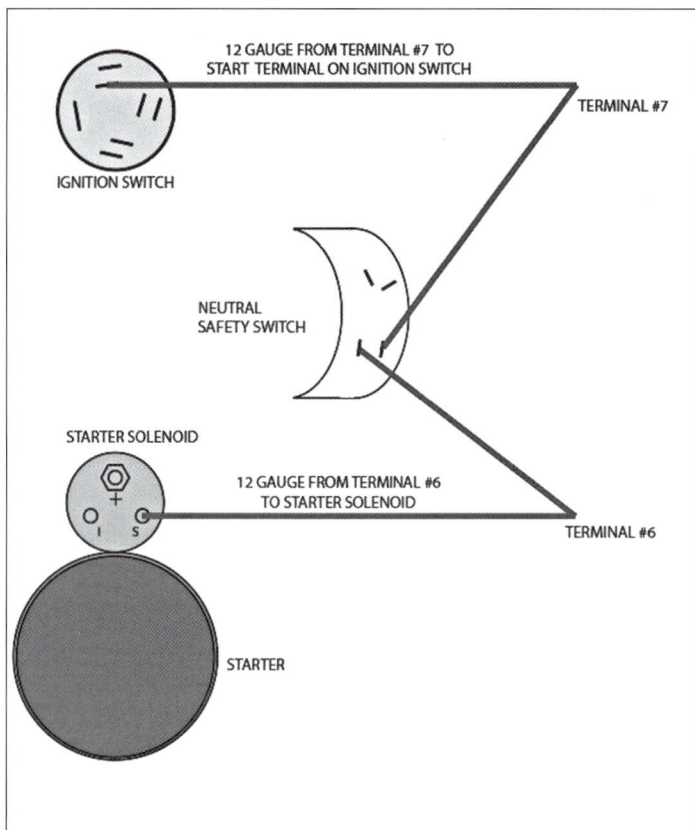

The 12-gauge wires from terminals 6 and 7 are used for the neutral safety switch to work correctly. From terminal 6, run one wire to the "S" terminal on the starter solenoid and another wire to one terminal on the neutral safety switch. From terminal 7, run one wire to the "start" terminal on the ignition switch and another wire to the remaining terminal on the neutral safety switch.

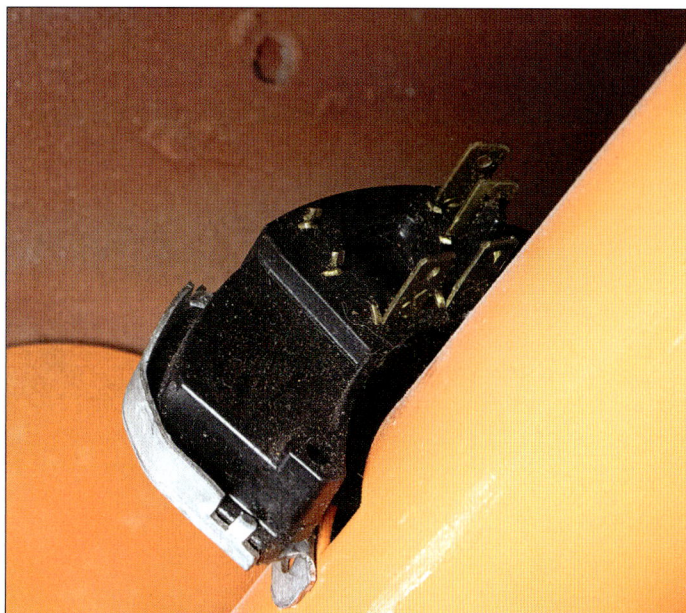

The most difficult part of wiring the neutral safety switch is determining which terminals are for it and which ones are for the reverse-light switch, as both sets of terminals are on the same switch. How do you figure it out? See chapters 2 and 7. Connections to the neutral safety switch and the reverse-light switch are typically made with a female spade terminal on the wire that fits over a male spade terminal on the switch. So, the connections can easily be disconnected and reconnected if/when you find they are not correct.

On the starter solenoid, the two small connections are labeled "S" and "R." The neutral safety switch should connect to the "S" terminal, with the battery cable connecting to the much larger lug.

This is what the wires at the starter would look like. The battery terminal connects to the largest lug on the starter solenoid. The neutral safety switch wire connects to the "S" terminal.

Terminal 8: Brake Feed

A 14-gauge wire connected to this terminal connects to and provides power to the brake-light switch. This terminal is protected by the 15-amp brake-feed fuse. As with terminal 1, this terminal is battery hot, meaning that when the battery is connected and charged, anything connected to this wire has power. However, that power is coming directly off the battery, meaning that the battery could run down quickly. The occasional use of the brake lights is not going to use much power, but almost anything else could.

Whether using a lever-type, plunger-type, or hydraulic pressure–type brake switch, the connections are the same. On the 1955 truck, a pressure-type switch is being used, and two 14-gauge wires are used. One comes from terminal 8 and the other comes from terminal 24 (with one wire going to each terminal).

Terminal 9: Battery Feed

This terminal is also battery hot but is not fused. It is used mainly as a connection point while the wiring panel is being assembled. It may be useful during troubleshooting, as it will always have power if the panel is connected to the battery.

Terminal 10: Battery Feed

This terminal has the same characteristics as terminal 9: battery feed. However, when using a GM steering column with the ignition switch on the column, it will be a necessity, as those ignition switches require two separate hot wires. With the addition of part number WRM20101 (available through Affordable Street Rods), this terminal can provide the required secondary power source.

Although the neutral safety switch/ reverse switch may be configured somewhat differently, it is commonly found near the base of the steering column on vintage GM pickups. Do some testing with a multimeter or test light to determine which terminals are for the neutral safety switch and which ones are for the reverse switch.

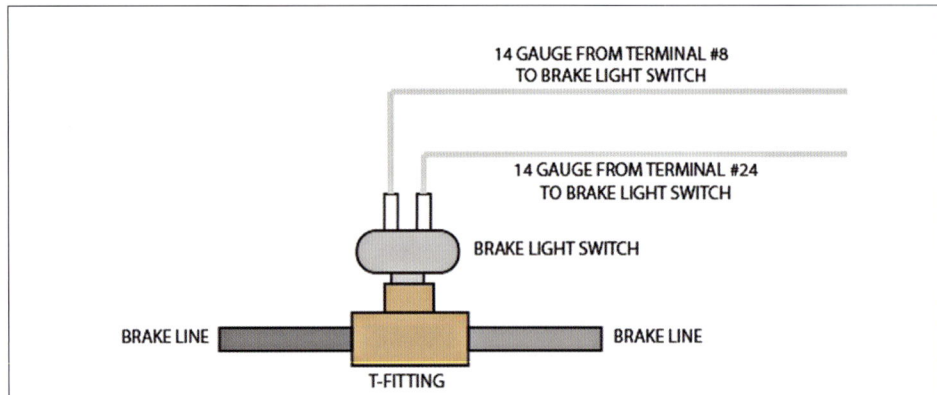

Connect a 14-gauge wire from terminal 8 to one terminal of the brake-light switch. Connect a 14-gauge wire from terminal 8 to the remaining terminal of the brake-light switch.

Terminal 11 provides power back to circuits that are protected by the radio, turn signal, wiper, and fan/accessory fuses. These circuits have power when the ignition switch is in the run or accessory position. Likewise, terminal 12 provides power back to circuits that are protected by the fuel pump, reverse lights, and heat/air fuses. These circuits have power when the ignition switch is in the run, accessory, or start position.

Terminal 11: Accessory Feed 1

This terminal provides power to the radio, turn signals, wipers, and fan/accessory fuses whenever the ignition switch is in the run or accessory position.

Terminal 12: Accessory Feed 2 (not on Power Panel II)

This terminal provides power to the fuel pump, rev LTS, and heat/air fuses whenever the ignition switch is in the start, run, or accessory position.

Terminal 13: Heat/Air

A 16-gauge wire connected to this terminal is used to provide power to the relays of the air-conditioning system or to the blower/fan switch of the heater. This terminal is hot whenever the ignition switch is in the start, run, or accessory position. This terminal is protected by a 25-amp heat/air fuse.

Terminal 14: Fan/Accessories

A 16-gauge wire connected to this terminal provides power to an electric fan via a relay. With the ignition key in the run or accessory position, this wire will provide power to a 70-amp relay. Due to the high draw of an electric fan, a relay must be used. This terminal is protected by the 25-amp fan/accessory fuse.

The electric fan can be wired in a few different ways, depending on when you want the electric fan to be able to run. When the electric fan is connected to terminal 14, it will run when the key is in the accessory

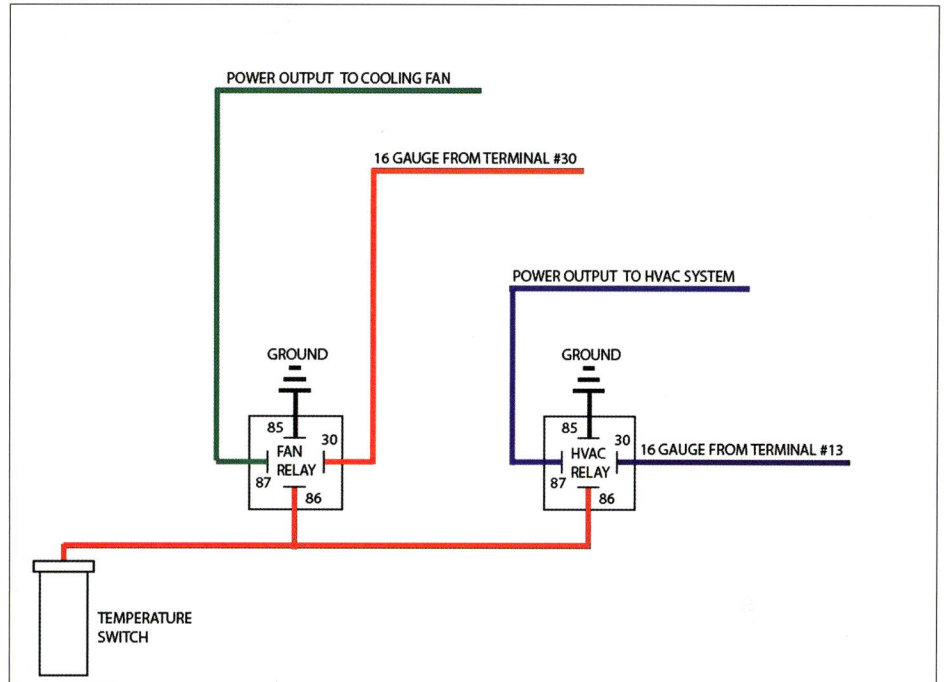

For the HVAC connections, use a relay to avoid burning up the switch. Connect a 16-gauge wire from terminal 13 of the fuse panel to terminal 30 of the electrical relay. Use a 16-gauge wire from the temperature switch to power the relay at terminal 86. Connect terminal 85 to the ground and terminal 87 to the HVAC system.

The HVAC control panel used in the 1955 Chevy truck fits into a removeable panel that is part of the center console.

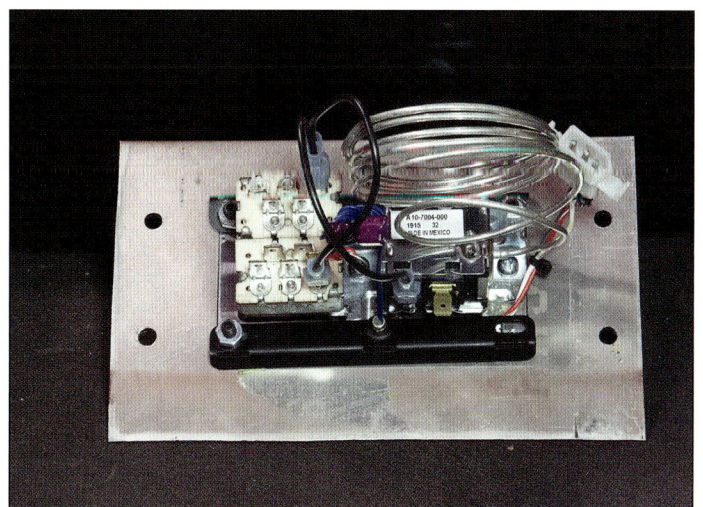

This is the backside of the HVAC control panel that was used in the 1955 Chevy truck. It has more electronic gadgetry than the similar unit used in the 1970 truck.

position, even when you may simply be listening to the radio. To control this, implement an adjustable fan thermostat that will shut the electric fan off after the coolant system cools down to a preset temperature.

If the goal is for the electric fan to run when the key is in the accessory position, use terminal 28 or 30, instead of 14 to provide power to the electric fan.

A 16-gauge wire connected to this terminal can be used to connect power to an electric choke on the carburetor.

Terminal 15: Wiper

A 16-gauge wire connected to this terminal provides power to the windshield wiper when the ignition switch is in the run or accessory position. On many aftermarket wiper systems, this wire connects to the wiper switch. On

For the electric fan connections, use a relay to avoid burning up the switch. Connect a 16-gauge wire from terminal 30 of the fuse panel to terminal 30 of the electrical relay. Use a 16-gauge wire from the temperature switch to power the relay at terminal 86. Connect terminal 85 to ground and terminal 87 to the electric fan.

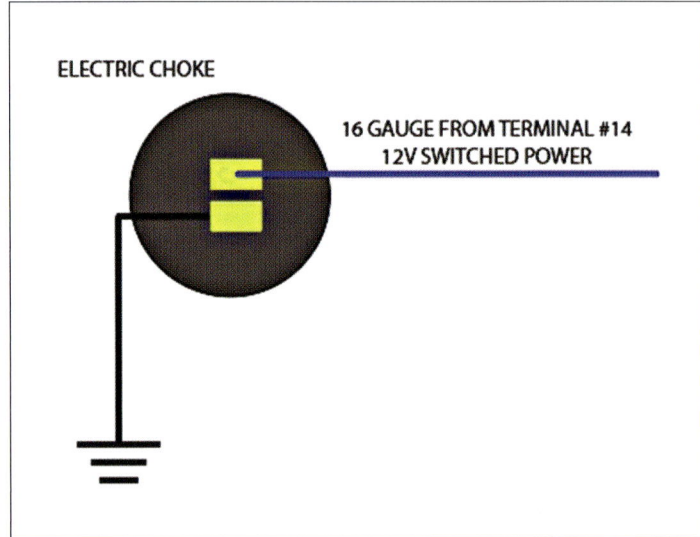

When using a carburetor with an electric choke, connect a 16-gauge wire from terminal 14 to the positive terminal on the electric choke. Connect the negative side of the electric choke to ground.

The symbols may be difficult to see, but the black cover on the electric choke typically indicates which connector is positive and which is negative. The blue wire in this photo is positive, and no ground wire has been installed yet.

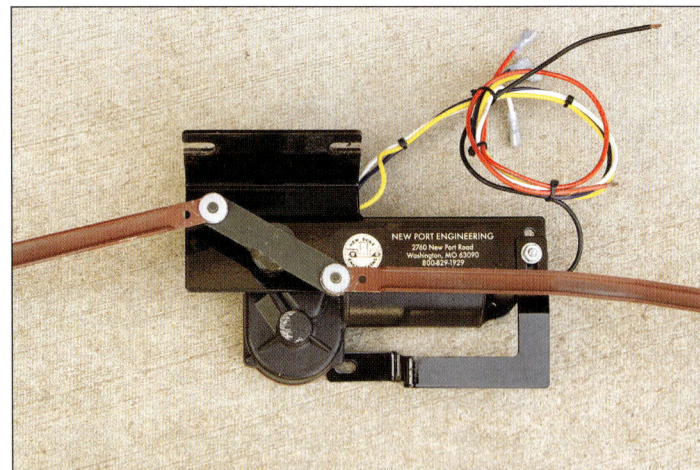

Anyone who has driven a vehicle equipped with vacuum wiper motors knows that electric wiper motors are significantly more reliable. New Port Engineering manufactures vehicle-specific electric wiper motor kits that are a true bolt-in. Kits feature a two-speed wiper motor and a washer pump. Simply mount the kit and connect the power and ground wires.

many stock wiper systems, this power wire connects directly to the wiper motor. This circuit is protected by the 5-amp wipers fuse.

Terminal 16: Horn

A 14-gauge wire connected to this terminal provides 12-volt power to the horn via the horn relay built into the wiring panel. This terminal is always hot; however, the horn will operate only when the circuit is grounded.

Terminals 17 through 24 are used to provide electrical power to brake lights, turn signals, hazard flashers, and the horn button, all of which are controlled through the steering column. Wires from the terminals are routed to one side of a quick-disconnect plug that is near the base of the steering column. The corresponding wires begin at the opposite side of the quick-disconnect plug and are then routed to their destination.

Terminal 17: Horn Button

Connect this terminal to the horn button (typically on the steering wheel but could be a remotely operated button or switch) to provide a method of grounding the horn. When the horn button or switch is depressed, the horn circuit is closed and the horn sounds.

Terminal 18: Left Front Turn Signal

A 16-gauge wire connected to this terminal provides power to the left front turn-signal lights. A second 16-gauge wire connects this terminal to the left turn-signal-indicator light on the dash.

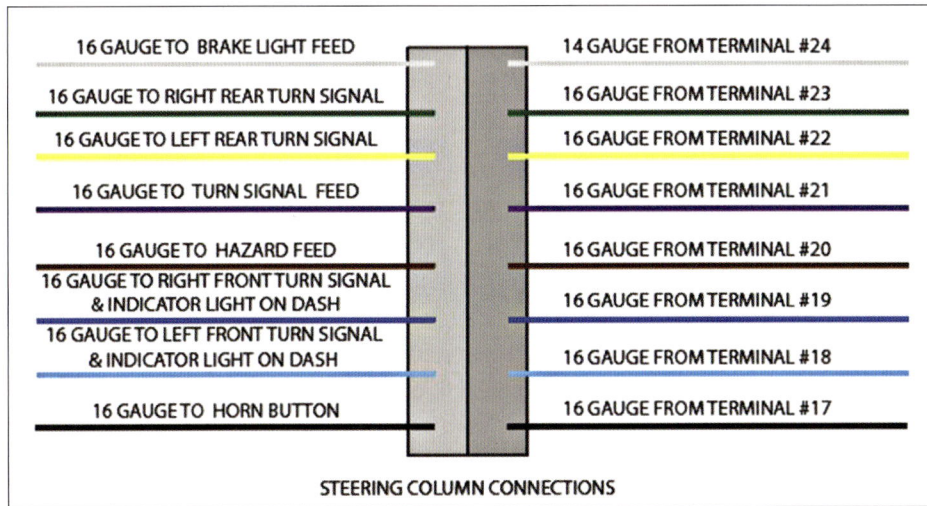

Left side	Right side
16 GAUGE TO BRAKE LIGHT FEED	14 GAUGE FROM TERMINAL #24
16 GAUGE TO RIGHT REAR TURN SIGNAL	16 GAUGE FROM TERMINAL #23
16 GAUGE TO LEFT REAR TURN SIGNAL	16 GAUGE FROM TERMINAL #22
16 GAUGE TO TURN SIGNAL FEED	16 GAUGE FROM TERMINAL #21
16 GAUGE TO HAZARD FEED	16 GAUGE FROM TERMINAL #20
16 GAUGE TO RIGHT FRONT TURN SIGNAL & INDICATOR LIGHT ON DASH	16 GAUGE FROM TERMINAL #19
16 GAUGE TO LEFT FRONT TURN SIGNAL & INDICATOR LIGHT ON DASH	16 GAUGE FROM TERMINAL #18
16 GAUGE TO HORN BUTTON	16 GAUGE FROM TERMINAL #17

STEERING COLUMN CONNECTIONS

When using a wiring kit, the steering-column pigtail is typically a matter of connecting wires of the same color on corresponding sides of the quick disconnect. However, when using an older steering column, the colors may not match.

After both sides of the pigtail have the wires installed, push both sides together until they lock. There will typically be some type of latch mechanism that secures both halves together but will also release them when required. The wire tie in this photo is simply securing the connection to the underside of the steering column/dash support.

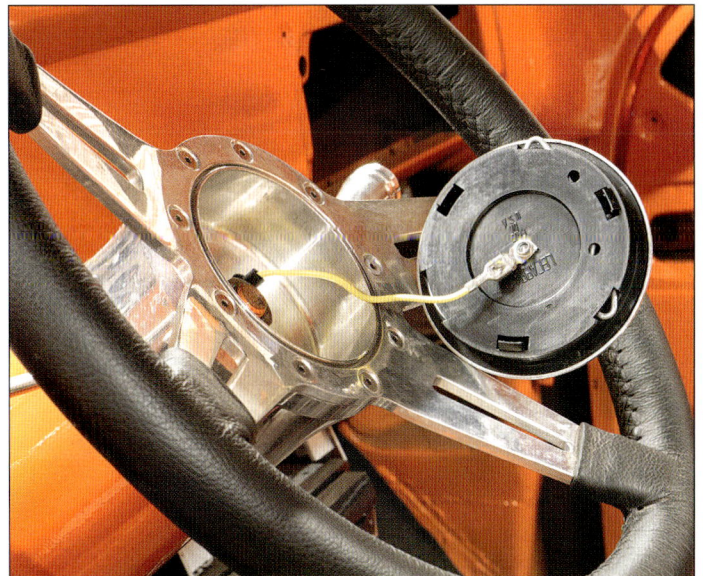

On aftermarket steering columns, the horn wire passes through the center of the steering-wheel hub and connects to the back side of the horn button.

Terminal 19: Right Front Turn Signal

A 16-gauge wire connected to this terminal provides power to the right front turn-signal lights. A second 16-gauge wire connects this terminal to the right turn-signal-indicator light on the dash.

Terminal 20: Hazard Flasher

This terminal is constantly hot and is protected by the 10-amp hazard fuse, making it a battery-hot flashed power source. When a load from the front and rear turn signals is attached to this terminal, it will trip the flasher, causing the turn signals to flash.

A troubleshooting note is that LED turn signals do not require enough current to cause a mechanical flasher to operate properly. When using LED turn signals that illuminate

Each of the turn-signal indicators on the back of the instrument panel receives a wire from the fuse panel, as well as a ground.

A flasher is the device that causes the turn signal to flash when activated. When the wiring is connected correctly and there is a proper ground, a faulty flasher is most likely the culprit if the turn signals or hazard flashers are not working correctly.

The front left and right turn signals are wired using two wires for each signal. One 16-gauge wire originating from terminal 18 connects to the left front turn signal, with another wire originating at terminal 18 connecting to the left front turn-signal indicator on the dash panel. In a similar fashion, two wires originating from terminal 19 connect to the right front turn-signal and right turn-signal indicator.

When using LED turn-signal lights, it may be necessary to use an LED flasher (also known as a no-load flasher) to get the turn signals and the flashers to operate correctly. It simply plugs into the fuse panel where the original flasher was located. Some LED flashers have a ground wire and some do not. If one exists, connect it to a ground source.

but do not flash, replace the mechanical flasher with an electronic flasher.

Terminal 21: Turn-Signal Flasher

This terminal is hot only when the ignition switch is in the run or accessory position, making it a key-on flashed power source. It is protected by a 10-amp turn fuse. Otherwise, this terminal is identical to the hazard flasher terminal. The differences between battery-hot flashed and key-on flashed power sources are an important item to remember when wiring any auxiliary emergency lighting.

Terminal 22: Left Rear Turn Signal; Terminal 23: Right Rear Turn Signal

The taillight housings serve not only taillights but also turn signals and the brake lights. The taillights are powered by a 16-gauge wire from the headlight switch. This wire is also used to provide power to the license-plate lights.

For the rear turn signals, connect them to the appropriate terminal with a 16-gauge wire. The left rear turn signal connects to terminal 22 and the right rear turn signal connects to terminal 23.

For the brake lights, one side of the brake-light switch receives constant 12-volt power from terminal 8. When the driver applies the brakes, this 12-volt power continues through the brake-light switch to terminal 24 and then to terminals 22 and 23. This then illuminates the left and right brake lights simultaneously. There is no separate brake-light wire to run to the brake lights, as the turn lights also function as the brake lights.

Terminal 24: Brake Switch

A 16-gauge wire connected to this terminal connects the brake switch

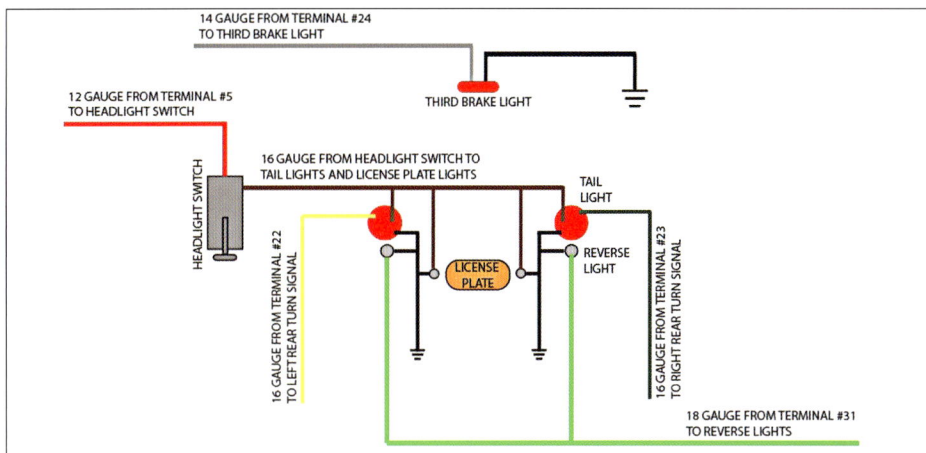

Taillights receive power through a 16-gauge wire from the headlight switch. The left rear turn signal and right rear turn signal receive power from terminals 22 and 23, respectively. The third brake light receives power through a 14-gauge wire from terminal 24.

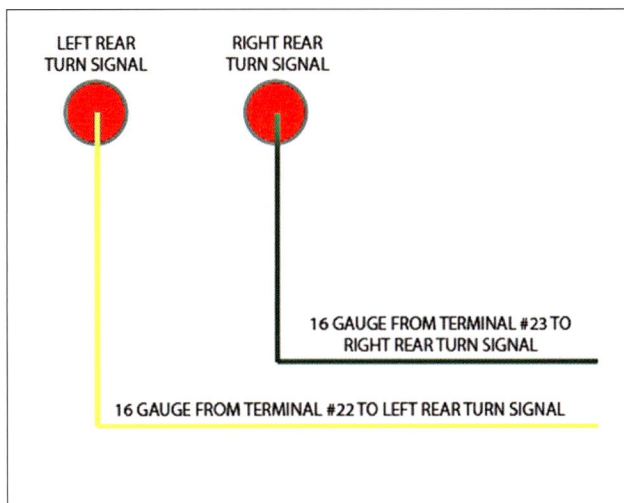

Provide power to the left rear turn signal by running a 16-gauge wire from terminal 22 to the left rear turn signal. Provide power to the right rear turn signal by running a 16-gauge wire from terminal 23 to the right rear turn signal.

These are aftermarket LED taillights for a 1958–1959 Fleetside bed. The connection for the taillight looks to plug into the stock-type receptacle.

to the turn-signal switch, which allows the rear turn lights to also function as brake lights. With the activation of the brakes, terminal 8 sends constant 12-volt power to this terminal. From here, that electric current is sent to the left and right rear turn-signal terminals (22 and 23 respectively). A 14-gauge wire from terminal 24 connects to a third brake light when used and provides power to the third brake light when the brakes are activated.

Terminal 25: Power Seats
(not on Power Panel II)

This terminal is battery hot and used to provide power to the power seats. It is protected by the 25-amp P/S-P/W fuse. A 12-gauge wire connected to this terminal provides power to the power seats. The shop truck will not have power seats, so this terminal simply will not be used.

Terminal 26: Accessory
(not on Power Panel II)

This terminal is battery hot and protected by the 25-amp P/S-P/W fuse. It can be used for accessories that require constant power, such as a remote-entry system, or any accessory that is designed to be powered by a cigarette lighter, such as a cell-phone charger. If off-roading or trailering is your thing, this circuit could be used to power a winch.

Terminal 27: Power Windows
(not on Power Panel II)

This terminal is battery hot and used to provide power to power windows. It is protected by the 25-amp P/S-P/W fuse. A 12-gauge wire connected to this terminal provides power to the power windows.

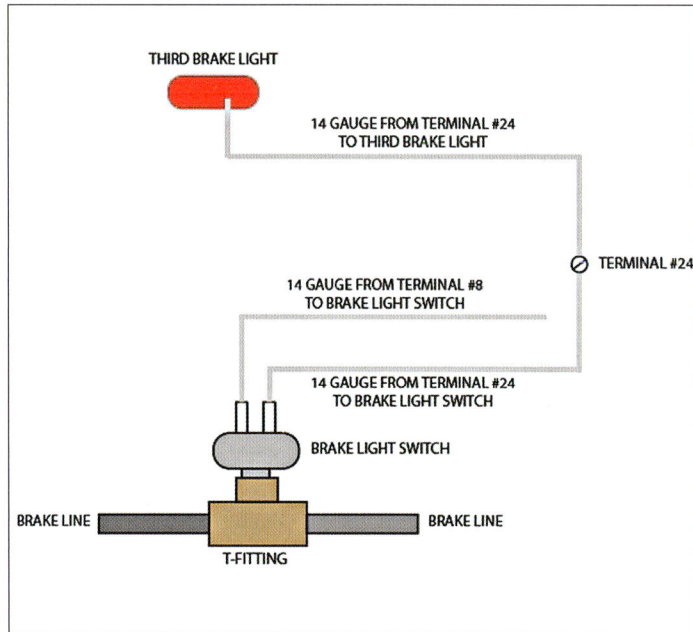

Terminal 24 serves as a connection point for the brake-light switch and the third brake light.

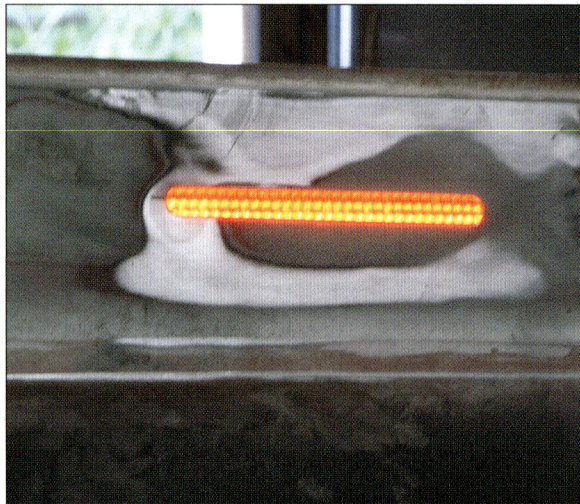

The LED third brake light has been mounted inside the sheet metal below the rear window and sanded smooth with the surface. It can be seen but not felt. Most of the circuits can be tested with a battery charger by connecting the charging cable to the positive terminal or wire and the negative cable to the ground source for the circuit.

A battery charger can be used to test electrical circuits prior to completion of all wiring. Testing the third brake light in this fashion shows that the LED third brake light is indeed bright.

Terminal 28: Accessory
(not on Power Panel II)

This terminal is hot when the ignition switch is in the start or run position and is protected by the 15-amp fuel-pump fuse. When using an electric fuel pump, be careful to not overload this circuit. A blown fuse will prevent the fuel pump from operating, which will prevent the engine from starting.

When using the Power Panel, a 16-gauge wire connected to terminal 28 provides power to the electric choke. When using the Power Panel II, a 16-gauge wire connected to terminal 14 provides power to the electric choke.

Terminal 29: Fuel Pump
(not on Power Panel II)

This terminal is hot when the ignition switch is in the start and run position and is protected by the 15-amp fuel pump fuse. This terminal should be used to provide power to a 30-amp fuel-pump relay via a 16-gauge wire. You must not connect the fuel pump directly to this terminal, as that will fail.

A mechanical fuel pump is being used on the shop truck, so this terminal will not be used. However, if fuel injection is installed at a later date, this terminal will provide power to an electric fuel pump.

Terminal 30: Accessory
(not on Power Panel II)

This terminal is identical to terminal 28 in that it is hot when the ignition switch is in the start or run position and is protected by the 15-amp fuel-pump fuse. When using an electric fuel pump, you must be careful to not overload this circuit, as a blown fuse will prevent the fuel pump from operating and prevent the engine from starting.

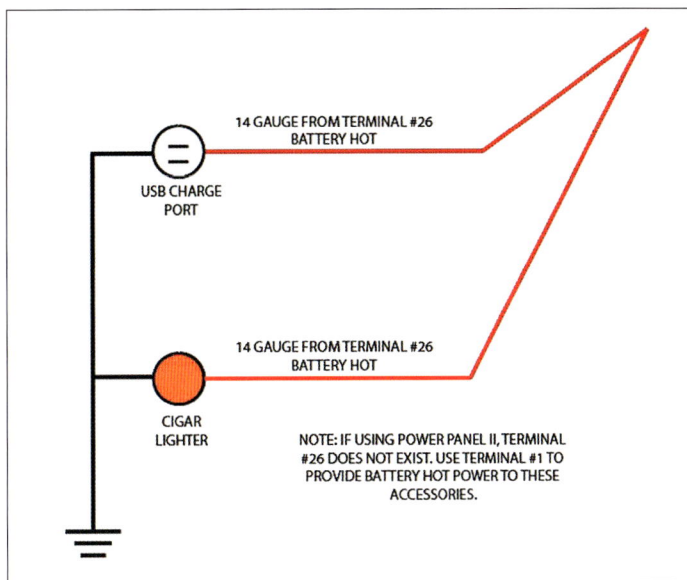

USB CHARGE PORT

14 GAUGE FROM TERMINAL #26 BATTERY HOT

CIGAR LIGHTER

14 GAUGE FROM TERMINAL #26 BATTERY HOT

NOTE: IF USING POWER PANEL II, TERMINAL #26 DOES NOT EXIST. USE TERMINAL #1 TO PROVIDE BATTERY HOT POWER TO THESE ACCESSORIES.

To provide constant battery power to an accessory power source, such as a cell phone charger or remote-entry system, run a power wire from terminal 26 to the input side of the accessory. There must also be a connection to ground for the device.

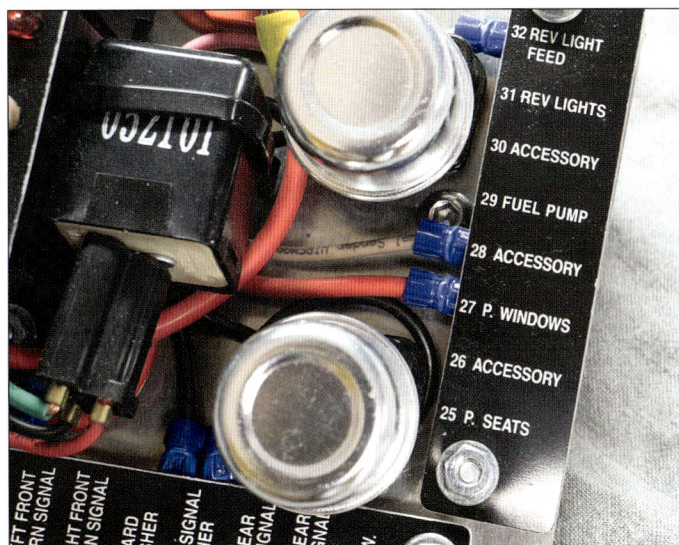

32 REV LIGHT FEED
31 REV LIGHTS
30 ACCESSORY
29 FUEL PUMP
28 ACCESSORY
27 P. WINDOWS
26 ACCESSORY
25 P. SEATS

Terminals 25 through 32 are not included on the Wiremaster Power Panel II. These terminals are designed for use with power seats, power windows, the electric fuel pump, and backup lights. However, they can be used for other circuits.

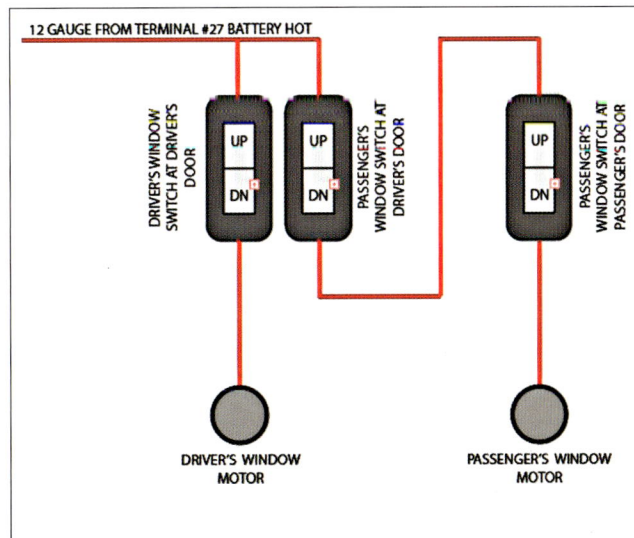

12 GAUGE FROM TERMINAL #27 BATTERY HOT

DRIVER'S WINDOW SWITCH AT DRIVER'S DOOR
PASSENGER'S WINDOW SWITCH AT DRIVER'S DOOR
PASSENGER'S WINDOW SWITCH AT PASSENGER'S DOOR

UP / DN

DRIVER'S WINDOW MOTOR
PASSENGER'S WINDOW MOTOR

In this truck, there are two DPDT switches mounted in the driver-side door and one DPDT switch mounted in the passenger-side door. One switch on the driver's side controls the window in that door, while the two remaining switches control the passenger-side window.

A 16-gauge wire connected to this terminal provides power to an electric fan via a relay. With the ignition key in the run or accessory position, this wire will provide power to a 70-amp relay. Due to the high draw of an electric fan, a relay must be used. This terminal is protected by the 25-amp fan/accessory fuse.

Terminal 31: Reverse Lights (not on Power Panel II)

A 16-gauge wire provides power to the backup-light switch. This switch is commonly located on the steering column when the shifter is on the column. When the shifter is on the floor, the backup-light switch is commonly located on the shifter.

There will not be any reverse lights on this truck, but there could be if desired. Power would come from terminal 31 via an 18-gauge wire. Even though reverse lights will not be installed, this wire could be used to provide power for a backup camera that may be installed in the future.

Terminal 32: Reverse Light Feed (not on Power Panel II)

This terminal is hot when the ignition switch is in the start or run position and is protected by the 10-amp reverse-lights fuse. When the transmission is shifted into reverse, a 16-gauge wire provides power to the backup-light switch, through terminal 31, and then to the backup lights.

Pigtails

Pigtails are intermediate wiring connections that are made in line between the fuse panel (or electrical source) and the electrical component that requires electrical power. These are often used to connect multiple wires to a component that may be discon-

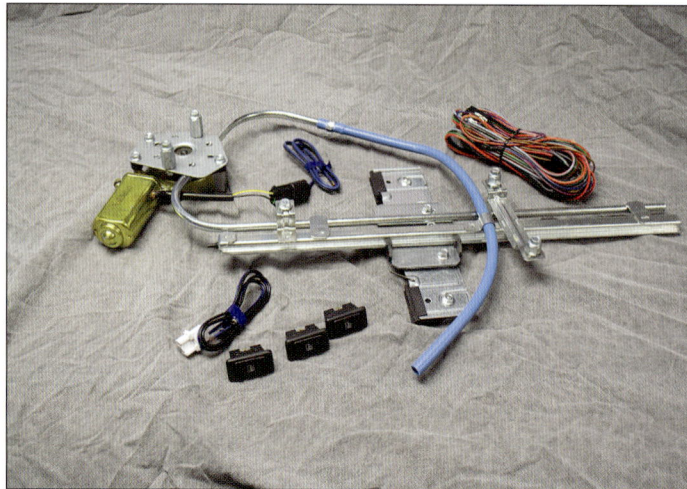

This is the motor and window riser for one door glass, along with switches and plenty of wire. Refer to the instructions provided with whatever power window kit you are using because they vary.

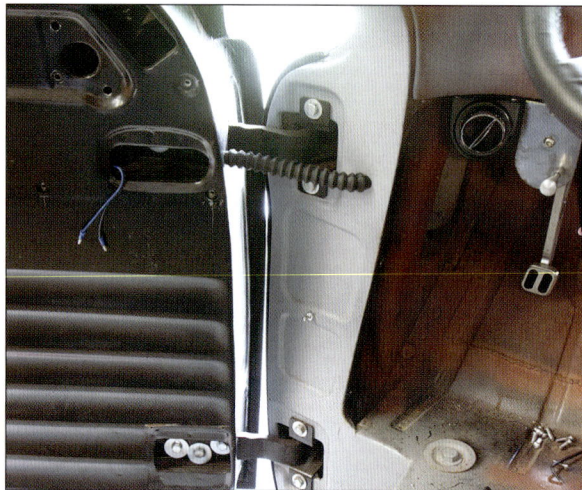

Any time that wires pass from the cab into a door, the wires must be protected by some sort of flexible conduit. At this point, the power window motors are installed in the doors, which is evidenced by two wires sticking out the door. Those will later be connected to power wires and the passenger-door window motor.

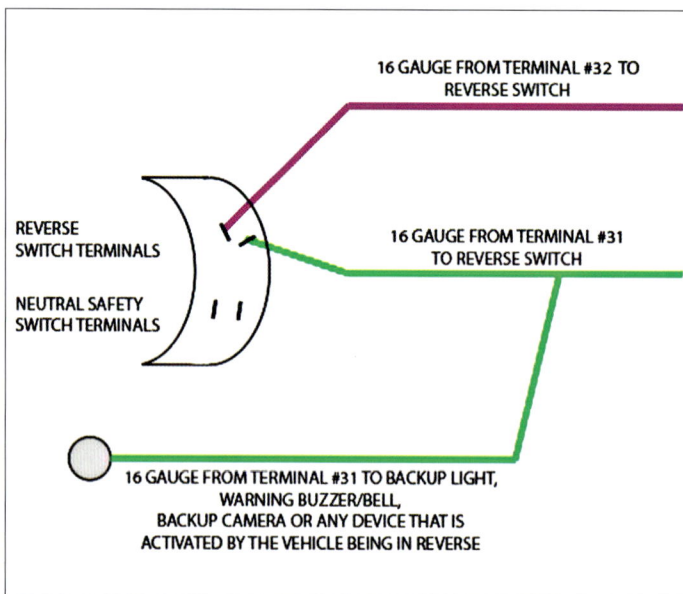

16 GAUGE FROM TERMINAL #32 TO REVERSE SWITCH

REVERSE SWITCH TERMINALS

16 GAUGE FROM TERMINAL #31 TO REVERSE SWITCH

NEUTRAL SAFETY SWITCH TERMINALS

16 GAUGE FROM TERMINAL #31 TO BACKUP LIGHT, WARNING BUZZER/BELL, BACKUP CAMERA OR ANY DEVICE THAT IS ACTIVATED BY THE VEHICLE BEING IN REVERSE

To provide power for backup lights, a backup camera, or any other device when the truck is in reverse, use a 16-gauge wire to connect terminal 32 to one terminal of the reverse switch. Connect a 16-gauge wire from terminal 31 to the remaining terminal of the reverse switch.

Run a 16-gauge wire from terminal 31 to the activated device.

nected for service. Quite often, a switch of some sort is involved. For automotive purposes, the steering column, ignition switch, and neutral safety switch are commonly wired using pigtails.

Steering Column

Since the turn-signal indicator and horn are typically located on the steering column and steering wheel, respectively, these wires are commonly terminated in a quick-disconnect plug that can be connected to the other half of the pigtail that runs wires to the electrical components. The fuse-panel terminal, wire gauge, and electrical components included in the steering-column pigtail are shown in Table 7-2.

To have the correct electrical connector, know the origin of the steering column that is being used. For purposes of this discussion, it will be a pre-1977 GM, 1977-or-later GM, aftermarket, or something else. The steering-column pigtail with the Wiremaster kit includes the 1977-or-later GM-style connector. When using this

style of steering column, installation is as simple plugging the pigtail into the column.

For other steering-column styles, install the wires into both halves of a steering-column connector. To do so, strip a 1/4 inch of insulation from each wire and insert the stripped wire into a brass terminal. Then, fold each of two forward ears over the stripped wire. Fold both rear ears over the insulation and then crimp both sets of ears for a secure connection.

With brass terminals installed on each wire, insert each wire into the correct position in the steering-column connector. Ensure that the wires are properly aligned with the matching wire in the opposite half of the connector. Route the pigtail away from

any pedal movement and cut the wires to length. Strip 1/4 inch of insulation off the opposite end of each wire, crimp on a fork terminal, and connect each wire to the appropriate terminal on the fuse panel.

Ignition

Multiple wires run between the fuse panel and the ignition switch. While these can be connected using a quick-disconnect plug, they are commonly wired directly between the fuse panel and the appropriate terminal on the ignition switch.

Since the ignition switch may need to be removed for service, it makes sense to leave the wires a little bit long. Be sure to use a wire tie to neatly tie the wires up behind the dash

Table 7-2: Steering Pigtail Connections		
Fuse Panel Terminal	Wire Gauge	Electrical Component
24	14	Brake-Light Feed
23	16	Right Rear Turn Signal
22	16	Left Rear Turn Signal
21	16	Turn-Signal Feed
20	16	Hazard Feed
19	16	Right Front Turn Signal
18	16	Left Front Turn Signal
17	16	Horn Button

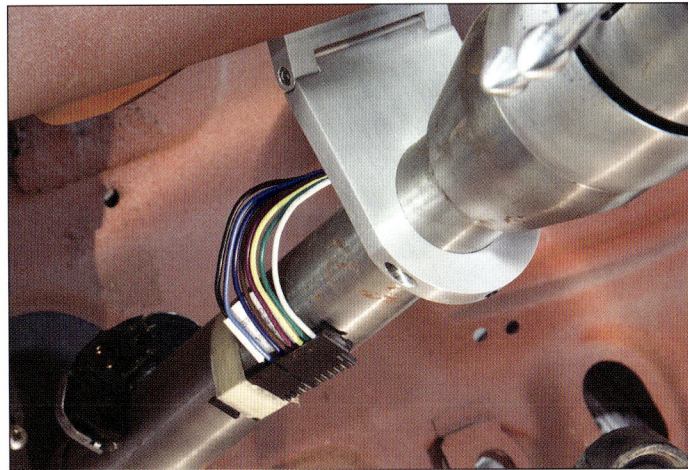

Many aftermarket steering columns include the steering-column pigtail, making for easy installation. Simply use the appropriate connector from the wiring kit and connect the wires.

This ignition switch was purchased through my local auto parts store. Instructions with the switch identified the terminals.

(rather than to leave them dangling in plain sight). The fuse-panel terminal, wire gauge, and electrical connection points included in the ignition pigtail are shown in the following table.

Table 7-3: Ignition Pigtail Connection		
Fuse-Panel Terminal	Wire Gauge	Electrical Connection Point
Power Terminal	10	Ignition Switch (BATT Terminal)
4	12	Ignition Switch (IGN Terminal)
7	12	Ignition Switch (START Terminal)
12	12	Ignition Switch (IGN Terminal)
11	12	Ignition Switch (ACC Terminal)
Power Terminal	8	Starter (BATT Terminal)

Neutral Safety

The neutral safety pigtail simply connects the two neutral safety terminals on the fuse panel to the neutral safety switch. Whether using a truck's stock steering column or an aftermarket column, if it is a column shift, this switch is normally located near the base of the column.

On an automatic transmission with a floor shift, the neutral safety switch is commonly located on or near the transmission. Some manual transmissions have a neutral safety switch located on the clutch pedal. Regardless of where the neutral safety switch is located, be sure that it is wired properly and used, as it is critical to safe operation.

Engine Compartment

Within the engine compartment, there are multiple wires and cables between various individual components that do not connect directly to the fuse panel. Still, they are every bit as important.

Coil

Connect terminal 3 on the fuse panel to the positive side of the ignition coil with a 12-gauge wire. When using an HEI ignition, this wire plugs directly into the battery terminal of the distributor cap. When using a points-style ignition, this wire connects to the ballast resistor that connects to the positive side of the coil. In addition, a cable (commonly included with the spark-plug wires) from the center of the distributor cap connects to the center terminal of the coil. Lastly, connect the negative side of the ignition coil to a known ground with a 12-gauge wire.

Tachometer

When using a tachometer, use a 16-gauge wire to connect the positive side of the coil to the signal-input terminal on the tachometer. When using an HEI-type distributor and coil, use the 16-gauge wire to connect the tachometer terminal on the distributor cap to the tachometer. Use a 16-gauge wire to connect the negative side of the coil to the tachometer.

A/C Compressor Clutch

When installing an air-conditioning unit, use a 12-gauge wire to connect terminal 13 on the fuse panel to the A/C compressor clutch.

A traditional coil is being used with the 1955 Chevy truck. The center terminal of the coil receives a wire from the distributor. The negative post of the coil connects to the tachometer, while the positive side connects to terminal 3 of the fuse panel.

Read the instructions provided with the distributor before connecting any wires so that you know how it should be connected to the ignition system.

This will allow the air-conditioning system to operate while the ignition switch is in the start, run, or accessory position.

Alternator

Use an 8-gauge wire to connect the power terminal on the fuse panel to the stud on the back of the alternator. Connect the 8-gauge wire of the alternator plug to this stud. The remaining wire of the alternator plug contains a diode and should be connected to a 16-gauge wire that connects to terminal 4 on the fuse panel. This diode allows the alternator to charge at low engine RPM.

Reverse Switch

When using backup lights, use a 16-gauge wire to connect terminal 31 of the fuse panel to each reverse light. Connect another 16-gauge wire between the reverse switch to terminal 32 of the fuse panel. Whenever the ignition switch is in the start or run position, this will provide power to the reverse-light switch, causing the backup lights to illuminate.

Interior

The balance of the interior wiring includes the gauges and instrument panel wiring and the wiring for controlling the HVAC system.

Instrument Panel

The gauges and their lighting can be wired ahead of time and on a table or workbench to make things easy. Mount the gauges in the dash panel and secure them with the hardware provided with the gauges. Refer to the instructions provided with the gauges before wiring them.

Connections vary from one manufacturer to another. However, the

gauges typically require a switched 12-volt power source, a ground, and a signal from whatever they are monitoring. They will also require a switched 12-volt power source and a ground for the dashboard lights for that paradise effect. In addition, there will typically be a high-beam-indicator light and left/right turn-signal indica-

tors. Be sure to leave the wires long enough for the wires to be terminated in a quick-disconnect plug that can be plugged into the other respective wires.

Coolant-Temperature Sending Unit

The coolant-temperature sending unit is typically included with the

The quick-disconnect plug allows for quick and simple connections between the distributor and the ignition system.

The wire with the bullet connector ultimately connects to a 12-gauge wire from terminal 13 on the fuse panel to provide power to the A/C compressor clutch.

The black wire in the photo connects the power terminal on the fuse panel to the alternator. The red wire connects the charge terminal of the alternator to the plug adjacent to where the wire from terminal 4 connects to the alternator.

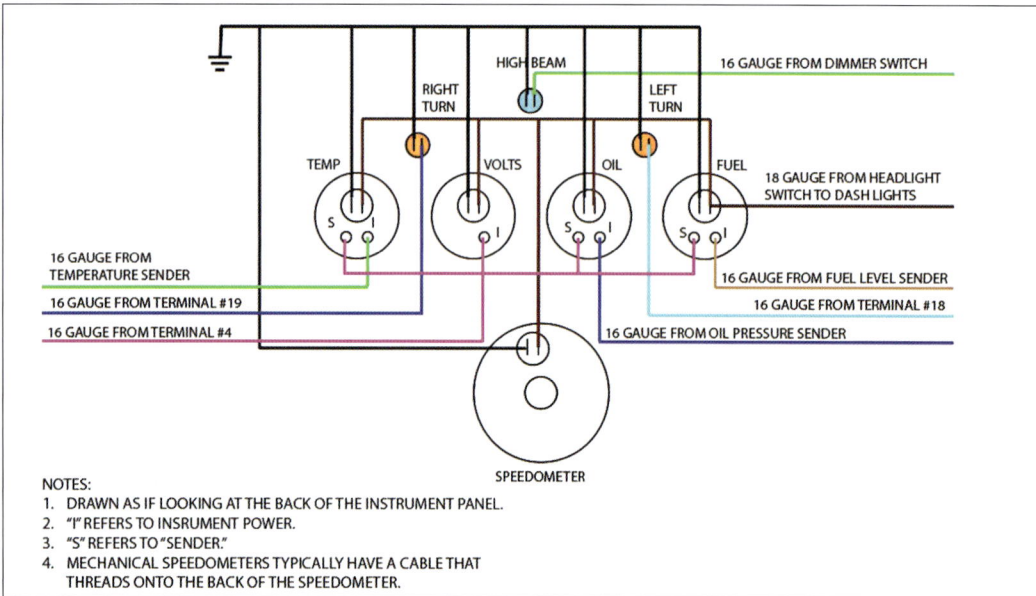

This is a generic schematic for electric gauges. In addition to a switched 12-volt power source and the proper senders, all gauges and lights will require a ground source.

Within the schematic:

HIGH BEAM — 16 GAUGE FROM DIMMER SWITCH

RIGHT TURN — LEFT TURN

TEMP — VOLTS — OIL — FUEL

18 GAUGE FROM HEADLIGHT SWITCH TO DASH LIGHTS

16 GAUGE FROM TEMPERATURE SENDER
16 GAUGE FROM TERMINAL #19
16 GAUGE FROM TERMINAL #4

16 GAUGE FROM FUEL LEVEL SENDER
16 GAUGE FROM TERMINAL #18
16 GAUGE FROM OIL PRESSURE SENDER

SPEEDOMETER

NOTES:
1. DRAWN AS IF LOOKING AT THE BACK OF THE INSTRUMENT PANEL.
2. "I" REFERS TO INSRUMENT POWER.
3. "S" REFERS TO "SENDER."
4. MECHANICAL SPEEDOMETERS TYPICALLY HAVE A CABLE THAT THREADS ONTO THE BACK OF THE SPEEDOMETER.

Wiring the dash panel with a quick disconnect allows for it to be wired in a more comfortable position than laying on the floor of a truck while reaching up to the dash.

A custom dash panel, simple electronic gauges, indicator lights, a coolant-temperature sending unit, and an oil-pressure gauge provide a reliable monitoring system for the truck's vitals.

temperature gauge. It can be threaded into various locations on the engine, with a convenient location being atop the intake manifold. The sending unit grounds in its mounting location, so do not use any type of sealant on the threads.

Oil-Pressure Sending Unit

The oil-pressure sending unit must be threaded into an oil gallery. On a small-block Chevy engine, that is conveniently located atop the engine near the distributor. Installing

it into the engine prior to installing the engine in the truck makes this an easy task.

Fuel-Level Sender

The fuel-level sender must be assembled in accordance with the included instructions to calibrate it for the size of the fuel tank. The sender is then inserted into the fuel tank and secured with screws. The sender wire that runs to the fuel-level gauge typically connects to the terminal closest to the center of the cap of

the fuel-level sender. A ground wire connects to the remaining terminal.

Ground Wires

When all accessories have been wired, verify that each electrical component has a proper ground. It does not matter whether a ground wire is connected as you are connecting power or if you go back and connect all the grounds as the final step, but you must verify that each component is grounded.

Depending on the mounting location and the sender being used, it may be necessary to use an adapter to achieve the correct fitment. These adapters may be included with the sender, but if they are not, they should be available at any reputable auto parts store.

Just like the coolant-temperature sending unit, an adapter may be required when mounting the oil-pressure sending unit. Again, do not use any sealant, as this will affect the operation of the gauge.

A ring terminal crimped onto a wire running directly to the oil-pressure gauge fits over the stud on the oil-pressure sending unit. Use a washer and a nut to secure it in place.

After assembling and calibrating the fuel-level sender, insert the float through the gasket, and then the rest of the sender into the fuel tank. Secure it in place with self-tapping screws.

The tan wire that connects closest to the center of the fuel-level sender runs to the fuel-level gauge. The dark wire that connects to one of the mounting screws connects to a ground stud.

In this application, the fuel tank is mounted behind the rear axle and below the bed. At the lower left of the photo is the installed fuel-level sender with the filler being to the right. Near the center of the photo is a fitting that receives a vent hose that connects to a rollover vent valve. Hiding behind the filler neck is the fuel pickup tube that connects to the rubber fuel hose that runs forward to the fuel pump.

TROUBLESHOOTING TIPS

Troubleshooting electrical problems can be frustrating. However, trying the simple stuff first and using a test light and/or a multimeter to test for voltage, current, and ground makes troubleshooting tasks go much smoother. The following problems and solutions are by no means all-inclusive.

Problem	Probable Cause	Solution
Points-type ignition not starting	Points are fouled or out of adjustment	Replace and/or adjust points
	Faulty ballast resistor	Replace or install ballast resistor
Switch failure in high-current items such as fan, fuel pump, headlights, and horn	Accessories are drawing more current than the switch can handle	Rewire the accessories using a relay
Fuses keep blowing	The circuit cannot handle the overall load needed for all the accessories	Use relays to minimize the current within the circuit and/or run some of the accessories on a separate circuit
Light bulb not illuminating	Faulty bulb	Check bulb with a multimeter or by trying it in another circuit and replace if defective
	Faulty connection between bulb and bulb socket	Clean the contacts on the bulb and the socket
Oil-pressure gauge reads full pressure, even if the engine is not running	Faulty oil-pressure sending unit	Replace oil-pressure sending unit
Power seats do not work	Obstruction beneath seat is preventing movement	Remove obstruction
	Blown fuse	Replace fuse; if fuse blows again, check for other problems within the circuit
	Faulty power seat motor or switch	Turn the ignition switch on, but do not start the engine. Operate the power-seat switch and listen for motor noise. If there is no motor noise, check the switch. If there is motor noise, inspect the drive assembly, transmission, gears, and tracks. Repair or replace as required.
Key will not turn in ignition switch	Faulty ignition lock cylinder	Replace ignition lock cylinder
Warning lights on the instrument panel do not turn on when the ignition key is turned to the on position	Faulty ignition switch	Replace the ignition switch
Intermittent cooling from the air-conditioning system	Faulty low pressure cutout switch	The refrigerant level is probably low; have the A/C system recharged
	Faulty compressor clutch	Less than adequate battery voltage is reaching the compressor. Check wiring connections. Test for proper voltage with a multimeter.
	Faulty compressor clutch relay	Check wiring connections. Test for proper voltage with a multimeter. Replace the relay if it is faulty.
	Faulty A/C control switch	Check electrical connections for good contact. If connections are good, replace A/C control switch.